The Theory and Reality of Democracy

The Theory and Reality of Democracy

A Case Study in Iraq

SUMAN GUPTA

continuum

Continuum
The Tower Building
11 York Road
London SE1 7NX

80 Maiden Lane
Suite 704
New York, NY 10038

British Library Cataloguing-in-Publication Data
A catalogue record for this book is available from the British Library.

ISBN: PB: 0-8264-9638-5

Library of Congress Cataloging-in-Publication Data
A catalog record for this book is available from the Library of Congress

Typeset by RefineCatch Limited, Bungay, Suffolk
Printed and bound in Great Britain by MPG Books Ltd, Bodmin, Cornwall

Contents

This book is dedicated to all Iraqi non-combatants who were killed in 2003 and 2004

Introduction

1 The Politically Realist Methodology

A politically realist approach to international politics is associated with conviction in the agency of states and an interest in conflict situations. Perhaps such an approach is as much the product of circumstances where agency of states is tested and conflict is in the air, as a conceptual position that myopically attends to these. In assuming a politically realist *methodology* here I depart from some of these associations, but accept that this study is the product of fraught circumstances which encourage recourse to the realist tradition. This study both attends to and derives from the post-11 September 2001 world . . . or should I say the post-Cold War world, or the post-industrial world in which forces of globalization are poised (largely) uneasily against local interests? However characterized, the prevailing context is one in which my theme (democracy in the international and transnational domain) and the socio-historical context that I eventually focus on (the 2002–2004 invasion and occupation of Iraq), spiral out into ever-expanding political discord and uncertainty. There are no limits to where a theme like democracy in the international/transnational domain might apply, and there is no way in which the 2002–2004 invasion of Iraq can be seen as a historical singularity; together my theme and context permeate into and crystallize from a world where conflicts seem to be both particular and pervasive, continuous and consecutive.

Against that influential aspect of modern political realism, 'neorealism' (represented by Kenneth Waltz, Robert Keohane, Robert Gilpin), it was sometimes argued that globalizing processes undermine the agency of states and that dominant phases of accord are more revealing than phases of discord.[1] Such arguments had enough weight for neorealists to seek to defend their theoretical position as a baseline from which complex situations can be realistically gauged.[2] In post-11 September 2001 circumstances, however, neorealist defensiveness has evaporated to some degree. If some globalization of accord may be perceived, more emphatic is the pervasiveness of discord. Each conflict, irrespective of its centre, ripples outwards through various means into the daily life of the planet; the twin faces of terrorism and security shadow the international domain; a 'continuous revolution' for peace, based ultimately on strong or weak agency of states, seems to be underway. Neorealists are congratulating themselves on the evidence of these turns now,[3] and it seems to me quite possible that my recourse to a politically realist methodology here is encouraged by prevailing circumstances.

I would like to begin this study, however, by clarifying the differences of the politically realist methodology assumed here from the wider tradition of realism in international politics. Naturally, that also entails delineating the connection between the realist tradition and my methodology.

A loose but popular perception of realism in international politics is implicit in the following statement by Francis Fukuyama. Here he reflects on the aftermath of the widely criticized 2002–2004 invasion of Iraq from the perspective of the US establishment:

> It is clear . . . that a very large part of the world, including many people who are normally inclined to be our friends, did not believe in the legitimacy of our behaviour towards Iraq. This is not because the Security Council failed to endorse the war, but because many of our friends did not trust us, that is the Bush Administration, to use our huge margin of power wisely and in the interests of the world as a whole. This should matter to us, not just for realist reasons of state (our ability to attract allies to share the burden), but for idealist ones as well (our ability to lead and inspire based on the attractiveness of who we are).[4]

One striking feature of those three sentences is the emphatic avowal of collective identity – the collective us/we/our appears no less than nine times in that space. The collective identity merges seamlessly with the neoconservative fold that Fukuyama announces himself as speaking from and to in the quoted paper (entitled 'The Neoconservative Moment'). His neoconservative credentials are impeccable – he has recently argued that a world wide convergence on liberal democracy is leading towards the end of history[5] – and it behoves him to take on the burden of speaking for (and thereby conflating) the American polity, the American nation-state, the American establishment, American neoconservatives, and (despite a subtle holding-apart) the Bush Administration. This self-positioning allows Fukuyama to make a distinction, pertinent to this study, between realist and idealist considerations. Realist considerations have to do with maintaining strategic and collective self-interest through the state; idealist considerations have to do with the aspirations of the collective self (embodied, at least for Fukuyama, in the state). Both draw from the collective self (we/us/our), but as the syntax of the last sentence suggests, realist considerations are usually at odds with idealist considerations.

Such a popular notion of realism in international politics informs a great deal of mass media discussion, political rhetoric and public debate. It has the advantage of appearing to be consistent with other, not unrelated, kinds of realism. It chimes in, for instance, with usually conservative appeals to political realism within nation-states:[6] as a compromise between contending interest groups, or between principles and practicalities, in favour of *status quo* or paths of least resistance. Organizational or institutional realism is akin to the above too. Legal positivism appeals to an ends-oriented realism as the defined function of judicial institutions and eschews ethical idealism – indeed, it sometimes seeks to redefine normatively loaded terms like 'democracy' accordingly.[7] With regard to the management of capitalist corporations, it is widely accepted that realist ends (the need to maintain or increase profit margins) may supersede idealist hopes (such as security of employment or investment in a greener environment). Philosophical moral realism, i.e. deriving and applying moral principles strictly in terms of the given human condition/natural order rather than in terms of some higher order or some constructed order, can also be associated with the above. More to our purpose, Fukuyama's popular notion of realism, as opposed to idealism, also has a family resemblance to more elaborate and carefully considered realist theories of international politics – but the differences are germane, and in fact the superficial resemblance is undercut by complexities of theory and method.

A couple of conventions of academic methodology[8] complicate the kind of popular version of realism (and idealism) that Fukuyama works with. One, trying to arrive at a realist theory of international politics enjoins a need to go beyond the enunciation of realist considerations for particular situations from specific collective positions for given self-interests. In academic convention a *theory* aspires to general or universal application. Two, in proposing a realist theory of international politics it is considered expedient (another convention) to position that theory in historical terms and/or to contextualize it persuasively against other similar or different theories. Increasingly through the latter part of the twentieth century, to assume or apply a realist theory of international politics has entailed ever more careful adherence to these methodological conventions.

To elaborate briefly on the effects of those two conventions in this area:

THE FIRST CONVENTION

The nuances of adopting a coherent and general realist position are influentially discussed in Hans Morgenthau's first chapter in *Politics Among Nations* (1954), Kenneth Waltz's *Theory of International Politics* (1979), Robert Gilpin's first chapter in *War and Change in World Politics* (1981), and, say, Barry Buzan *et al.*'s *The Logic of Anarchy* (1993). It is not my intention to engage in separate analyses of these – I particularly mention them because they demonstrate distinct methodological ploys with a view to elaborating distinct politically realist theories. Morgenthau's six principles of a realist theory of international politics enable a carefully defined 'objective' position and identify a neutral key concept ('interest defined in terms of power').[9]

Waltz tries to erase both the acknowledgement of a position, however objective, or a key concept, however neutral (he regarded both as 'reductive'), in favour of a systems-based approach built around key agents (states) which could accommodate increasing or accruing degrees of complexity.[10] Gilpin follows Waltz's neorealist terminology, but pares it down to certain dualities (equilibrium/change, costs/benefits) that are suitable for a particular category of international political events.[11] And Buzan *et al.* depart from neorealism by proposing a structural realism which treats the processes of international politics as a metaphor (understood through a Romantic concept of the metaphor).[12] Of greater interest than the distinctions here though are the similarities that arise from methodological conventions attached to engaging with theory. There are two noteworthy similarities, both of which have proved usefully vulnerable for detractors. (1) The *over-determination of key abstractions* in such theories, such as Morgenthau's 'human nature' and 'interest defined as power', Waltz's agency of states at the core of the international system, Buzan *et al.*'s device of metaphor as enabling structuring of international politics. Each of these abstractions and consequent theoretical frames is unequal to the complexity that can obtain in international politics. It is always possible to find a complex of historical, social and cultural details that simply do not fit within theories that follow from key abstractions. The only argument against such unwieldy details is that the theories they undermine nevertheless aid conceptualization and clarification – as positions to depart from as much as frames to apply. But such a justification can attach to any theory. Ultimately every theory competes with its rivals by claiming a superior embrace rather than by acknowledging a tenuously applicable usefulness – which leads to the second similarity. (2) Giving, where necessary, selective attention to and amenable interpretation of historical, social and cultural complexes to validate a theory – or *the over-determination of the perceptual field.* Every realist theory of international politics, particularly such influential ones as Morgenthau's and Waltz's, has been accused of this. This means: once the theory is persuasively elaborated, either everything is seen as inferable from it, or that which isn't is regarded as negligible or of marginal interest. In other words, the more theoretically embedded the realist becomes the more schematic or less rigorous his documentation of the real sphere appears – which undermines the very weight of the appellation 'realist'.

THE SECOND CONVENTION

Placing the historical position of a realist theory and/or contextualizing it persuasively against other theories are essentially processes of self-advocacy. However committed to avoiding extrinsic idealist considerations (often associated with strong or absolute moral principles) a realist may be, and however determined to be objective or non-reductive, by arguing strenuously against those the realist tends to get defined by opposition. Thus, the lineage through Machiavelli's ideas, concepts of human nature and utilitarianism and *Realpolitik* that modern realism in international politics sometimes claims, brings also a lineage of moral battles and accusations which have little to do with it. To guard against such polarization, later twentieth-century political realists have chosen not just to argue against moral positions which distort analysis of the real world (in doing which they easily attract 'criticism' for being amoral or immoral), but also to acknowledge and actively embrace the moral distinctiveness of political realism. In fact, the popular opposition between the idealist and the realist seldom applies in well-formulated and rigorous political realist theory. What are often regarded as idealist considerations are now well within the ken of realist thinking; they interpenetrate and overlap, merge and separate, within realist thinking in rather more complicated ways. The final three of Morgenthau's six principles, for example, enjoin on political realism an awareness of the 'moral significance of political action', recognition of 'moral laws that govern the universe', and cultivation of a 'distinctive intellectual and moral attitude to matters political'.[13] This doesn't amount to an enunciation of moral principles which the realist claims to adhere by; it is more the exercising of a moral attitude and the recognition of the significance of morality within realist thinking. A more extended consideration of the idealism, so to say, that is implicit in political realism appears in R. N. Berki's contemplation of political realism. Drawing on strains of argument normally associated with (unpopular) concepts of naturalism, the *Realpolitik* and opportunism, Berki proposes a synthetic notion of political realism consisting of three features. One, political realism incorporates a particular 'awareness of self-limitation' – 'knowledge in the proper sense and not an uncritically accepted article of faith; one can be aware of one's limitations only if one is aware of one's possibilities; the frontier is never reached in one's dreams, only in active life, in the waking hours . . .'.[14] Two, the recognition that 'change and action with a view to improvement are not only possible but morally obligatory in politics . . . unless we understand resistance *as* resistance, obstacles *as* obstacles and contradiction *as* contradiction, we are not realists, but conservative defenders of the *Realpolitik*'.[15] And three, 'a synthetic concept of political realism must include a clear argument regarding the choice of means in the execution of political designs'.[16] More searching forms of reconciling idealist and realist political thinking, such as Reinhold Niebuhr's,[17] are of less interest in this context because they seem to me to assert rather violently the supremacy of allegedly universal idealist (Christian) considerations and muscle them into realistic theory without fully recognizing their cultural specificity and the vested interests they serve.

These observations on the manner in which realist theories of international politics differ from popular notions of realism, allow me to clarify the precise aspirations of the politically realist *methodology* that is assumed in this study. My methodology goes further than the expectations of the popular notion of realism but doesn't go as far as a fully fledged realist theory in international politics. By using a politically realist methodology I do wish to associate this study with the spirit of political realism, and some of its aspirations: i.e., cultivate the sort of moral attitude that is described by Morgenthau and Berki; not be taken in by moral principles that distort analysis of the real world; be especially cautious about moral claims made on the basis of a higher order/a constructed order/a narrowly defined context; be attentive to the real world in all its complexity and detail (however unwieldy); be attentive also to the impact of the conceptual – especially the idealist sort – in the real world. At the same time, in assuming the politically realist methodology I do not wish to present the usual vulnerabilities of realist theory: I do not intend to commit myself to the defence of key abstractions (agency of states, human nature, primacy of conflict, etc.); I am determined not to limit my perceptual field in any but methodologically pragmatic ways; I do not expect to be able to come up with formulations that can claim to apply in all directions and contexts (I will limit myself to the retrospective and the contemporary and the possibilities arising from these).

Another way of presenting the politically realist methodology of this study is in terms of certain schematic observations about methodology in political analysis generally, rather than in terms of the realist tradition in itself.

In taking this alternative tack, I assume that the methodology of political analysis – whether as a process of erecting a general or limited theory, or whether to illuminate a particular context or theme – is determined by rational objectives (i.e. what analysis hopes to achieve). Several putative objectives cover the field (some of these may gesture towards or lead into others, and some may rest satisfied in their achievement) and one or some or all of these may be called upon within a particular analytical effort. The putative objectives in question are: *explanative*, *predictive*, *visionary* and *prescriptive*. Brief discussions of each below ascertain the methodological processes that go into their realization, establish the linkages between these, and enable a reasonably precise delineation of the politically realist methodology.

EXPLANATIVE ANALYSIS

Explanative analysis aims to obtain a rational understanding of a particular context/subject, or to arrive at general formulations which enable rational understanding of a wide range of contexts/subjects. There are a large number of complicated and much discussed methods through which such analysis can be initiated: e.g., by questioning the nature of rationality; by focusing on key factors such as class, system, action; by constructing on the foundation of first principles (an original contract, for instance); by drawing upon analogues with other fields of knowledge; and so on. Insofar as I touch on this to clarify the politically realist methodology, the manner in which various explanative methods call upon (perhaps construct) notions of reality is of particular interest. In fact, to be persuasive, even the most abstruse method has to take recourse to some sort of appeal to reality. It appears to me that on the whole two kinds of recourse can be discerned. The first kind appears in analysis that develops with reference to *hypothetical* situations – which can be checked for realism or plausibility. That is the spirit in which, for example, John Rawls constructs his well-ordered society from a hypothetical original contract, or Robert Nozick uses a hypothetical original condition of anarchy followed by the hypothetical emergence of protective agencies as precursors of the political state.[18] The second kind of appeal to reality is found in analysis that tests itself through *descriptions* of complex socio-historical situations. This is used effectively, for example, in Joseph Schumpeter's analysis of the possibilities of democracy and socialism in the mid twentieth century, or Ernest Mandel's assessment of the political economy of late-twentieth-century capitalism.[19] Both kinds of appeals to reality (hypothetical and descriptive) may be used within a single analytical approach (usually the case), but often one is emphasized more than the other. Thus, analysis from first principles often tends to appeal predominantly to hypothetical situations, while analysis drawing upon analogues between different fields of knowledge generally prefers a descriptive appeal to reality. With regard to these, admittedly rather schematic, observations about explanative analysis, the politically realist methodology of this study situates itself as follows: in this study I focus primarily on the second kind of appeal to reality, description of a complex socio-historical situation. Insofar as I engage in explanative analysis I do not develop arguments in terms of hypothetical situations. Insofar as I am attentive to conceptual positions which have a bearing on this study, I naturally consider carefully the appeals to hypothetical reality made in them, and examine their claims of realism and plausibility.

PREDICTIVE ANALYSIS

Predictive analysis extends on the aims of explanative analysis by charting out future possibilities arising from or for a given context/subject, or a wide range of contexts/subjects (including assessments of the future of the world or the human species). Predictive analysis is thus conditional on the explanative analysis that it follows. Most political theory and research engage, implicitly or explicitly, in predictive analysis. Predictive analysis is confined to discerning how a present situation (understood through some explanative method) *could* unravel or unfold (if that explanative method continues to apply). I do not mean that term to extend to considerations of how a present situation *should* progress – that is where this is distinguished from visionary and prescriptive analyses. Good examples of predictive analysis are: Marx's prognosis of the failure of capitalism through its own contradictions, Carl Schmitt's doubts about the future of parliamentary democracy against the advantages of authoritarianism, Schumpeter's forecast of the inevitable spread of socialism, and prevailing expectations (both fatalistic and hopeful) of the emergence of a global democratic capitalist world-order.[20] The politically realist methodology of this study engages in predictive analysis only insofar as permitted by my explanative analysis of a socio-historical context. This naturally includes taking account of predictive analyses from other conceptual positions which have a role to play in this context.

VISIONARY ANALYSIS

Visionary analysis aims to conceptualize the most desirable or ideal political condition, and understand prevailing contexts/subjects and contending conceptual positions accordingly. This may follow from any of the approaches mentioned in describing explanative analysis – building upon certain first principles, focusing on key social or political factors, drawing upon analogues to other fields, etc. Undertaking visionary analysis usually involves calling upon hypothetical tests of realism or plausibility (a tendency inaugurated in Plato's *Republic*). Such analysis very seldom coheres with predictive analysis – usually these develop along separate lines, and may be brought together in a mutually interrogative fashion. So, in Marxist thinking the predictive analysis of exacerbation of class conflict in capitalist society is interrogated against the discrete visionary analysis of the ideal condition of a classless egalitarian ethos. Or, in neoliberal thinking the visionary analysis of a minimal state giving free play to market forces may be critically juxtaposed against the predictive analysis of the consequences of welfare economics in majoritarian democracies. Very rarely predictive analysis may lead into visionary analysis. This only happens when the predictive analysis is based on an explanative analysis of a socio-historical context which appears to have primarily desirable or ideal possibilities in it (necessarily a conservative attitude). This occurred in Hegel's teleology of history, where the politically self-conscious culture of the Germany of his time was given as a final aspiration of world history.[21] More recently, deliberately assuming a Hegelian attitude, Fukuyama's thesis that the world is converging on Western liberal democracy presents an attempt to turn predictive analysis into visionary analysis.[22] As far as the politically realist methodology of this study goes, no visionary analysis will be attempted. The primary explanative focus on a particular socio-historical reality precludes utopianism to a large degree. Methodologically,

I can think of no reason to favour a conservative evaluation of the socio-historical context in question, such as may enable visionary analysis. This doesn't imply that visionary analysis of democracy in the international/transnational domain cannot be undertaken with illuminating effect;[23] visionary analysis is simply outside the prerogatives of the politically realist methodology. As before, in this study I am alert to visionary analysis in other relevant conceptual positions.

PRESCRIPTIVE ANALYSIS

Prescriptive analysis either aims to find solutions for political practice out of a variety of explanatory analyses, or aims to correct departures between predictive and visionary analyses in a pragmatic fashion. Examples of the former are: Morgenthau's prescriptions of diplomacy, Anthony Giddens's thoughts about 'life politics' between left and right ideologies, conditions that apply in forums of rational deliberation in democratic practice suggested by Jürgen Habermas and others.[24] The strand of prescriptive analysis bridging predictive and visionary analyses has a more interesting history. Advocacy of contending prescriptive analyses for that end was famously debated between revolutionary socialism and democratic socialism (between Eduard Bernstein and Lenin, or Karl Kautsky and Lenin[25]). Contending positions taken by Karl Mannheim (as advocate of holistic planning) and Karl Popper (as an advocate of piecemeal incremental change)[26] were also essentially a confrontation of two kinds of prescriptive analyses. In both cases it is at the level of the prescriptive that differences are enunciated, rather than the visionary; and in both cases differences derive from divergences in explanative analyses. An intriguing position that is sometimes taken in prescriptive political analysis is that of inaction, or rather the recommendation that the exercise of rational agency be muted or made compliant with large spontaneous processes. This is implicit in certain strands of systems theory (Habermas's critique of Niklas Luhmann's position was an interrogation of this tendency[27]), and is explicit in management theory that accepts an evolutionary view of organizations.[28] The politically realist methodology of this study does not extend to prescriptive analysis in the sense of trying to find a bridge between visionary and predictive analyses. Again, this is purely a self-imposed methodological constraint rather than an ideologically determined decision; since I have imposed such a constraint already on visionary analysis here, the possibility of extending to this sort of prescriptive analysis is forestalled. However, I may, reluctantly, engage in prescriptive analysis in the sense of mediating between divergent explanatory analyses, but only for strictly contextualized and exigent matters. This possibility follows from the interest that the politically realist methodology has in extant conceptual positions.

These clarifications of the politically realist methodology (in schematic terms, apropos general objectives of political analysis) lead to three tasks in this study, which are presented in two parts here and a conclusion:

1. A politically realist critical engagement with the prevailing conceptual field that pertains to the main theme of this study – democracy in the international/transnational domain. The emphasis is on the different kinds of explanative analyses, the different modes of appeal to reality and pragmatic practice which are found in the field. In other words, the emphasis is on applying the realist methodology to the field rather than developing a realist conceptual position or ideology. This forms the substance of Part I.
2. A politically realist engagement with the socio-historical context that this study addresses – the invasion and occupation of Iraq between September 2002 and June 2004. The emphasis here is on pertinent details of the processes involved, and the manner in which these may be positioned in terms of the conceptual field discussed in Part I, or may fail to be so positioned, or demand modifications within that conceptual field. This forms the substance of Part II.
3. A concise synthesis of the observations and questions that arise from Parts I and II taken together. This step may lead to some immediate predictive and possibly even prescriptive insights. The observations and questions here, in other words, are presented with the understanding that, 'It is impossible to describe the process of political deliberation without at the same time contributing to it in some measure.'[29] This forms the substance of conclusion.

This study may be regarded as possessing an inordinate interest in the conceptual field for a realist approach to a particular socio-historical context. That is largely the point here. It is assumed that the contemporary conceptual field presents the limits of possibilities within which complex socio-historically located political actions and perceptions unfold. The conceptual field determines in a variety of ways both the planning and undertaking of actions and the efficacy of those actions. Conversely, in a mutually modifying fashion, such actions, perceptions and effects feed back and stretch the conceptual field in necessary ways. The hugely significant theme of democracy – the idea of democracy and the reality of democracy – in our world has to be approached through a convergence of the conceptual and the socio-historical.

A few final words remain in this introductory chapter to explain why I have chosen to bring together the theme of democracy in international/transnational politics with the socio-historical context of the recent invasion and occupation of Iraq. As a frame, the context in question provides extraordinary facilities for a politically realist engagement with my theme. It is one in which a sheer concentration of events *in extremis* allowed for an almost spontaneous deployment and dissection of ideas of democracy. Political justifications for and against military invasion were constantly couched in terms of ideas of democracy (in a range of speeches, and formal and informal debates), negotiating connotations of democracy with both national and international/transnational effect. The democratic credentials and legitimacy of international organizations such as the United Nations or supranational alignments such as the European Union were tested to the full. In this context the scale of interest in political affairs was such, and the contingency of political self-locations so pressing, that the vast resources of the national and international mass media converged in addressing these events with unprecedented concentration. These let loose both the possibilities of democratic responsiveness and the manipulation of democratic expression in a particularly revealing fashion. International democratic responsiveness, for instance, was evidenced in the extraordinary simultaneous massing of protestors around the world. The after-the-event political discourse of 'democratization' in Iraq, which was deployed by different political alignments and in the media, alludes to another facet of the idea of democracy in international/transnational politics. On the whole, the context from September 2002 to June 2004 provides an exploitable frame for a political realist apprehension of democracy in international/transnational politics.

Further, this socio-historical context is also amenable to this study because of the agonized intellectual effort at documentation and conceptualization that was undertaken at every phase of its unfolding. The extent to which the conceptual field – centrally with regard to the claims of Western democracy – tested and was tested by, impinged and was impinged upon, during the period in question was momentous. The proliferation of scholarly and analytical books within the period speaks for itself. A small selection would include: Milan Rai and Noam Chomsky, *War Plan Iraq* (2002); William Rivers Pitt and Scott Ritter, *War on Iraq* (2003); Gwynne Dyer, *Ignorant Armies* (2003); Tariq Ali, *Bush in Babylon* (2003); Sheldon Rampton and John Stauber, *Weapons of Mass Deception* (2003); Nafeez Mosaddeq Ahmed, *Behind the War on Terror* (2003); David Miller, John Pilger and Mark Thomas, *Tell Me Lies* (2004); Slavoj Zizek, *Iraq: The Borrowed Kettle* (2004); Hans Blix, *Disarming Iraq* (2004); Dilip Hiro, *Secrets and Lies* (2004); Bob Woodward, *Plan of Attack* (2004).[30] The appearance of these and similar works within the socio-historical context in question naturally gave them an emphatically interventionist agenda in addition to documentation and analysis. Documentation and analysis were expected to work in these as weapons of advocacy to disturb the course of the political process as it unfolded. Indubitably, this field of scholarship has itself become written into the interstices of that socio-historical context – usefully so for this retrospective study with a measured politically realist methodology.

NOTES

1 E.g., Terry Nardin, *Law, Morality and the Relations of States* (Princeton, NJ: Princeton University Press, 1983); Friedrich V. Kratochwil, *Rules, Norms and Decisions: On the Conditions of Practical and Legal Reasoning in International Relations and Domestic Affairs* (Cambridge: Cambridge University Press, 1989); James C. Hsiung, *Anarchy and Order: The Interplay of Politics and Law in International Relations* (Boulder, CO: Lynne Reinner, 1997).

2 The debate was aired most revealingly in Robert O. Keohane (ed.), *Neorealism and Its Critics* (New York: Columbia University Press, 1986). Neorealist analysis as a baseline of political analysis was given persuasive treatment in Keohane's *After Hegemony: Co-operation and Discord in the World Political Economy* (Princeton, NJ: Princeton University Press, 1984). However, a defensive tone characterized sympathetic overviews of the realist tradition at the end of the 1990s, as in Robert Jervis, 'Realism in the Study of World Politics', in Peter J. Katzenstein, Robert O. Keohane and Stephen D. Krasner (eds.), *Exploration and Contestation in the Study of World Politics* (Cambridge, MA: MIT Press, 1999), pp. 331–52.

3 A collection of essays – Ken Booth and Tim Dunne (eds.), *Worlds in Collision: Terror and the Future of the Global Order* (Basingstoke: Palgrave, 2002) – bringing together responses from a range of intellectuals to the terrorist attacks of 11 September 2001 in the US, includes indicative pieces by both Robert Keohane ('The Public Delegitimation of Terror and Coalitional Politics', pp. 141–51) and Kenneth Waltz ('The Continuity of International Politics', pp. 348–53).

4 Francis Fukuyama, 'The Neoconservative Moment', *The National Interest* 76, Summer 2004, pp. 63–4.

5 Francis Fukuyama, *The End of History and the Last Man* (Harmondsworth: Penguin, 1992).

6 Globalization studies often assert that it is now inappropriate to characterize the domestic sphere as distinct from the international sphere, given the ever closer degrees of overlap, interdependence and continuity that have come to exist between these traditionally distinguished spheres. On this point see Ian Clark, *Globalization and International Relations Theory* (Oxford: Oxford University Press, 1999), Ch. 1 ('The Great Divide'). Political studies that concede this point, on the understanding that the nation-state is in a process of erosion, are as numerous as those that feel that this is a myth. In realist terms it can hardly be gainsaid that while many of the factors pointed to and arguments given by globalization studies do justify their position in this regard the distinction between the domestic and the international or supranational or transnational continue to enjoy wide everyday currency and provide the rationale behind many aspects of ongoing political process.

7 As is attempted in Richard A. Posner, *Law, Pragmatism and Democracy* (Cambridge, MA.: Harvard University Press, 2003). This is in the tradition of legal positivism, associated primarily with Hans Kelsen.

8 In alluding to 'conventions of academic methodology' I do not wish to question the rational considerations on which they are based; the idea is not that such conventions are arbitrary or dispensable, but that they mark the distinctiveness of academic discourse. I also thereby wish to be alert to the complexity of calculations underlying such conventions, which has been the subject of much research from various perspectives: sociological (e.g., Pierre Bourdieu, *Homo Academicus* [Cambridge: Polity, 1988]), educational (e.g., Tony Becher, *Academic Tribes and Territories*, 2nd edition [Buckingham: SRHR and Open University Press, 2001]), psychological (Marjorie Garber, *Academic Instincts* [Princeton, NJ: Princeton University Press, 2001]), and discourse analytical (e.g., Ken Hyland, *Disciplinary Discourses* [Harlow: Pearson, 2000]).

9 Hans J. Morgenthau, *Politics Among Nations: The Struggle for Power and Peace* (New York: Knopf, 1954), Ch. 1.
10 Kenneth N. Waltz, *Theory of International Politics* (Reading, MA.: Addison-Wesley, 1979).
11 Robert Gilpin, *War and Change in World Politics* (Cambridge: Cambridge University Press, 1981), particularly Ch. 1.
12 Barry Buzan, Charles Jones and Richard Little, *The Logic of Anarchy: Neorealism to Structural Realism* (New York: Columbia University Press, 1993), Part 3.
13 Morgenthau, *Politics Among Nations*, pp. 8–10.
14 R. N. Berki, *On Political Realism* (London: Dent, 1981), p. 26.
15 Ibid., p. 27.
16 Ibid., p. 28.
17 Reinhold Niebuhr's numerous books in this vein include: *The Children of Light and the Children of Darkness* (London: Nisbet, 1945); *Christian Realism and Political Problems* (London: Faber & Faber, 1954); *Nations and Empires* (London: Faber & Faber, 1960); *The Democratic Experience* (London: Pall Mall, 1969).
18 John Rawls' formulations are discussed in Ch. 4; Robert Nozick, *Anarchy, State and Utopia* (Oxford: Blackwell, 1975).
19 Joseph A. Schumpeter, *Capitalism, Socialism and Democracy* (London: Allen & Unwin, 1943); Ernest Mandel, *Late Capitalism*, trans. Joris de Bres (London: Verso, 1978).
20 Marx, *Capital*, Vol. 3, trans. Samuel Moore and Edward Aveling, ed. Frederick Engels (London: Lawrence and Wishart, 1959); Carl Schmitt, *The Crisis of Parliamentary Democracy*, trans. Ellen Kennedy (Cambridge, MA.: 1985); Schumpeter, *Capitalism, Socialism and Democracy*, ibid.
21 G. W. F. Hegel, *The Philosophy of History* (New York: Dover, 1956).
22 Francis Fukuyama, *The End of History and the Last Man* (Harmondsworth: Penguin, 1992).
23 In *Corporate Capitalism and Political Philosophy* (London: Pluto, 2002), I had argued that a rational and provisional utopianism is desirable in contemporary political theory. This is a view I still subscribe to; but the international/transnational context has moved on since I had taken up that study, and it now seems to me that the conceptual preconditions for that step need more careful consideration than I had allowed then. In subscribing to the politically realist methodology of this study I therefore do not make any unnecessary concessions to utopian possibilities.
24 Morgenthau, *Politics Among Nations*, Chs. 31–2; Anthony Giddens, *Beyond Left and Right: The Future of Radical Politics* (Cambridge: Polity, 1994); Jürgen Habermas's contribution to discussions about prescriptions for deliberative democracy are examined at some length in Chapter 5 below.
25 Bernstein–Lenin debate: Eduard Bernstein's revisionist position was stated in 1898 in *Evolutionary Socialism*, trans. Edith Harvey (New York: Schocken, 1961), and criticized in V. I. Lenin's 1902 book *What Is to be Done?* – which appears in Vol. 1 of his *Selected Works* (Moscow: Progress, 1963).

Kautsky–Lenin debate: despite initial agreement between the two about the role of intellectuals and the undesirability of Bernsteinism, they fell out after the Second International on how colonialism and the First World War should be addressed, and as Karl Kautsky gradually moved towards revisionism himself. Kautsky's pamphlet *The Dictatorship of the Proletariat*, trans. H. J. Stenning (Manchester: National Labour Press, 1918), was vigorously attacked by Lenin in *The Proletarian Revolution and the Renegade Kautsky* (1918) – it appears in Vol. 3 of his *Selected Works* (Moscow: Progress, 1964).
26 Both Karl Mannheim and Karl Popper were concerned with the functioning of democratic society. Whereas Mannheim was inclined to support holistic planning, as in *Man and Society in an Age of Reconstruction* (London: Routledge & Kegan Paul, 1940) and *Freedom, Power and Democratic Planning* (London: Routledge & Kegan Paul, 1950),

Popper was sceptical of this approach – see *The Open Society and Its Enemies Vol. 2* (London: Routledge & Kegan Paul, 1945), Ch. 23.

27 Niklas Luhmann's social systems theory is most completely laid out in *Social Systems* (1984), trans. John Bednorz and Dirk Baecker (Palo Alto, CA: Stanford University Press, 1995). Jürgen Habermas's critique of Luhmann is lucidly expressed in *The Philosophical Discourse of Modernity* (Cambridge, MA: MIT Press, 1987), pp. 368–85. For useful overviews of the Habermas–Luhmann debate see Kenneth C. Bausch's 'The Habermas/Luhmann Debate and Subsequent Habermasian Perspectives on Systems Theory', *Systems Research and Behavioral Science* 14: 5, September–October 1997, pp. 315–30; and Loet Leydesdorff's 'Luhmann, Habermas and the Theory of Communication', *Systems Research and Behavioral Science* 17: 3, May–June 2000, pp. 273–88.

28 As in C. Wailand, 'Evolutionary Systems Management of Organizations', *World Futures* 36: 2–4, pp. 141–54; Larry E. Geiner, 'Evolution and Revolution as Organizations Grow', *Harvard Business Review* 1998, pp. 55–68; Kathleen M. Eisenhardt and V. Ramaswamy, 'Coevolving: At Last, A Way to Make Synergies Work', *Harvard Business Review* Jan.–Feb. 2000, pp. 91–102; Suzanne Kelly, 'What Business Can Learn from the Simple Science of Complexity', *Journal for Quality and Participation* 22: 5, September–October 1999, pp. 44–6.

29 Buzan, Jones and Little, *The Logic of Anarchy*, p. 177.

30 Milan Rai and Noam Chomsky, *War Plan Iraq* (London: Verso, 2002); William Rivers Pitt and Scott Ritter, *War on Iraq* (San Francisco, CA: Context, 2003); Gwynne Dyer, *Ignorant Armies* (Toronto: McClelland & Stewart, 2003); Tariq Ali, *Bush in Babylon* (London: Verso, 2003); Sheldon Rampton and John Stauber, *Weapons of Mass Deception* (London: Constable & Robinson, 2003); Nafeez Mosaddeq Ahmed, *Behind the War on Terror* (Gabriola Island, BC: New Society, 2003); Dilip Hiro, *Secrets and Lies* (New York: Thunder's Mouth, 2004); David Miller, John Pilger and Mark Thomas, *Tell Me Lies* (London: Pluto, 2004); Slavoj Zizek, *Iraq: The Borrowed Kettle* (London: Verso, 2004); Hans Blix, *Disarming Iraq* (New York: Pantheon, 2004); Dilip Hiro, *Secrets and Lies* (New York: Nation, 2004); Bob Woodward, *Plan of Attack* (New York: Simon & Schuster, 2004).

Part I

2 *Democracy and Political Realism*

This part consists primarily in a survey, using the politically realist methodology, of the conceptual field wherein democracy in international/transnational politics is theorized. The emphasis on the international/transnational domain necessarily comes with certain cautions: for instance, that it is often difficult to discern distinct domestic and international/transnational domains, or that the manner in which international and transnational is collided here (with an oblique) underplays significant distinctions between them. Definitions may be useful here: the domestic domain alludes to political institutions and systems that operate primarily with regard to members of a polity (usually, citizens of a nation-state); international politics alludes to political institutions and arrangements whereby different nation-states conduct their bilateral or multilateral relations to each other; transnational politics applies to a level of interactions which operate outside formal national and international arrangements and have an effect on a wide range of nation-states and widely dispersed citizenry. Such definitions are necessarily provisional; in fact there is little agreement on the supportability or desirability of such distinctions, and the overlaps and interpenetrations involved are of a complexity that renders them unsustainable beyond providing an initial analytical foothold. But they are useful nevertheless, not just because they provide a simple initial structure which can then be complicated, but also because they are embedded in linguistic usage at all levels (not least academic) and aid immediate comprehension. So the definitions are provisional and no more than a momentary convenience here; they are registered mainly to recognize that these terms come with a linguistic advantage which is given. More importantly than the definitions though, in this study these terms are distinguished and clarified by the context and effect with which they are used.

Since such definitions do not characterize adequately the field this study engages with, the scope of this discussion can be rephrased as follows: this part presents a politically realist survey of ways in which current thinking about democracy accommodates or negotiates with political boundaries – especially nation-state boundaries, but also ethnic and cultural boundaries. There are several conveniently available appellations for different strands in this field: cosmopolitan democracy, well-ordered liberal democracy, deliberative democracy, radical democracy, and democratization studies (especially in relation to comparative politics). Subsequent chapters in this part address these in that order, with a particular focus on the matter of crossing or rising above (nation-state) boundaries and with the politically realist methodology in hand.

Much writing in this area has struggled with the urge to define democracy, however tentatively. Insofar as subsequent chapters of this part go, each works with certain definitive or descriptive notions of democracy which I pick up where relevant. What the various implications of, and manoeuvrings surrounding, that term amply demonstrate is its fluidity and contextual flexibility. To urge a single definition of democracy in the face of that would be inconsistent with a realist methodology, and is not attempted here. However, there is no denying that democracy appears to have an immediate and effective meaning in linguistic practice, and that there is some sort of embedded linguistic core beneath all the fluidity when it is evoked, whether for rigorous analysis or everyday expression. Broadly speaking, there are several given and received implications of democracy which are not consistent with each other, which seem to loosely work in various combinations according to linguistic practice, and which impinge upon sophisticated theorizations of democracy. The ones that are both embedded in general linguistic practice and constantly available in analytical positions explored here are: the minimum linguistic meaning; normative connotations; legislative denotation. Brief elaborations of each follow.

THE MINIMUM LINGUISTIC MEANING

A reminder of the etymologically rooted minimal meaning of democracy, government by people (*demos*, people, and *kratos*, rule/strength), may seem redundant in this context, except that it plays an unremitting role in linguistic practice – even conceptually rigorous linguistic practice. The *demos* are uncompromisingly inclusive: everyone is included whose humanity is recognized by others. It is the sticky absoluteness of this minimum meaning which confers on the term both unwieldiness and effectiveness. Any procedural qualification of democracy (parliamentary, majoritarian, representative) is less than democracy; any drawing of boundaries where democracy applies (in states, forums, communities) is less than democracy; any possible exclusion of anyone who may claim inclusion among the *demos* is less than democratic. Every attempt to make the term coherent with political practice is an unsatisfactory compromise; anyone who claims to be democratic is claiming too much; each attempt to give the term some sort of analytical or theoretical weight has to begin with an apology for inevitable failure.

For pragmatic reasons the always self-defeating minimum meaning of the term should have been abandoned at its inception, and has always been and is constantly being abandoned whenever the matter is given any thought, but has equally always stuck. Attempts are made to dissociate democracy from its minimum linguistic meaning by giving purely procedural definitions (Joseph Schumpeter's influential two definitions of democracy, for instance, were such[1]); and occasionally, alternative terms are proposed to absorb some of the pragmatic connotations of democracy without aspiring to the minimum meaning (Robert Dahl used *polyarchy* in that spirit[2]). But the success of these manoeuvres is always limited. When Norberto Bobbio observed that 'democracy is subversive'[3] (before proceeding to a distinctly moderate view of the pragmatics of democracy) he had hit upon a resonant phrase that encapsulates the inherently uncompromising, unwieldy, unforgotten, uncontainable inclusiveness of the term. The minimum linguistic meaning of the term works against all instituted and given borders.

A constant and uncomfortable awareness of the minimum linguistic meaning of democracy runs through all the conceptual positions discussed below, both as something to hold at arm's length (e.g. when defending an ostensibly democratic order) and as something to appeal to (e.g. when seeking a stronger or a pluralistic or a reconceived democratic order).

NORMATIVE CONNOTATIONS

To a significant extent, Schumpeter-like or Dahl-like attempts to take democracy beyond the minimum meaning fail because of the normative *weight* of democracy. While the minimum meaning is always inadequate for utilitarian considerations, it nevertheless always evokes an implicit and unavoidable normative value. Any potentially utilitarian realization of democracy is tacitly measured against the implicit normative weight of its minimum meaning. In possessing implicit normative connotations, the term *democracy* is by no means unique in politics; indeed political discourse appears to operate on the basis of a large number of such terms (e.g. freedom, absolutism, totalitarianism) – terms that are constitutionally not neutral. The normative weight of such political terms derives from the field of linguistic consensus and application – however rough and ready and unanalytical that might be. It is the field of everyday political discourse, where politicians use terms with rhetorical and manipulative effect, where people take up and respond to terms according to the histories associated with their popular usage, and where such terms become loosely associated with other normatively loaded discourses (religious, for instance). The normative weight of such political terminology is productively discussed by William E. Connolly:

> Concepts such as 'democracy', 'politics', and 'freedom' are bounded by normative considerations; to use these concepts in our society is to characterize arrangements and actions from a normative angle of vision. And if we were to exorcise the evaluative point from any of these concepts,

> we would be at a loss as to how to clarify or refine its boundaries when new and unforeseen situations arose. . . .
>
> If we say that a society is undemocratic or that a practice does not meet democratic standards, we are typically characterizing that practice or society critically; we are describing it from the vantage point of accepted standards of political participation, debate, and accountability.[4]

This statement is framed by Connolly's argument that the implicit normative character of terms like *democracy* renders them less amenable to descriptive definition than might be expected, and constantly leaves them open to debate. In Connolly's characterization of the normative content of *democracy* the term is understood to generally possess a positive character (democracy is good). This has not always been the case: from Plato to Mencken,[5] a large number of thinkers have assumed that democracy may generate undesirable social and political tendencies. Such allocations of a negative character to democracy are distinct from arguments where democracy is itself not given a negative characterization, but is seen as being misappropriated or used with mendacious intent (markedly in socialist critiques of bourgeois democracy, for instance). Arguments that straightforwardly saw democracy as negative are, with hindsight, easily unpacked and dispensed with for being anachronistic or leading to undesirable political outcomes. In this study I go along with Connolly's characterization, which is indubitably the dominant one in our time.

Sociolinguistic attentiveness to the normative connotations of terms like *democracy* is also useful in providing ways of assessing their contingent and pragmatic deployment. John Wilson's pragmatic analysis of political speech identifies three arguments attached to the enunciation of political terms: one, which he calls an L-pragmatic argument, focuses on how contextual meaning is encoded in the language system; two, a P-pragmatic argument, where terms and their usage are accounted on the basis of 'rules or general principles of behaviour which although generally reflected in the linguistic system, may be found beyond this'; and three, an O-pragmatic argument, 'where meaning is constructed through the orderly negotiation of talk within contexts'.[6] Insofar as the evocation of democracy in the L-pragmatic and P-pragmatic arguments goes, chains of normative equivalences are easily established given its inherently normative character. So, arguments like 'because ours is a democratic country the people are happy' or 'democracy goes hand-in-hand with freedom and respect for human rights' seem immediately plausible because normatively similar terms are drawn together. When placed in an O-pragmatic argument though, democracy invariably becomes a more ambiguous matter.

LEGISLATIVE DENOTATION

The above kind of pragmatic linguistic attentiveness to implicitly normative political terms has to be exercised with more than usual caution for the specific case of *democracy*, because it is rather different from examples like *free* or *totalitarian*. The latter are primarily normatively descriptive terms which come with *connotative* effect: a given alignment or system is regarded as being free or totalitarian (and thereby associated with other normatively equivalent terms). Democracy can be used *connotatively* (e.g. a given system or alignment is or isn't democratic, which suggests that it is or isn't open, is or isn't free, and so on), but significantly democracy can also *denote* a particular institutional arrangement (e.g. India or the US are parliamentary democracies). The conflation of connotation and denotation that constantly occurs in the deployment of the term *democracy* results often in interesting conceptual obfuscations and ambiguities.

Denotatively, democracy now commonly alludes to a political state wherein the government is elected through universal adult suffrage (is therefore representative of the majority) from a range of political parties, and which is characterized by and supports institutions whereby citizens can express opinions regarding government and different interest groups can protect their interests. This is a fairly specific realization of democracy's connotations in political practice. From a conceptual point of view, it is always understood that this realization does not exhaust democracy's normative connotations – almost all subsequent chapters here attest to hopes of evolving further or other kinds of realizations of democracy. The possibility of contemplating and trying to realize other or further models is always open; the question is how to approximate the minimum meaning and normative connotations of democracy in terms of legislative procedure given the current condition of political organization (so that other denotatively democratic models may emerge).

To clarify this point, it is worth contemplating a specific attempt at theorizing democracy with a view to examining procedural possibilities. Schumpeter's two doctrines of democracy provide a useful example here, not so much because these represent a pioneering effort (the substantive terms of the two doctrines were available in prior theorizations by, for instance, Mill, Weber or Michels[7]), as because of the paradoxical clarity and ambiguity manifest in these formulations and the influence they exercised in post-Second World War political studies.

I am referring to the distinction Schumpeter made between two doctrines of democracy in *Capitalism, Socialism and Democracy* (1943). The first he regarded as an eighteenth-century philosophical concept of democracy which is unrealistic:

> The democratic method is that institutional arrangement for aiming at political decisions which realizes the common good by making the people itself decide issues through the election of individuals who are to assemble in order to carry out its will;[8]

and the second he proposed as the more realistic and pertinent for modern polities and states:

> the democratic method is that institutional arrangement for arriving at political decisions in which individuals acquire the power to decide by means of a competitive struggle for the people's vote.[9]

It is interesting that Schumpeter's distinction attracted as much attention as it did subsequently, because it was clear to most that this was a rather hasty summative exercise in a book with other preoccupations (a celebratory critique of capitalism as an economic-historical process, and a careworn discernment of how that process logically ensures the eventual victory of socialism). John Plamenatz, for instance, doubted whether any eighteenth-century thinker adhered to Schumpeter's classical doctrine;[10] and Danilo Zolo saw in it a confused attempt to bridge two classical doctrines (the participative and the representative).[11] In a more approbatory vein, the second doctrine came to be regarded as gesturing towards future explorations of leadership and oligarchic formations in parliamentary democracies (by Ralf Dahrendorf, Raymond Aron and Robert Dahl,[12] among others). The appeal of Schumpeter's doctrines, however, went deeper than that; it lay in the consecutive presentation of both with a consistent procedural emphasis. In presenting the classical doctrine, Schumpeter probably wasn't aiming at authenticity to particular statements (such as Rousseau's,[13] for instance), but positing a more or less hypothetical precursory *democratic* procedure (with some resemblance to a number of classical ideas) so that continuity to a recognizably current *democratic* procedure becomes available. Both doctrines of democracy are based on the centrality of the elective procedure: only, in the former, election is purely for the implementation of a democratic decision (i.e. for the appointment of an executive); whereas, in the latter, election is a legitimizing measure for both decision-making and executive functions ostensibly on behalf of people (i.e. for the appointment of representative government). That the placement of procedural coherence and continuity between the two doctrines rather confuses the issue of democratic participation and democratic representation, and seems to entail two quite different constructions of *demos*, are arguments that did not particularly concern Schumpeter – but that is where the minimum meaning and normative connotations of democracy in relation to the denotative are negotiated.

Schumpeter's own recognition of these gaps is revealing. In shifting from the classical to the new doctrine he expressed some anxiety about the continued usefulness of the term *democracy*. Pondering the decoupling of the 'will of the people from its utilitarian connotations' involved in moving to the new doctrine, Schumpeter remarks that the 'will of the people' (apparently close to the minimum meaning of democracy) is an unrealistic trigger because in practice it is indeterminable.[14] In assuming a procedural emphasis and making his two doctrines consecutively linked in procedural terms, Schumpeter, in other words, was deliberately and gradually pushing democracy away from its minimum meaning and normative connotations. He wasn't dealing with *democracy* as the term is usually received, but with a separate issue, *democracy as a utilitarian matter*. To avoid confusion on this score, Schumpeter distanced his efforts clearly from the normative connotations of democracy which are apparently closer to the classical doctrine. Greater allegiance to something like the classical doctrine arises, he observes, from its perceived closeness to normative discourses – to religious belief, so that democracy becomes 'an ideal or rather an ideal scheme of things';[15] to popular conceptions of nationhood and national histories;[16] and because 'politicians appreciate a phraseology that flatters the masses and offers an excellent opportunity not only for evading responsibility but also for crushing opponents in the name of the people'.[17] It is the minimum meaning and normative idealism associated with democracy that bothers Schumpeter when he wonders whether his new doctrine of democracy should be thought of as *democracy* at all:

> It would however be better not to retain the term because this tends to obscure the fact that as soon as we have severed the will of the people from its utilitarian connotation we are building not merely a different theory of the same thing, but a theory of a completely different thing.[18]

The brief examination of Schumpeter's two doctrines conveys to some degree the ways in which the three shades of democracy – the minimum meaning, normative connotations and legislative denotation – are apt to run into, interchange with and obfuscate democracy even in conceptually rigorous practice. In less rigorous usage, the interchanging of the three shades and confusion between them is an everyday matter.

With these clarifications in mind, and the realist methodology in view, an appropriate beginning for this survey of current conceptual engagement with democracy in the international/transnational domain is with political realism itself. I mean political realism as a developed conceptual position rather than simply limited to certain methodological decisions. As might be expected from a conceptual position that usually accepts the agency of states as determinative in the international sphere, neorealists (coming back to the most influential recent 'school' of realism) have by and large accorded democracy an almost exclusively denotative understanding. Indeed, a commonplace of realist thinking in this area is that *democracy* is a denotative misnomer. States with multi-party elective systems that are usually referred to as democratic invariably limit choice to a fixed range of party policies and ideologies; are amenable to manipulation by financial and elite interests; and cede governance to bureaucracies and party formations with, for the most part, remote access to people. Thus, what passes as a democracy is actually more precisely an oligarchy – it is oligarchies that we see in operation in our world when we refer to democracies. With this specific qualification in mind, neorealists engage with the international level, especially *vis-à-vis* the anarchic (primarily conflictual) politics thereof. Some of the early works of Kenneth Waltz in this area give reasonably clear indications of the manner in which this occurs. With reference to real political events, Waltz finds that democratic states behave much as any other kind of state in international politics, and that neither the minimum meaning nor the normative associations of democracy play a significant role (though they are always expected to or are claimed to). Thus, after examining the widely prevalent conviction that democratic states are inherently peaceful, on the grounds that the direct involvement of people operates as a restraint, Waltz finds that historical evidence shows otherwise: 'faith in the uniformly peaceful proclivities of democracies has proved utopian'.[19] However, debate on the democratic peace concept continues (especially with an empiricist thrust) and is updated in Chapter 8 here. His conclusion on this question provocatively plays with normative terms to deliberately distance them from the denotative sense of democracy (seen as 'the internal structure of [certain] states'):

> Bad states lead to war. As previously said, there is a large and important sense in which this is true. The obverse of this statement, that good states mean peace in the world, is an extremely doubtful proposition. . . . The actions of states, or more accurately, of men acting for states, make up the substance of international relations. But the international political environment has much to do with the ways in which states behave. The influence to be assigned to the internal structure of states in attempting to solve the war–peace equation cannot be determined until the significance of the international environment has been reconsidered.[20]

Another turn to the neorealist take on this area is given in Waltz's follow-up study of the manner in which the domestic politics of two democracies, the American and the British, impinged upon foreign policy. Without trying to summarize the findings of this essentially empirical study (which confirmed the observation that modern democracy has an oligarchic nature), one of the briefly stated and somewhat surprising conclusions Waltz reached here conveys the thrust of his approach: that 'democratic governments of the Western type are well able to compete with authoritarian states',[21] and that authoritative and democratic rulers work with similar calculations when it comes to foreign policy. Critiques of the neorealist penchant, well demonstrated in Waltz's works, for overlooking larger-than or other-than state players in international politics, have led to more complex neorealist expositions of war and peace.[22] Most of these manage to evade the normatively loaded associations of democracy. However, in the wake of conflicts arising from the terrorist attacks in the USA on 11 September 2001, Waltz has pointed out that his perspective clearly remains as valid as ever.[23]

A politically realist approach (with more an applied realist view, and less invested in the theoretical coherences that neorealists seek) which tries to come to grips with the nuances of democracy in an increasingly interpenetrative, overlapping and therefore complex international/transnational domain is Danilo Zolo's. Zolo's consideration of democracy under late twentieth-century conditions announces its realist allegiances through a particular take on social complexity. The realist understanding of social complexity is differentiated from Luhmann's evolutionary characterization of complex social systems[24] by an insistence on 'the analysis of the *actual* level of complexity of *contemporary* political systems' (my emphases).[25] Zolo's analysis addresses the prevailing relationship between two sides of the perennial political equation, between society and government. So, on the one hand, the disposition of contemporary society is pondered, and on the other hand, the manner in which democratic states operate with regard to contemporary society is examined. The growing complexity of contemporary society is characterized by ever more variegated and autonomous specialist territorializations and simultaneously growing interdependence between these, by constant exacerbation of abstraction and depersonalization, and by increasing social mobility. For Zolo, these lead to a 'radical *dispersal of the public sphere*' (author's emphasis).[26] The result is the 'removal of the horizon of the "political city" itself as the domain of "citizenhood" '.[27] This observation has an obvious bearing on the boundary issue: increasing complexity is fragmentation of operational boundaries (into specialist autonomous territories) at the expense of the conventional political constituency, but without the emergence of other boundaries (since there is nevertheless increasing interdependence). Simplistically, boundaries within which democratic practice can be contained are simply not delineable any longer – they constantly slip away between fragmentation and interdependence. This paradox is further complicated by the observation that this situation, while apparently undermining the operations of democracy, also raises demands for democracy. At the other side of the equation, the ostensibly democratic political state finds that notions of democracy on which it is instituted (liberal individualism, representativeness and gradations of participativeness) are simply not equal to dealing with the increasing complexity outlined above. The only response that is available to such democratic states is to impose structural simplicity on the complex situation, but that inevitably leads to the devolution of democracy even in its own limited and questionable terms. Structural simplicity is imposed by constantly reducing the choices that are open to people (by strengthening prerogatives of and limiting numbers of political parties, reducing electoral choice, allowing only negative freedoms, devolving responsibility for public interest services to market-led corporations, etc.), which means that the state increasingly becomes characterized less as representative government and more as guardian – in fact, now 'the regimes that are known as democratic are more properly *differentiated and limited autocratic systems*, that is, in traditional terminology, liberal oligarchies'.[28] There is a catch-22 here: increasing social complexity manifests itself in greater and greater desire for democracy and can only be responded to by a diminution of democratic freedom and choice as these are understood now.

The logic of this realist approach seems to lead to some sort of despair; a rational bind that can only spiral towards ever-reduced possibilities of realizing democracy (i.e., there's a constantly increasing distance between the denotative and connotative aspects of democracy). But along with this logic also comes a whiff of politically realist obscurity. Zolo appears not to be able to simply stand by and accept the inevitable failure of democracy; his realist critique comes laden with the kind of moral obligation that Berki has placed within it. He seems to gesture towards prescriptive analysis, even desire prescriptive analysis, without being able to undertake it. It is a Beckettian situation, or a Marcusian situation.[29] Zolo constantly makes prescriptive gestures such as the following:

> [In] order that the recursive mechanism of democracy can function effectively . . . a far-reaching alteration of the institution of authority will be necessary and a substantial alteration of the very logic of the political code. In place of the linear simplicity of the traditional mechanisms for reducing fear, it will be necessary to substitute a nexus of interdependencies within which the need for order and security would be held constantly in balance with the opposite need for the preservation of complexity and political and economic 'freedoms'. In place of the structures of vertical power there will need to be political mechanisms of a reflexive type, capable of subordinating, through a powerful retroactive circle, both the sovereign political will to the will of the citizens (i.e. the limitation and democratic constitutional legitimizing of power) and the will of the citizens to the sovereign will (i.e., the guarantee by bureaucratic administration of security and order). Herein lies the great challenge in defence of social differentiation which the bourgeois requirement of a democratic constitutional state makes against the power of unlimited political protection, i.e. against the unlimited reduction of complexity.[30]

Several interesting strategies are layered over each other in the obscurity of such gestures. The prescriptive tone (note phrases like 'it will be necessary' or 'the great challenge') confers an air of optimism on Zolo's cogitations. However, the lack of precision therein simultaneously defers optimism – it can't yet be said what exactly substituting 'a nexus of dependencies', having 'political mechanisms of a reflexive type' or achieving a 'powerful retroactive circle' actually consist in. The need to maintain the effective functioning of the 'recursive mechanism of democracy' or 'the preservation of complexity' seems to be an impulse that comes with the normative connotations of democracy; but these connotations are immediately counterbalanced by coeval procedural qualifications (such as 'economic "freedom" ' with those eloquent quotation marks, or '*bourgeois requirement* of a democratic constitutional state' [note my emphasis]). The obscurity of these political realist gestures lies in subtle linguistic shifts and ploys. The overall effect of Zolo's argument is more or less as follows: realistically speaking there is an impermeable logic that relates contemporary state to society only in a relationship of diminishing democracy without ever having started from a position of achieved democracy at all; this realization comes with the desire to change this situation; the desire to change has to be realistic too, otherwise why bother with expressing the realization and the desire; this calls for a politically realist effort at prescriptive analysis, and such a call is effectively made and indicatively imminent . . . and it stays imminent after the argument has ended. Some may say that nothing more than despair is reached, and others that nothing less than the imminence of the realistic prescription has been indicated.

This position seems to me worth dwelling on because, in the midst of all the fissures and subtle shifts and obscurities, it is an essentially honest and complete expression of a position. It effectively explains why the issue of boundaries has always been complicated and is becoming more so. Zolo's understanding of social complexity defeats democratic government within boundaries (for him, a coherent meeting of polity and political state); increasing social complexity only diminishes the practice of democracy within boundaries. And yet, how else can democratic government be denoted (without boundaries, with many boundaries, with new boundaries, nevertheless with the same boundaries)? That question is the spur for prescriptive analysis. The question is easily posed. But, if one's eyes are firmly fixed on the intricate intermeshing and containment – what Luhmann might call the continuity of an *autopoietic* social system[31] – of contemporary society as it actually seems to, so to say, carry on, it is difficult to see an answer or way out. But social complexity also demands a way out and one has to look for a way out. This is the position. It seems to me that Zolo states it well; that he expresses a prescriptive desire without offering solutions serves to delineate the position all the more clearly.

Insofar as Zolo's later writings go, he moves on to realist engagement with particular conflict situations (the Gulf War, the Kosovo War)[32] which manifest the kind of complexity and reductiveness – with the evident but carefully disguised vested interests of so-called Western democratic states – that are theorized in *Democracy and Complexity*. These are also critiques of conceptual positions which conflate the normative and denotative aspects of democracy, and proceed on that basis to prescriptive analysis. I return to Zolo's later writings briefly in the context of cosmopolitan theorists (next chapter).

It is, I think, self-evident that what Zolo describes as social complexity, or what I understand as a problem of boundaries, is either synonymous with or encompasses familiar discussions of *pluralism* and *globalization* in political theory. If this doesn't appear to be self-evident I hope it will become so as I progress. In my discussion of influential conceptual positions apropos democracy below I trace out how ideas like pluralism and globalization essentially devolve into a preoccupation with boundaries.

In closing this chapter, I would like to note occasional attempts to invest apparently realist views of democracy with predominantly normative understandings of democracy – especially through the inspiration of Niebuhr's attempt to wed Christian theological principles with realist considerations. Thus, in an article on the realist attitudes of E. H. Carr, Winston Churchill and Reinhold Niebuhr by Robert G. Kaufman (which not insignificantly appears in a collection entitled *Roots of Realism*, drawn from the journal *Security Studies*) one finds the following statement of conviction (in many ways the enterprise of the collection as a whole and the journal it draws from):

> My main argument is that realism's salutary emphasis on the importance of power, geopolitics, man's eradicable flaws, and the constraints of anarchy needs supplementing with additional factors drawn from the idealist tradition: the necessity for transcendent moral standards by which to judge relative degrees of moral and geopolitical evil; a recognition of the pacifying effects of stable liberal democracies vis-à-vis one another; the importance of the domestic determinants of foreign policy for promoting cooperation or exacerbating international conflict.[33]

Further consideration of the kind of idealist factors named here is taken up in subsequent chapters. In an immediate way, the suggestion that there is any realist (or realistic) expectation of finding 'transcendent moral standards' to gauge 'geopolitical evil', or realist consensus about the 'pacifying effects of stable liberal democracies', seems to me to be not just untenable but invidious. This has the air of an ideologically partisan idealism disguised as well-grounded realism, or of contextually specific normative beliefs disguised as universal axioms. Insofar as the aspiration of realism is to derive from, apply to, and generalize about domains that are materially available, empirically documented, epistemologically rational, and discursively analysable the insertion of such idealistic factors into realism is hopelessly destructive.

NOTES

1 Joseph A. Schumpeter, *Capitalism, Socialism and Democracy* (London: Allen & Unwin, 1943), p. 250.
2 Robert Dahl, *Polyarchy: Participation and Opposition* (New Haven, CT: Yale University Press, 1971).
3 Norberto Bobbio, *Which Socialism? Marxism, Socialism and Democracy*, trans. Roger Griffin (Cambridge: Polity, 1987 [1st publication 1976]), p. 74.
4 William E. Connolly, *The Terms of Political Discourse*, 3rd ed. (Oxford: Blackwell, 1994/1974), p. 29.
5 Plato, *The Republic*, trans. Desmond Lee (Harmondsworth: Penguin, 1955), part 9: Bk VIII – 'Imperfect Societies'; H. L. Mencken, *Notes on Democracy* (New York: Knopf, 1926) or, with G. J. Nathan, *The American Credo* (New York: Knopf, 1920).
6 John Wilson, *Politically Speaking: The Pragmatic Analysis of Political Language* (Oxford: Blackwell, 1990), p. 4.
7 John Stuart Mill, 'Considerations on Representative Government', *On Liberty and Other Essays*, John Gray (ed.) (Oxford: Oxford University Press, 1991); Max Weber, *Economy and Society*, Guenther Roth and Claus Wittich (eds.) (Berkeley, CA: University of California Press, 1978), Vol. 1: Ch. 3 and Vol. 2: Ch. 10; Robert Michels, *Political Parties: A Sociological Study of the Oligarchic Tendencies of Modern Democracy* (New York: Dover, 1911).
8 Joseph A. Schumpeter, *Capitalism, Socialism and Democracy* (London: Allen & Unwin, 1976 [1st publication 1943]), p. 250.
9 Ibid., p. 269.
10 John Plamenatz, *Democracy and Illusion* (London: Longman, 1973), pp. 96–9.
11 Danilo Zolo, *Democracy and Complexity* (Cambridge: Polity, 1992), pp. 65–6.
12 Ralf Dahrendorf, *Class and Class Conflict in Industrial Society* (London: Routledge & Kegan Paul, 1959), esp. part 2; Raymond Aron, *Democracy and Totalitarianism*, trans. Valance Ionescu (London: Weidenfeld and Nicolson, 1968/1st French edition 1965); Robert Dahl, *Polyarchy: Participation and Opposition* (New Haven, CT: Yale University Press, 1971).
13 See Jean Jacques Rousseau, 'The Social Contract', *The Social Contract and Discourses*, trans. G. D. H. Cole (London: Dent, 1913), especially Book IV.
14 Schumpeter, *Capitalism, Socialism and Democracy*, p. 253.
15 Ibid., p. 266.
16 Ibid., p. 266.
17 Ibid., p. 268.
18 Ibid., p. 253.
19 Kenneth N. Waltz, *Man, the State and War: A Theoretical Analysis* (New York: Columbia University Press, 1954/2001), p. 102.
20 Ibid., pp. 122–3.
21 Kenneth N. Waltz, *Foreign Policy and Democratic Politics: The American and British Experience* (London: Longman, 1968), p. 308.
22 Robert O. Keohane, *After Hegemony* (Princeton, NJ: Princeton University Press, 1984); Robert Gilpin, *War and Change in World Politics* (Cambridge: Cambridge University Press, 1981).
23 Kenneth Waltz, 'The Continuity of International Politics', in Ken Booth and Tim Dunne (eds), *Worlds in Collision: Terror and the Future of the Global Order* (Basingstoke: Palgrave, 2002), pp. 348–53.
24 Detailed in Niklas Luhmann, *Social System*, trans. John Bednarz Jr. and Dirk Baecker (Stanford, CA: Stanford University Press, 1995/ 1st German edition 1984).

25 Danilo Zolo, *Democracy and Complexity: A Realist Approach*, trans. David McKie (Cambridge: Polity, 1992), p. 5.

26 Ibid., p. 114.

27 Ibid., p. 114.

28 Ibid., p. 181.

29 The literary equivalent is Samuel Beckett's inability to express along with an obligation to express (the general tenor of much of his writing, made explicit in his 'Three Dialogues With Georges Duthuit', *Proust and Three Dialogues* [London: Calder, 1965]); the closer equivalent in political theory is to Herbert Marcuse's discernment of the all-encompassing scope of advanced capitalist one-dimensionality coupled with the call for an oppositional Great Refusal, cf. *One-Dimensional Man: The Ideology of Industrial Society* (London: Sphere, 1964), p. 13.

30 Zolo, *Democracy and Complexity*, p. 61.

31 Luhmann, *Social Systems*, pp. 34–6 gives the first description of *autopoeisis*, and then *passim*.

32 Danilo Zolo, *Invoking Humanity: War, Law and Global Order*, trans. Federico and Gordon Poole (London: Continuum, 2002); Danilo Zolo, *Cosmopolis: Prospects for World Government*, trans. David McKie (Cambridge: Polity, 1996).

33 Robert G. Kaufman, 'E. H. Carr, Winston Churchill, Reinhold Niebuhr, and Us: The Case for Principled, Prudential, Democratic Realism', in Benjamin Frankel (ed.), *Roots of Realism* (London: Frank Cass, 1996), p. 315.

3 *Cosmopolitan Democracy*

Possibly the most optimistic and apparently pragmatic conceptual attempt to extend democracy to the international/transnational domain in recent years has come from theorists of cosmopolitan democracy. In general these possess both explanative analysis of globalization processes, and a prescriptive effort to direct those processes in a democratic direction. A number of political theorists (Norberto Bobbio, Richard Falk) appear to have converged on cosmopolitanism, but this area is associated primarily with the individual and collaborative (with Archibugi and McGrew) researches of David Held. In this chapter it is mainly in Held's terms that the central arguments in favour of cosmopolitan democracy are presented and briefly interrogated. From a realist perspective, Danilo Zolo engages in a sustained critique of cosmopolitan ideas. These too are brought into the examination of cosmopolitan democracy here.

The argument regarding cosmopolitan democracy as laid out by Held is taken up half way here to enable an immediate focus on the international/transnational domain – the argument as a whole draws upon ideas that are discussed in following chapters. I am not therefore attempting a linear or chronological survey of ideas here; this is more a symptomatic clarification of prevailing views of democracy in the international/transnational domain, the connections and fissures between which emerge gradually. In a more systematic vein, it is a chronological approach to Held's work which reveals important presumptions in theorizing cosmopolitan democracy. Towards the end of a textbook style historical survey of ideas of democracy, *Models of Democracy* (1987), Held offers a view of politics and a corresponding view of citizenship which underlie later cosmopolitan formulations:

> . . . politics is a phenomenon found in and between all groups, institutions (formal and informal) and societies, cutting across public and private life. It is expressed in all the activities of cooperation, negotiation and struggle over the use and distribution of resources. It is involved in all the relations, institutions and structures which are implicated in the activities of production and reproduction in the life of societies. Politics creates and conditions all aspects of our lives and it is at the core of the development of problems in society and the collective modes of their resolution. . . .

> If politics is conceived in this way, then the specification of the conditions of enactment of the principle of autonomy amounts to the qualification of the conditions for the participation of citizens in decisions about issues which are important to them (i.e. us). Thus, it is necessary to strive towards a state of affairs in which political life – democratically organized – is, in principle, a central part of all people's lives.[1]

This is one of the few passages in the book where Held departs from a referential mode (summarizing, criticizing terms used in existing and contextualized texts) to a direct proclamative one (presenting decontextualized formulations with universal effect). The passage also encapsulates, through that syntactic twist, a move from the explanative to the prescriptive. Politics is given as both *a priori* (continuously recognizable as that which underlies all processes) and *a posteriori* (continuously available as that which can be instrumentalized for change). By giving this particular turn to the concept of politics, and then proceeding to associate citizenship and the search for autonomy with it, and presenting that as democratic organization (or democratic aspiration), the latter become decontextualized and general in a similar fashion. The unfolding of all politics becomes a teleological reaching towards greater democracy. The shift from the referential to the proclamative mode (or from the explanative to the prescriptive), in other words, involves a tacit and unquestioning acceptance of the minimum meaning and normative connotations of democracy, and to some extent of the denotative aspect of the term (though there are many contending models of democracy), and represents another drive towards imbuing these with more procedural potency (reaching towards a more democratic model which brings connotative and denotative nuances closer). Such essentially syntactically performed moves from explanation to prescription lie at the core of cosmopolitan theorization; in the process, interestingly, agency is both allocated (to and for us) and dispersed (we are everyone, with the absolute stickiness of the minimum meaning contained).

Models of Democracy goes no further in its conclusion than recognizing a number of prevailing polarities and yearning for rational synthesis – a way forwards. A path is sought between the New Right, championing the inviolability of the individual, and the New Left, hoping for equalitarian and consensual collective institutions and legislation; between civil society, a potent sphere of informal associations and actions, and states/corporations, formally organized and effective; between private and public, both in the narrow application to organizations and as marking broad domains of human existence. The binary development of the argument opens out briefly to the recognition of multiple overlapping spheres of belonging which loosens the legalistic connotations of citizenship. The expectations raised by these conceptual steps coalesce into further definite explanations and prescriptions in identifying the international/transnational domain as the one where democracy needs to be taken forwards. The decision to do so is based on the recognition of increasing limitations and dispersal of state prerogatives; the decision also effectively evades slippages between legislative denotation and normative connotation that apply to what are thought of as liberal democratic states. By the late 1980s Held had elaborated on the polarities that he was trying to find his way through, and was focused on the international/transnational domain for his prescriptive efforts.[2]

The programme of cosmopolitan democracy is clarified fully by the mid-1990s, partly in terms of relevant globalization trends (the explanative background), and partly in terms of the structures through which it could be implemented (the area where prescriptions could apply). Two succinct summary quotations cover each respectively. Regarding the explanative background:

> . . . the meaning and place of democratic politics have to be rethought in relation to a series of overlapping local, regional, and global processes and structures. At least three elements of change are essential to recognize: first, the way processes of economic, legal, political, and military interconnectedness are altering the nature, scope, and capacity of the sovereign state from above, as its 'regulatory' ability is challenged and reduced in some sphere; secondly, the way local and regional groups, movements, and ethnic communities are questioning the liberal democratic state from below as a representative and accountable power system; and, thirdly, the way global interconnectedness creates chains of interlocking political decisions and outcomes among states and their citizens, reconstituting in the process the relationship between sovereignty, democracy, and territorial political community.[3]

And for the prescriptive application:

> In my view, the problem of democracy in our times is to specify how democracy can be secured in a series of interconnected power and authority centres. For democracy involves not only the implementation of a cluster of civil, political and social rights (freedom of speech, press and assembly, the right to vote in a free and fair election, a universal and free education), but also the pursuit and enactment of these rights in intergovernmental and transnational power structures. Democracy can only be fully sustained in and through the agencies and organizations which form an element of and yet cut across the territorial boundaries of the nation-state. The possibility of democracy today must, in short, be linked to an expanding framework of democratic states and agencies. I refer to such a framework as 'the cosmopolitan model of democracy', by which I mean a system of governance which arises from and is adapted to the diverse conditions and interconnections of different peoples and nations.[4]

There are several interesting features in these programmatic statements of cosmopolitan democracy. The complex consideration of contextualized and contending models of democracy through which democracy was approached in Held's research in the 1980s has become reduced to a decontextualized and general and primarily normative understanding of democracy – essentially democracy as the participative and representative protection and exercising of certain basic rights. In other words, the kind of syntactic twist through which Held had moved from the referential frame to the proclamative frame in *Models of Democracy* has reached a culmination here, whereby the proclamative has become the dominant mode and the referential the supplementary mode. Now, the concept of democracy is simply there (and has the uninterrogable weight of its minimum meaning and its salutary normative connotations), and the task is to make an all-embracing referential frame (an increasingly complex global domain) consistent with that. Also (perhaps more) interestingly, the agencies through which the prescribed ways of making consistent would or should be exercised have an implicit exclusion, while appearing not to or while appearing to be presented on behalf of all (the absolute *demos*). What the second quotation above gestures to is not a programmatic dissolving or radical restructuring of the nation-state-based structure of the international/transnational domain (it is averred that this is happening in a more or less spontaneous fashion, but this is not what cosmopolitan democracy prescribes), but to bring the agency of democratic nation-states in line with parallel and overarching agencies in that domain ('agencies and organizations which form an element of and yet cut across the territorial boundaries of the nation-state'). What is sought is an alignment between already democratic nation-states (denotatively identified) with such agencies to fulfil the normative connotations of democracy and international/transnational effect ('an expanding framework of democratic states and agencies'). This, of course, implies also the exclusion, in terms of such agency as states may still have, of states which are not denotatively recognized as democratic (e.g. communist and theocratic and autocratic states) while including their peoples in the normative aspirations of democracy. In short, this could well come to be appropriated into a programme for some sort of unilateral extension of the normative connotations of democracy in the international/transnational domain (of giving normative democracy transnational effect), by organizations and agencies that are perceivably democratic in alignment with denotatively understood democratic nation-states (as if they already embody normative connotations). This also entails dissolving principles of multilateralism (irrespective of the denotative associations of member states) in the international/transnational domain that are legislatively enshrined, for instance, in some parts of the United Nations (UN).

Held's contribution to the volume from which the latter quotation is taken, *Cosmopolitan Democracy: An Agenda for a New World Order*, goes on to briefly outline some measures towards establishing cosmopolitan democracy; notably, by bringing the UN in line with its Charter, creating regional parliaments along the lines of the European Union, and entrenching a cluster of rights at national and international levels. The larger part of the rest of that volume unsurprisingly lives up to its agenda-setting title by focusing primarily on the UN. Norberto Bobbio's 'Democracy and the International System', Richard Falk's 'The World Order between Inter-State Law and the Law of Humanity', and Daniele Archibugi's 'From the United Nations to Cosmopolitan Democracy' are included in this vein. Bobbio's recruitment to the cause of cosmopolitan democracy is an indicative and in many ways representative one, for it came from more ambiguous prior theorizations. Bobbio's earlier theorizations of democracy apparently originated in a sympathetic disenchantment with socialism and led to a reluctant championing of liberal democracy as pragmatically operative in denotatively democratic states. Bobbio had somewhat bitterly realized that there could be no automatic connection between socialism and democracy because the former is agenda-driven (seizing and then using the mechanisms of state power) and the latter implicitly subversive. According to Bobbio:

> [Democracy] is subversive in the most radical sense of the word, because, wherever it spreads, it subverts the traditional conception of power, one so traditional it has come to be considered natural, based on the assumption that power – i.e. political or economic, paternal or sacerdotal – flows downwards.[5]

Bobbio's inability to discover an automatic connection between socialism and democracy dovetailed into his essential acceptance of democracy as representative government which can only sustain a liberal politics. Though Bobbio seemed to be aware of all the difficulties with accepting the latter position (because in practice this inevitably departs from the normative connotations of democracy in worrying ways that he outlined), he seemed equally determined not to try to conceptualize any other way.[6] Bobbio thus worked with an either-or logic which allowed him only a choice between democracy-and-socialism and democracy-and-liberalism, and he went for the latter as the least bad option. It can be argued that Bobbio's either-or logic actually revealed, despite rhetorical gestures, an ultimately uncritical and predeterminedly friendly approach to liberal democracy – Antonio Negri's critique of Bobbio made this argument,[7] as did Perry Anderson's assessment that Bobbio was sympathetic to a conservative variety of political realism.[8] Bobbio's failure to theorize the relationship between socialism and democracy just before the onset of the crucial period of upheavals in the 1980s, was however linked to more hopeful reconceptualizations of socialism and democracy. The latter usually worked on the Bobbio-like assumption that there is no automatic connection between democratic and socialist theory, and any attempt to bring them together would have to be a planned bridging exercise. As Cunningham was to put it: 'The democratic socialist is confronted with a dual task: to secure socialism against capitalist opposition and to do so in a way that will develop socialism's democratic potentials.'[9] By and large, as in Bobbio, the association of socialism with the centrality of the political state meant that attempts at reconceptualizing democracy with a socialist commitment have limited democracy to the boundaries of political state control – as a monologically conceived nation-state, community, society.

In Bobbio's essay 'Democracy and the International System', included in *Cosmopolitan Democracy*, he moves to a different arena – neither the socialist nor the denotatively liberal democratic state in an either-or equation, but the UN as the key actor in international/transnational politics – in a way that can be recruited to the aspirations of the cosmopolitan agenda. Somehow leaping from the inventive characterization of democracy as subversive to a happy acceptance of the usual minimum meaning and normative connotations of democracy, he here finds that in the international domain the formation first of the League of Nations and then of the UN was in the direction of a realization of true democracy; in his words:

> A great step forward has been made . . . in terms of not only universality of the pact, but also of its democratic inspiration. This is plain in the UN's recognition of human rights, which prejudicially limits the authority born of the agreement without endowing it with unlimited power comparable with that of autocratic governments. It is also clearly visible in its creation of an institution typical of any democratic society: the Assembly in which all contracting parties are equally represented and all decisions taken by a majority vote.[10]

Here two compromises implicit in UN structures are observed: the compromise whereby universal normative democracy (in the Human Rights declaration) and denotative procedural *multilateral* democracy (in the constitution of the General Assembly) uneasily shoulder each other; and the compromise whereby the procedural multilateral democracy of the General Assembly is undercut by the undemocratic prerogatives of the UN Security Council. The details of these are elaborated briefly in Chapter 8 below. Bobbio notes these schisms to conclude that democratic inspiration has not materialized into democratic functioning in the UN yet (if this could happen the UN would rise above its international status and bring together the international and the transnational). He observes that 'the principal effect of the unfinished process of democratization of the international order is that, in the final analysis, the only way of resolving conflicts that arise in the international system is by recourse to reciprocal violence'.[11] Bobbio has been inclined to justify the role of primarily Western states on these grounds in the context of the first Gulf War and the Kosovo War, for instance.

The characterization of the UN as manifesting a 'democratic *inspiration*', and of the reasons why '*reciprocal* violence' sometimes occurs with UN sanction are noteworthy because they demonstrate effectively the superseding weight of the normative connotations of democracy in Bobbio's thinking. Since his entire argument is against the principle of multilateralism, the *democratic* inspiration must refer to the minimum meaning of and the usual decontextualized normative connotations of *democratic*. The casual manner in which 'reciprocal' is inserted before 'violence' with UN sanction is surely to make this violence consistent with the normative connotations of the UN's democratic inspiration – he doesn't closely examine whether UN sanctioned aggression has been uniformly reciprocal or not. The switching of the denotatively legislative and connotatively normative aspects of democracy which occurs here, and which Held was observed to indulge above, sets the tone for the volume of essays *Cosmopolitan Democracy* (after all, Bobbio's is the first paper in the collection). The manner in which Bobbio-like apprehensions of the UN are recruited to the agenda of cosmopolitan democracy is best exemplified in Archibugi's (co-editor with Held) paper in the collection, 'From the United Nations to Cosmopolitan Democracy'. In this the agenda is given its clearest expression: essentially, one that both suggests maintaining the centrality of states in international relations, and proposes a strengthening of the UN and a resolution of the contradictions within its current structures. For the latter, it is recommended that the UN be made the frame within which sovereign states could act as a true confederacy, and which could support an extensive experiment in getting individual states to operate together in a federal fashion. This would entail first and foremost shifting the balance of power within the UN to the General Assembly, reform of the Security Council, enabling more effective international judicial power thereby, with a view to giving 'voice to citizens in the world community in an institutional mode parallel to states'.[12] Giving voice to citizens in the world community has a salutary equivalence with the minimum meaning of democracy and its normative connotations; the structural adjustments whereby this can be achieved appear to be no more than a few practical twitches to procedures that already pertain in denotatively democratic states. By focusing on the matter of transforming the UN from an international forum to a parallel transnational government, Archibugi, like Held, evades explicit announcement of the uncomfortable matter of excluding states that are not regarded as democratic. Also by glossing very quickly over the manner in which states and inter-state relations play in the history and practice of the UN, he makes the task of adjusting the character of the UN to realize cosmopolitan democracy seem unquestionably feasible. Briefly, with Archibugi the issue rests as follows: cosmopolitan democracy would be realized by retaining the *status quo* of state boundaries (presumably of parliamentary democracies and others) as an international sphere, and adding an overlapping transnational level of universal democracy without boundaries. It is effectively consistent with Held's or Bobbio's implicit insertion of unilateral democracy against multilateralism, only it seems to achieve this in a tactful manner – with a sleight of hand, so to say.

Held's own work after this returned to further elaboration and charting out of globalization trends that appear to render a move towards cosmopolitan democracy not just necessary but imminent. He returns, in other words, to the explanative effort that goes hand in hand with the prescriptive in the build-up of cosmopolitan democracy. In the monumental *Global Transformations* therefore he sets out to examine globalization in an empiricist spirit, as:

> a process (or set of processes) which embodies a transformation in their spatial organisation of social relations and transactions – assessed in terms of their extensity, intensity, velocity and impact – generating transcontinental or interregional flows and networks of activity, interaction, and the exercise of power.[13]

This ambitious and wide-ranging project is realized in usefully detailed and connected discussions of political, military, cultural and economic (in terms of trade/markets, finance and corporate power) globalization, and the effect of globalization on the environment. A consideration of the detailed observations of this is outside the scope of this study. It persuades by a wealth of detail and analysis that there has emerged at an international/transnational level, in the latter part of the twentieth century particularly, a set of processes whereby traditional emphasis on domestic politics and state-centred arrangements cannot be sustained and has already been eroded or systematically undermined. Similar to a host of researchers and political analysts who feel uneasy about such globalization processes (such as Samir Amin, Saskia Sassen, Naomi Klein, Noam Chomsky, George Monbiot, Colin Leys and others), Held also finds that globalization processes have led to new kinds of disenfranchisements and inequities, and that conventional state-centred and unilateral and multilateral arrangements are often abused to shroud these. But, unlike those named in parenthesis, and more in common with Anthony Giddens, Ulrich Beck and other third way enthusiasts who can discern promise and progress in such developments, Held ends on an optimistic note – by returning to cosmopolitan democracy. Unlike other kinds of projects which are cognisant of globalization processes and seek to reform the international/transnational domain accordingly (with familiar binaristic ease, Held disposes them as either liberal internationalist or radical [more in allusion to radical democracy theorists, who are addressed here in Chapter 6, than the earlier left radicals] projects), promise is found again in the cosmopolitan project. It is presented as the panacea to the problems that have surfaced in this detailed examination of globalization, which may finally attain procedurally the normative connotations of democracy, or at least restore such democratic legitimacy as had been achieved within nation-state domains before globalization processes undermined them. Held sees the cosmopolitan project as attempting 'to specify the principles and institutional arrangements for making accountable sites and forms of power which presently operate beyond the scope of democratic control'.[14]

The cosmopolitan democracy project of course continues to be elaborated and extended[15] with explanative support and prescriptive zeal, but the above critical summary presents I think its main contentions. A sustained critique of these arguments, as it happens from a politically realist perspective, has been undertaken by Danilo Zolo. A particular engagement with some of Held's presumptions, already available (as observed above) in *Models of Democracy*, was presented by him in an essay published in *Prospects for Democracy*, edited by Held. In this Zolo expressed scepticism about the decontextualized and thereby generalized view of rights and citizenship to which Held attaches the normative connotations of democracy. Zolo's scepticism is not as attentive to the linguistic turns involved as I have been, but attacks exactly the same consequence – the decontextualization of ideas to enable ultimately unilaterally effective normative claims in the name of democracy. After giving a brief outline of the historical contexts and development of ideas of citizenship and rights, Zolo questions therefore Held's extended scope of citizenship:

> It is doubtful whether, from the stand point of a coherent theory of citizenship, this concept can usefully include any new category of interests which may become publicly acknowledged. In my view this normative inflation of the concept of citizenship runs the risk of diluting its historical and functional significance, of ignoring the formal and substantive differences which distinguish the various kinds of rights and, above all, of ignoring the tensions existing between them.[16]

In the essay Zolo returns instead to his own earlier perceptions of paradoxes arising with regard to democratic practice (which he regarded as essentially oligarchic anyway) due to increasing complexity. From a slightly different perspective, David Chandler has also examined the rationale underlying cosmopolitan global citizenship, to conclude that 'the moral and ethical premises of cosmopolitan democracy necessarily lead advocates of this perspective to downgrade the rights framework of democracy and political equality',[17] and that it is based, in fact, on the concept of 'sovereign inequality'.[18]

Subsequent studies of what Zolo regards as cosmopolitan thinking, particularly in his books *Cosmopolis* and *Invoking Humanity*, extend these initial doubts about its decontextualized normative basis in a systematic manner. More importantly, these doubts are themselves contextualized against ongoing conflicts in the real world which reveal and give flesh to the implicit unilateral aggressiveness noted above. These are no longer specific engagements with particular arguments of certain theorists, but critiques of widespread intellectual tendencies in which Bobbio, Habermas, Falk, Held and others appear in a symptomatic fashion. Contextualizing *Cosmopolis* against the first Gulf War, Zolo carefully unravels the manner in which cosmopolitan democratic aspirations to transform arrangements in the international/transnational domain have become aligned with a reinvented notion of just war[19] in the name of universal humanity and democracy. He also demonstrates through a historical-political analysis that the cosmopolitan democratic aspiration of creating a reinforced UN and a normatively based global judicial system is inevitably undermined by the numerous debilitating contradictions in actual UN and international legal operations, wherein state-centred power politics proves determinative under the cover of universalistic rhetoric. His conclusion, diametrically opposed to the cosmopolitan one, is that:

> Far from being reformed and empowered in the cosmopolitan direction of 'world government', existing international and economic institutions – such as, in particular, the United Nations, the World Bank and the International Monetary Fund – will instead need to be subjected to substantial functional reduction.[20]

Invoking Humanity[21] takes this critique further, this time in the context of the Kosovo War. Zolo's analysis of the NATO military intervention in 1999, without UN sanction, in the Federal Republic of Yugoslavia is worth summarizing briefly here, not because it brings new arguments with regard to cosmopolitan democracy but in view of the interest in the US–UK invasion of Iraq in Part II of this study. The latter is also, as detailed in Part II, characterized by humanitarian claims and lack of UN sanction. In *Invoking Humanity*, Zolo examines the following: the causes of NATO intervention in Yugoslavia, the conduct of that intervention, and the results of that intervention (especially in relation to the setting up of the Hague tribunal to prosecute 'crimes against humanity'). He finds that each of these are threaded together by Western European claims of serving humanitarian interests or acting on behalf of humanity, while actually serving their own hegemonic interests and blatantly subverting international legal principles and human rights. The alleged cause of NATO intervention was the 'ethnic cleansing' of Albanians by Serbian militia. Zolo looks to the history and historiography of the Balkan region to understand the brutal ethnic conflicts that have been experienced there. He observes that historians have generally tended to explain such conflicts in terms of regional cultural characteristics, and have often underplayed the historical role of imperialist intervention and occupation by Western European powers. He also explains that the singling out of Serbians as being nationalist aggressors and Albanians as being victims of 'ethnic cleansing' was reductive given the complexities of ethnicity-based politics and violence in the region. The ambiguities of the Raçak massacre (the most publicized act of Serbian 'ethnic cleansing' and in many ways the immediate cause of NATO intervention), and the manner in which findings regarding this were distorted for propagandist purposes, is pondered. Against the ostensibly humanitarian justifications of the war, Zolo poses four other plausible and politically realistic theses: that the war was engineered to establish Western control on oil corridors that pass through the Balkans; that it was manoeuvred by the US to impede the process of European integration; that it was a crucial step in the US's post-Cold War strategy of creating a new NATO-centred hegemonic federalism; or that it was brought about to establish the control of the Atlantic Alliance over the whole Eurasian region. Zolo concludes that the ostensible humanitarian concern as cause of the war is unconvincing, and appears to be designed to shroud the more politically realistic causes that may be discerned.

If the ostensibly humanitarian cause of the Kosovo War is questionable, the conduct of the war by US-led NATO forces is shown to subvert and contradict humanitarian principles in all sorts of ways. The manner in which Albanian guerrillas, often espousing far-right ideologies, were co-opted into the war effort; the manner in which possible negotiations were deliberately sealed off; the disregard for Serbian and Albanian civilian life (exemplified in the deliberate bombing of the radio station in Belgrade, and numerous 'erroneous' bombings of civilians) and cultural artefacts and monuments; the illegality of the NATO action (conducted without UN sanction) in terms of international law – all these are explored in detail to present a compendium of the unholy strategies of superpower politics at their worst. Finally, Zolo examines the dismal and inconclusive outcomes of the war for Kosovo. Most relevant here is a close examination of the Hague Tribunal's so-called investigations and bringing to justice of perpetrators of crimes against humanity in former Yugoslavia. This is shown to have been partisan, ideologically motivated and dubiously conducted in numerous ways. The policing of the Hague Tribunal's jurisdiction by NATO, one of the parties in the conflict under investigation, itself presents an obvious contradiction. The financing of this body (heavily sponsored by the US) is questioned. The dismissive attitude toward claims that not just Serbian but NATO forces may also have committed crimes against humanity is interrogated. The penchant for creating laws in response to acts to define them as criminal (and indeed other contraventions of legal rationality) is discussed.

Such observations are, of course, familiar – for instance, Noam Chomsky, to name the best-known political analyst and critic of US foreign policy, has made similar observations with regard to a wide number of contexts, including those that Zolo addresses.[22] Chomsky's work is based on the interventionist possibilities of revealing and synthesizing information, and works with (rather than against) normative assumptions. What is different about Zolo's views is that they bring the conceptual and the contextual to inform each other, to demonstrate how ideas of democracy and political actions in the name of democracy determine and affect each other in complex ways. In short, Zolo's work comes with a theoretical investment which supersedes documentation, synthesis and intervention. This brings me back to the arguments of cosmopolitan democracy outlined above. Keeping (and adding to) critiques such as Zolo's in view, several summative observations are available. One, the arguments of cosmopolitan democracy circulate around switches between the decontextualized normative connotations of democracy and the contextually specific denotative ascriptions of democracy, which owe more to an amenable environment and linguistic practice (examined in the previous chapter) than to social, historical and political analysis. Two, the aspirations of creating an effective democracy in the international/transnational domain by reforming existing institutions (such as the UN) and frameworks (such as of international law) are based more on the allocation (however qualified) of normatively effective democratic credentials to the latter than analysis of their histories, financial dependencies, relationships to particular states and alignments, roles in specific events and contexts. Three, implicit in the cosmopolitan democracy argument is the possibility of allocating to denotatively understood democratic states and other international/transnational alignments a unilaterally effective ideological weight which may work aggressively against existing multilateral principles – with worryingly inconsistent and contradictory (undemocratic) real world outcomes. Four, the appeal of the cosmopolitan argument is not so much in that it can be usefully instrumentalized by dominant vested interests (Zolo shows that it can), but in that its normative character appeals to and appears sympathetic to those who feel disenfranchised or marginalized. Five, even if the normatively based prescriptions of cosmopolitan democracy are accepted (the explanative reasons given are persuasive) it remains unclear by what means they may become enactable. Ultimately it is optimistically based on the spontaneous moral will of democratic states and democratically inspired international alignments and democratically universal civil society to enfranchise all, without analysing how this moral will can overcome the logic and interests whereby these very states and alignments and peoples have brought about (or at least allowed) the perceived disenfranchisements in the first place.

In responding to those who are critical of or sceptical of cosmopolitan democracy, Held and McGrew, and Archibugi, have briefly addressed the reservations of political realists. Held and McGrew respond by reiterating dated doubts about realist overdetermination of the agency of political states.[23] Archibugi skims over realist observations and misgivings about power politics in the international/transnational domain by stating that all those whom Zolo associates with cosmopolitan unilateralism are explicitly against 'global integration of coercive force'.[24] They tend not to address the specific context-based syntheses and analyses by realists, and prefer to reiterate normative prescriptions with increasingly visionary emphasis – gradually the prescriptions seem to tend towards spontaneous realization through inevitably unravelling globalization processes. When they do register the more substantive politically realist anxieties, cosmopolitan democrats become as anxious as their critics.[25] In the wake of post-11 September 2001 conflicts, wherein cosmopolitan democratic legitimacy appears to be claimed by the US and the UK, Archibugi has tried to clarify both what is meant by humanitarian intervention and what the cosmopolitan position is regarding this in a dissenting spirit.[26] Unsurprisingly though, his understanding of humanitarian intervention comes predictably in a string of associated and decontextualized normative terms, and his recommendation is reforming the UN apparatus in certain ways to alleviate some of the problems in what now passes as humanitarian intervention in the name of democracy. Suggestive as Archibugi's suggestions are, he fails to take into account the realistic rationale of and purposes for which the UN has come to be constituted as it is, or suggest impetuses other than ethical goodwill to impel the reform.

The coherence between the conceptual position of cosmopolitan democracy and occurrences in the real world (especially aggression in the name of democracy and human rights) that Zolo, I think reasonably, perceives has much to do with the larger conceptual field that the cosmopolitan argument draws upon and is symptomatic of. Held's argument as I have outlined it above can scarcely be regarded as being specifically at the centre of the real world. Its merits (and my reasons for focusing on it) are precisely that it synthesizes in a deliberate way a number of disparate conceptual positions which have a sort of family likeness, with a straightforward apprehension of the international/transnational domain. Zolo's critique of cosmopolitan democracy above is therefore not simply a set of critical statements directed at particular thinkers like Bobbio, Falk, Held – it is directed against, so to say, a complex conceptual territory of which many features are brought together in cosmopolitan thinking. The argument of cosmopolitan democracy outlined above is a particular, rather coherent and well-conceived, compromise between various different conceptual positions.

A range of disparate conceptual positions come to mind as tangentially related to the synthesis of cosmopolitan democracy. Some are visionary and emphasize the future role of non-governmental associations, others examine the prospects of world government, some suggest confederal arrangements, and yet others move in the opposite direction and seek to reinvigorate the nation-state. David Miller's is one such: after abandoning the market socialist project with which he began,[27] his more recent writings champion the efficacy of the nation-state as the arena within which 'deliberative democracy' (which I come to soon) can be most coherently implemented – even with global effect.[28] Benjamin Barber's visualization of 'strong democracy' asserts the normative connotations of democracy more emphatically than cosmopolitan democrats do. However, when he gets down to outlining the institutions and practices that may embody 'strong democracy' it becomes clear that what he is ultimately proposing is the unilateral expansion of specifically American democracy – amongst other measures, he recommends: 'A program of universal citizenship service [which] would enlist every *American* citizen – male and female alike – in a service corps for one or two years of either military or non-military training and service' (my emphasis).[29] Takis Fotopoulos's attempt at visualizing a new kind of transnational democratic organization inflates the notion of citizenship in a manner reminiscent of Held's ideas; Fotopoulos suggests that distinct kinds of citizenship should be made contingency-based and lead to a range of confederal boundaries that would overlap with each other.[30] Martin Albrow does something similar in his visionary analysis of the coming Global Age; citizenship, he prophesies, would gradually become a matter of belonging to consumer associations, and democracy would become a matter of protecting consumer rights.[31] Albrow's future democracy, one might say, would be confined to pervasive consumption with no discernible influence in productive arrangements.

Though widely divergent in certain respects, it seems to me that reasonably clear lines of coherence exist between these examples and the synthesis that is achieved in cosmopolitan democracy. The decontextualized and ahistorical centrality of the normative connotations of democracy, the tendency to mix up the denotative and connotative aspects of democracy, a desire to define or redefine citizenship accordingly, the unthinking or passive condoning of unilateral aggression on these grounds, awareness of the international/transnational domain as key, negotiation or adjustment of some existing international/transnational institutions and arrangements to meet normative ends, claiming to speak for the disenfranchised and the marginalized – all these are common denominators. Cutting through all of these there's the norm-drenched neuterness of virtuous liberal political discourse.

Nevertheless, even seen as such cosmopolitan democracy is not the only – and arguably not even the most influential – territory in the conceptual field. It limits itself by tacking together description-based explanative analysis and prescriptive analysis uneasily: more by linguistically fulfilled desire than by a continuous rational method. Ultimately, the norms are assumed rather than argued in a stringently rationalistic fashion. Other conceptual positions lie alongside, sometimes underlie, cosmopolitan democracy; those that approach democracy in terms of philosophical first principles, for instance (as Rawls and Habermas do); those that perform the linguistic turns more deliberately (as theorists of radical democracy do); those that have a different take on the empirical field and democracy and procedure (democratization theorists) – and each of these negotiate the boundaries within the international/transnational domain. There are coherences which extend, I believe, across almost the entire conceptual field wherein democracy is considered with regard to the international/transnational domain.

NOTES

1 David Held, *Models of Democracy* (Cambridge: Polity, 1987), p. 277. Though the meaning of the term autonomy here is reasonably self-evident, it is worth noting that Held had stated a general principle of autonomy as follows: 'individuals should be free and equal in the determination of the conditions of their own lives; that is, they should enjoy equal rights (and, accordingly, equal obligations) in the specification of the framework which generates and limits the opportunities available to them, so long as they do not deploy this framework to negate the rights of others' (p. 271).
2 David Held, *Political Theory and the Modern State* (Cambridge: Polity, 1989), especially Ch. 6, 'The Contemporary Polarization of Democratic Theory: The Case for a Third Way', and Ch. 8, 'Sovereignty, Natural Politics and the Global System'.
3 David Held and Anthony McGrew, 'Globalization and the Liberal Democratic State', in Yoshikazu Sakamoto (ed.), *Global Transformation: Challenges to the State System* (Tokyo and New York: United Nations University Press, 1994), p. 79. Similar views were elaborated in David Held, 'Democracy: From City States to a Cosmopolitan Order?', in David Held (ed.), *Prospects for Democracy: North South East West* (Cambridge: Polity, 1993), pp. 13–52.
4 David Held, 'Democracy and the New International Order', in Daniele Archibugi and David Held (eds.), *Cosmopolitan Democracy: An Agenda for a New World Order* (Cambridge: Polity, 1995), p. 106.
5 Norberto Bobbio, *Which Socialism? Marxism, Socialism and Democracy*, trans. Roger Griffin (Cambridge: Polity, 1987/1st edition 1976), p. 74.
6 Both the shortcomings of existing democracy and the conviction that liberal representative democracy as it exists is the only available option are the substance of most essays in both *Which Socialism?* and Norberto Bobbio, *The Future of Democracy*, trans. Roger Griffin (Cambridge: Polity, 1987/1st edition 1984).
7 Antonio Negri, 'Is There a Marxist Doctrine of the State?', in Bobbio, *Which Socialism?*, pp. 121–38.
8 Perry Anderson, 'The Affinities of Norberto Bobbio', *New Left Review* no. 170, July/August 1988, p. 19.
9 Frank Cunningham, *Democratic Theory and Socialism* (Cambridge: Cambridge University Press, 1987), p. 273.
10 Norberto Bobbio, 'Democracy and the International System', in Daniele Archibugi and David Held (eds.), *Cosmopolitan Democracy*, pp. 28–9.
11 Ibid., p. 33.
12 Daniele Archibugi, 'From the United Nations to Cosmopolitan Democracy', in Archibugi and Held (eds.), *Cosmopolitan Democracy*, p. 135.
13 David Held, Anthony McGrew, David Goldblatt and Jonathan Perraton, *Global Transformations: Politics, Economics and Culture* (Cambridge: Polity, 1999), p. 16.
14 Ibid., p. 449.
15 Recent books by Held are essentially more succinctly prescriptive reiterations of points made in *Cosmopolitan Democracy* and *Global Transformations*: see David Held and Anthony McGrew, *Globalization/Anti-Globalization* (Cambridge: Polity, 2002), and

David Held, *Global Covenant: The Social Democratic Consensus to the Washington Consensus* (Cambridge: Polity, 2004). In both, the arguments are reframed in response to criticisms of cosmopolitan democracy, and with an attempt to engage in debate and include apparently opposed conceptualizations.

16 Danilo Zolo, 'Democratic Citizenship in a Post-Communist Era', in Held (ed.), *Prospects for Democracy: North South East West*, pp. 258–9.

17 David Chandler, 'New Rights for Old? Cosmopolitan Citizenship and the Critique of State Sovereignty', *Political Studies* 51, 2003, pp. 340.

18 Ibid., p. 343.

19 The original conceptualization of just war is usually attributed to Augustine, primarily on the basis of remarks on war in *City of God* Book XIX, trans. Henry Bettenseon (Harmondsworth: Penguin, 1972). The various ways in which the just war idea has been reconsidered can be gauged from Jean Bethke Elshtain (ed.), *Just War Theory* (New York: New York University Press, 1992).

20 Danilo Zolo, *Cosmopolis: Prospects for World Government*, trans. David McKie (Cambridge: Polity, 1997), p. 169.

21 Danilo Zolo, *Invoking Humanity: War, Law and Global Order*, trans. Federico and Gordon Poole (London: Continuum, 2002).

22 For instance, on the Kosovo War Noam Chomsky has written the following: *The New Military Humanism: Lessons from Kosovo* (London: Pluto, 1999); *A New Generation Draws the Line: Kosovo, East Timor and the Standards of the West* (London: Verso, 2000).

23 David Held and Anthony McGrew, *Globalization/Anti-Globalization*, pp. 16–17.

24 Daniele Archibugi, 'Cosmopolitan Democracy and Its Critics', in Bruce Morrison (ed.), *Transnational Democracy in Critical and Comparative Perspective: Democracy's Range Reconsidered* (Aldershot: Ashgate, 2003): the quotation is from p. 204, about realist critics pp. 203–4.

25 As in Daniele Archibugi, 'Demos and Cosmopolis', *New Left Review* 13, Jan./Feb. 2002, pp. 24–38 – written shortly after the 11 September 2001 attacks in the USA and the consequent bombing of Afghanistan and dislodging of the Taliban regime.

26 Daniele Archibugi, 'Cosmopolitan Guidelines for Humanitarian Intervention', *Alternatives* 29: 1, Jan.–Feb. 2004, pp. 1–22.

27 David Miller, *Market, State and Community: Theoretical Foundations of Market Socialism* (Oxford: Clarendon, 1990), p. 238.

28 David Miller, *Citizenship and National Identity* (Cambridge: Polity, 2000), particularly Ch. 10.

29 Benjamin Barber, *Strong Democracy: Participatory Politics for a New Age* (Berkeley, CA: University of California Press, 1984), p. 300.

30 Takis Fotopoulos, *Toward an Inclusive Democracy: The Crisis of the Growth Economy and the Need for a New Liberatory Project* (London: Cassell, 1997); his concept of citizenship is summarized on pp. 216–17.

31 Martin Albrow, *The Global Age* (Cambridge: Polity, 1996), p. 173.

4 *Rawls and Liberal Democracy*

Concepts of cosmopolitan democracy depend largely on explanative analysis based on description of real world processes (globalization trends), and undertake consequent prescriptive analysis that embraces more or less unexamined normative connotations of democracy (but which enjoy wide consensus and apparently cohere with its minimum meaning). I observed in the introductory chapter that description of the real world is one possible way of approaching explanative analysis; another possible way has to do with presenting plausible hypothetical situations and developing concepts accordingly. Since the latter necessarily entails greater awareness of the rationale underlying conceptual construction (constant attention to what make hypothetical situations plausible), typically such analysis presents a strong logical structure. In this and the next chapters, current conceptual positions apropos democracy are taken up which employ self-aware philosophical rationality. These approach explanative and prescriptive analysis of democracy in terms of philosophically rational first principles.

The widely accepted normative connotations of democracy are central to the business of identifying amenable first principles. The normative connotations are not written in an obvious manner into the minimum linguistic definition, but they are embedded in and emerge from the linguistic use of the term *democracy* in specific historically and culturally determined contexts. Following the cue from William E. Connolly, I observed that in our time – and indeed for about a century or so – there has been almost universal consent for a positive characterization of *democracy* (as in, democracy is good). Where conceptualizations of democracy begin with first principles, these first principles are usually also normative in ways that cohere with the positive normative characterization of democracy, and are chosen to be amenable to the conceptual realization of a plausible democratic society as the good or ideal society. This means that the identification of first principles to conceptualize democracy is usually the selection, rigorous definition and extension of a set of similarly characterizable normative terms, which are then seen to be mutually dependent and enhanced. In other words, an equivalence of coherent normative terms is used to enunciate first principles, and it is assumed that normative equivalence can give rise to substantive interrelationships between these terms, and ultimately lead to the fleshing out of an enhanced (in denotative terms) democratic system. These equivalent normatively loaded terms may be put into first principles such as these: 'a democratic society is one where all members are *free*', 'a democratic society is *not coercive*'; 'a democratic society is one where members *govern themselves*'; 'a democratic society is one where all members are *equal*'; 'a democratic society is *inclusive* or is one that accommodates *pluralism*'. The italicized terms – freedom, coercion, self-government, equality, inclusiveness, pluralism – are obviously terms that become complicated when rigorously examined (arguably unconditional freedom is undesirable, some inequalities are natural, there are rational limits to inclusiveness, and so on). Political theory has largely been and continues to be an ongoing and inconclusive debate about qualifying these terms. Equally obviously, these terms come, increasingly with almost universal consent, with an immediately recognized positive normative character – like democracy. To begin conceptualizing democracy by creating a chain of equivalence of normatively like terms, to pose these as first principles, and then proceed to work out the complications and interdependencies that arise and resolve them into a coherent system, appears to be a promising endeavour. This is what philosophers of 'liberal democracy' or 'deliberative democracy' do. I address these two positions in this and the next chapter, particularly insofar as they are relevant to the domain of international/transnational politics.

The insertion of *pluralism* or *inclusiveness* amongst those associated normative terms is worth pausing on; that is where the complexities of the boundary issue are posed in such conceptual positions. It is now the case that the condition of pluralism or inclusiveness is not merely a gesture towards accommodating divergent ideological positions (say, through a multi-party structure or through the institutionalization of discursive forums) but also towards encouraging the harmonious coexistence (some prefer the term 'toleration') of diverse cultural and ethnic and other identity-defined groups. Though the experience of the Jews and the Romany in Europe before and during the Second World War had sensitized political discourse to the implications of ethnic and cultural diversity, inclusiveness in the current encompassing sense has been till recently a piecemeal and particularistic idea (considered mainly in relation to specific identity-based claims in specific legislative and material terms). The generalization of *pluralism* to encapsulate both divergent ideological positions and the presence of multiple ethnic and cultural perspectives was still an unusual move when de Certeau, in *La culture au pluriel* (1974), included the following response to an interviewer's question (contextualized in terms of Breton and Basque separatist claims), 'how can a real, effective political organization be drawn from a cultural demonstration?':

> I believe it can be done only by getting rid of the idea of a cultural enclave, the idea that the problem involves Bretons and Bretons alone. If Basques and Bretons have been unable to win autonomy, it is because of the global

> organization of the society in which they live. In this sense, the problem concerns all French citizens; at stake is the impossibility imposed on each and every person to live in a society that admits a plurality of groups.[1]

Impressionistic and confused as this response was, it did fuse the ideological consideration of the 'global organization of society' with the universal import of admitting a 'plurality of groups' – the latter with cultural reference – in what was then a prescient fashion. The impetus for this generalization of pluralism then, as now,[2] was politically realist: dissent of internally marginalized cultural groups, civil liberties bids by racially or sexually defined underprivileged groups, the emergence of greater degrees of ethnic diversity due to large-scale migrations, and so on. The normative weight that the generalized term *pluralism*, or the idea of *inclusiveness*, has since acquired is a response to politically realist apprehension of the world – but the normative weight also allows it to become essentialized as a given condition, to be thrown in within that chain of equivalences in conceptualizing democracy, to be made a first principle itself. But, and this I follow up below, just as it has acquired an implicit normative weight, it has also retained a certain politically realist resonance which makes it particularly unwieldy. Pluralism inserts into such conceptual efforts from first principles self-defeating problems, usually in the shape of negotiations of boundary issues.

One of the most persistent conceptual developments of a liberal democratic system from first principles is undoubtedly John Rawls's, so much so that scarcely any liberal political argument can now be presented without some acknowledgement of his authority (the elaborations of democratic liberalism by Thomas Nagel, Amy Guttmann and others[3] are to significant degrees elaborations of Rawls's efforts). In discussing conceptualization of 'liberal democracy' from first principles therefore, it seems appropriate to focus on Rawls's efforts. I do not need to rehearse the manner in which Rawls establishes his first principles – they are essentially in line with the logic of associating norms and establishing a sequence of normative equivalences outlined above. In this instance the process is pushed forwards by a singular moral impetus, the concept of 'justice as fairness' (again, both ends of that come with terms that are already assumed to be of equivalent normative weight). It is worth noting, however, the methodological ploy that Rawls self-consciously employs. For Rawls, the sequence of normative equivalences is established by imagining an original contract. The status of the original contract is presented as follows:

> One should not be misled . . . by the somewhat unusual conditions which characterize the original position. The idea here is simply to make vivid to ourselves the restrictions that it seems reasonable to impose on arguments for principles of justice, and therefore on these principles themselves. . . .

> There is, however, another side to justifying a particular description of the original position. This is to see if the principles which would be chosen match our considered convictions of justice or extend them in an acceptable way. We can note whether applying these principles would lead us to make the same judgments about the basic structure of society which we now make intuitively and in which we have the greatest confidence; or whether, in cases where our present judgments are in doubt and given with hesitation, these principles offer a resolution which we can affirm on reflection.[4]

It is clear that the status of this methodological ploy is *not* based on an apprehension of political reality, but on the limits of the rationally conceptualizable, i.e. within the area of the ideal that is realizable *by* rational thought. This distinction is made clear later in *A Theory of Justice*, where Rawls speculates on an alternative approach which 'describes a certain kind of social order, or the aspect of the basic structure that is actually realized'[5] (though that immediately dissolves into an equally idealistic Plato or Hegel inspired notion of the 'private society'). The ideal area's relationship to a political reality, let's say the world Rawls lived in, is *only* insofar as it coheres with certain intuitive values that prevail therein (precisely what I meant by appealing to given normatively weighted terms as first principles). There is the obvious circularity involved here of trying to conceptually realize a 'good society' by simply carefully ordering and manipulating terms that are presumed to be good anyway: Rawls's argument could be seen as a careful affirmation of the goodness of that which is already given as good.

However, the circularity was no impediment to the usefulness of Rawls's ideas because of the way they impinged upon contending political theory in his time (within, let's say, the real world wherein conceptualization has material effects). What made Rawls attractive to many and aroused the hostility of some was the argument for democratic equality based on a difference principle, which allowed him to champion compensatory justice. This went against the grain of those libertarian or neoliberal thinkers whose assertion of the primacy of the individual in constitutional democracy led to the conviction that compensatory ideas were untenable, and who therefore preferred the 'invisible hand' of natural justice in uncontrolled markets. But this usefulness of Rawls's work in a sphere of politically real debates is, so to say, outside that work; Rawls's rationally conceptualized ideal system may have an ethical bearing on actually realized systems but is not derivable from or returnable to them.

To some extent approbation of Rawls's work came because, within his idealized 'well-ordered society', he was able to argue plausibly for positions that were close to the heart of the politically realist liberal-left. Thus the extension of the deliberative rationale of the original contract methodology, the apparent clarification of 'toleration' and 'toleration of the intolerant', the apparent clarification of just institutional structures, the apparent ability to accommodate a great deal of ideological difference and mediate between them all seemed to be salutary examples to follow with politically realist concerns in mind – very real and material concerns, like the increasing sensitivity to the evidence of pluralitic ideological and social constituencies. Ironically though, the possibility that these desirable (for some political realists) positions are only rationally maintainable within the constraints of Rawls's 'well-ordered society', and become a great deal hazier and contestable and perhaps even undesirable when juxtaposed on politically real domains, poses a constant problem. This is precisely the kind of contradiction that Mouffe gestures towards when she maintains that 'Rawls's "well-ordered society" rests on the elimination of the very idea of the political' by imposing conditions that actually remove pluralism as it is manifested and understood in our world.[6] The contradictions that Rawls's conceptual position gradually falls into, with increasingly worrying and irrational conservatism, are worth teasing out in detail – best done by paying close attention to his negotiation with the boundary issue.

When *A Theory of Justice* was published in 1972 the problem of boundaries was still a relatively uncomplicated matter. In trying to draw a just position for accommodating civil disobedience by minorities in his 'well-ordered society' (Rawls favours the rule of majority consensus in the institutional functioning thereof), Rawls clarifies that: 'For simplicity I shall limit the discussion to domestic institutions and so to injustices internal to a given society.'[7] From this limited perspective the onus of responding responsibly to injustice towards minorities is placed consistently on the minorities themselves:

> What seems called for is a political understanding among the minorities suffering from injustice. They can meet their duty to democratic institutions by coordinating their actions so that while each has an opportunity to exercise its right, the limits on the degree of civil disobedience are not exceeded.[8]

This seems reasonable given that with the conditions of a good and just order in place, it is unlikely that any perceived injustice to a minority could be regarded as a particularly heinous one or one that would be institutionally favoured. But Rawls did clearly feel some unease with this, and in fact further discussion of this was postponed by closing off the boundaries of the 'well-ordered society' for the moment, and leaving the consideration of multiple boundaries for later consideration:

> Now I assume that the boundaries of these schemes are given by the notion of a self-contained national community. This supposition is not relaxed until the derivation of the principles of justice for the law of

> nations, but wider problems of international law I shall not further discuss.[9]

This seemed plausible enough at the time, and given the ambition and scope of *A Theory of Justice* postponement was practical. Rawls's further investigations, which appeared as *Political Liberalism* in 1993, reveal that instead of 'relaxing' the supposition of a 'self-contained national society' as the 'well-ordered society' he had hardened it. Here he doesn't merely loosely assume that such a society is self-contained, he also assumes that it is 'closed', defined as follows:

> I assume that the basic structure is that of a closed society: that is, we are to regard it as self-contained and as having no relation with other societies. Its members enter it only by birth and leave it only by death. This allows us to speak of them as born into a society where they will lead a complete life. That a society is closed is a considerable abstraction, justified only because it enables us to focus on certain main questions free from distracting details. At some point a political conception of justice must address the just relations between peoples, as I shall say.[10]

A certain number of qualifications are given here: this is offered as a *basic* unit which can then presumably be complicated; this allows an appropriate focus on the main questions about justice in a 'well-ordered society'; this is temporary because there's another postponement – there's still the law of peoples forthcoming. At first glance this 'well-ordered society' might appear to be so conveniently wrapped up in self-containment and closure that the only precedent appears to be some sort of Fascist fantasy of *volk* bound to the land, defined collectively as a nation. But this would be inaccurate, because it is importantly and self-consciously presented as a convenient, abstract, idealized conceptual position *in response to* the appearance of pluralism, in the contemporary sense and with all normative weight in place, into political discourse on democracy. This mode of well-ordering society, as Rawls explains, allows him to take into account the nuances of reasonable *pluralism* as Joshua Cohen had discussed it (there's a useful reference to Cohen,[11] whose work I touch upon soon) as a manageable matter. One of the reasons for getting pluralism (albeit moderated by reasonableness and comprehensiveness) into the 'well-ordered society' in this fashion is, oddly enough, a politically realistic recognition:

> . . . the diversity of reasonable comprehensive religious, philosophical, and moral doctrines found in modern democratic societies is not a mere historical condition that may soon pass away; it is a permanent feature of the public culture of democracy. Under the political and social conditions secured by the basic rights and liberties of free institutions, a diversity of

> conflicting and irreconcilable – and what is more, reasonable – comprehensive doctrines will come about and persist if such diversity does not already obtain.[12]

This is probably the first point where Rawls seems to inadvertently let slip that actually he thinks of his abstract, idealized, basic 'well-ordered society' as roughly the same as those politically real, complex, ostensibly democratic, modern societies out there. Pluralism has to be inserted in the former as if it is the same as pluralism in the latter, Rawls says. But these pluralisms in these unrelated contexts cannot be the same, and the attempt to pose them as somehow coextensive is deeply disquieting. In *politically realist terms* the 'well-ordered society' is no more than a proto-Fascist myth, though as a conceptual idealization with good intentions it could be allowed to pass as a temporary convenience. The faint air of regret with which Rawls says that pluralism in modern democracies is 'not a mere historical condition that may soon pass away'[13] immediately acquires a different ring. Has there ever been a historical condition which had any resemblance to the self-contained and closed 'well-ordered society' without the inconvenience of pluralism? Or, for that matter, even with the inconvenience of pluralism? Thereafter gradually, and still with the terminology which endeared him to the liberal-left as a champion of compensatory and distributive justice, which provided the ammunition to argue against neoliberal or libertarian attempts to conceptually destroy social welfare and the public sphere, Rawls conducts an interesting attempt to address some of the recognizable political rhetoric of the American right in his conceptual efforts. This occurs remarkably in his reformulation of the 'clear and present danger rule' with regard to the restriction of political speech, so that it can only be invoked under very special circumstances. He analyses this with reference to real legal precedents in America where socialists were incarcerated for expressing unpopular political views, which he castigates; but he does this with the greatest confidence that: 'Never in our history has there been a time when free political speech, and in particular subversive advocacy, could be restricted or suppressed'.[14] The limited scope that he does leave for the 'free and present danger rule' is nevertheless suggestive given that this was written in 1982, at a time when that phrase had a particular resonance in US foreign policy (which he doesn't mention, naturally given the self-imposed blinkers of the closed 'well-ordered society'). By this time the confusion between the admittedly idealized, basic, highly abstract 'well-ordered society' and the real politics – actually *realpolitik* – of US democracy is presented without much fuss. And yet, even in the midst of these moves, Rawls came up with conceptual formulations that attracted the liberal-left. His proposed method for resolving pluralism within the 'well-ordered society', by negotiating 'overlapping consensus' (this he came up with in 1987) between advocates of rational and comprehensive but different ideologies, religions, cultures, has been given serious treatment by Habermas (I discuss this below), for instance.

Rawls's promised essay on 'The Law of Peoples' appeared in its finalized form in 1999. Here two noteworthy further moves with regard to the boundary issue are made:

1. Boundaries are hardened further, only in this instance not so much by the definition of closure in 'well-ordered societies', but by holding three differently characterized and equally idealized, basic and abstract constructions of society (one of which is identical to the 'well-ordered society') as clear and immiscible and independent formations in a strict moral hierarchy. At the top there are 'well-ordered people' living in 'liberal democracies', somewhere in the middle are 'decent hierarchical people' living under 'hierarchical consultative regimes', and at the bottom are indecently oppressed 'hierarchical people' living under 'totalitarian non-consultative hierarchical regimes' which have a tendency to become 'outlaw regimes'. Each of these is given a clear moral constitution in terms of the original contract of 'justice by fairness'. Each is implicitly closed; but the self-contained 'well-ordered liberal democracy' tries to extend to 'the decent hierarchical society' and generally tolerates the 'non-consultative hierarchical regime'. That is, until the latter, as an 'outlaw regime' (by nature evil), threatens either of the above, in which case 'just war' (much in the Christian terms given by St Augustine, but carefully removing the Christian allegiance to God) can be legitimately waged. Incidentally, the characterization of the 'decent hierarchical society' is insinuatingly presented by imagining an 'idealized Islamic people named "Kazanistan" '.[15] Rawls is confident that these three closed societies cover all the variations that can possibly obtain, and that the law of peoples that he accordingly lays down is 'universal in reach';[16] 'not ethnocentric';[17] and realizable in or at last reconcilable with 'our social world'.[18]
2. The obfuscation between the idealized and the real political is continued with problematic and contradictory effect, not by complicating the basic and abstract models but by either simply taking these as analogous to real societies or by subtle shifts in terminology. The conclusions which he reaches by reflecting on these idealized, basic, abstract – and, it is clear by now, polarized – peoples are constantly justified with reference to historical experience. Thus, the reductionism that is implicit in Rawls's conceptual idealized framework becomes a reductive interpretation of real history and politics itself. For instance, the contention that 'well-ordered democracies' as he understands them cannot, as a matter of principle, wage war against each other is seen to be borne out by historical experience: 'Though liberal democratic societies have often engaged in war against nondemocratic states, since 1800 firmly established liberal societies have not fought one another,'[19] he says, and dwells on it.[20] The

excessive normative inference made from this apparently historically informed observation is best questioned by registering that empirically led debate on this point is far from over.[21] He comments on the conduct of the Second World War, condemns the evil of Hitler's Nazism, excuses the British bombing of German cities and apologizes for American fire-bombing of Japanese cities as a failure of statesmen, cites figures on the economies of 'burdened states', and so on. Charting out the numerous historical inaccuracies and simplifications is not my thing here; noting that these are used mendaciously to promote the obfuscation of the idealized with the real is. It is analogous to Hegel's or Spengler's attempts at fleshing out a teleological universal history[22] to 'prove' their philosophy.

At any rate, it seems to me reasonably obvious that this liberal conceptualization of democracy in the international/transnational domain is so fraught with contradictions and failures that it is hardly worth dwelling on in itself. Its influence is however of some interest – both in the cosmopolitan democracy that I have discussed in the previous chapter, and in the deliberative democracy that I come to in the next. However, I shouldn't leave this reading of Rawls without noting that his work provides the closest philosophical underpinning of what has emerged as the dominant US – and essentially right-wing – political rhetoric from Ronald Reagan to George W. Bush in international politics. Counter-intuitively, it is more Rawls who presents this, than neoliberals like Nozick or neoconservatives like Fukuyama. As such, it is of particular significance to this study. I do not explore neoliberal and neoconservative views of individualist democracy because I have discussed this elsewhere,[23] and besides these have been critiqued with great perspicacity by others.[24]

NOTES

1 Michel de Certeau, *Culture in the Plural*, trans. Tom Conley (Minneapolis, MN: University of Minnesota Press, 1997), pp. 71–2.
2 On the implications of this generalization, with something of de Certeau's apprehension in it, see Charles Taylor, *Multiculturalism and 'The Politics of Recognition'* (Princeton, NJ: Princeton University Press, 1992).
3 Thomas Nagel, *Equality and Partiality* (New York: Oxford University Press, 1991); Amy Gutmann, *Liberal Equality* (Cambridge: Cambridge University Press, 1980). In her later writings Gutmann has adopted the terminology of 'deliberative democracy' – but still with some of the ethical prescriptive edge of Rawls – as in *Identity in Democracy* (Princeton, NJ: Princeton University Press, 2003) and, with Dennis Thompson, *Democracy and Disagreement* (Cambridge, MA: Harvard University Press, 1996).
4 John Rawls, *A Theory of Justice* (Oxford: Oxford University Press, 1971), pp. 18–19.
5 Ibid., p. 521.
6 Chantal Mouffe, 'Rawls: Political Philosophy Without Politics', in *The Return of the Political* (London: Verso, 1993), p. 51.

7 Rawls, *A Theory of Justice*, p. 371.
8 Ibid., p. 375.
9 Ibid., p. 457.
10 John Rawls, *Political Liberalism* (New York: Columbia University Press, 1993), p. 12.
11 Ibid., p. 36 – the reference is to Joshua Cohen, 'Moral Pluralism and Political Consensus', in David Copp and John Hampton (eds.), *The Idea of Democracy* (Cambridge: Cambridge University Press, 1993).
12 Ibid., p. 36.
13 This regret is echoed soon afterwards, this time with a clear sense of the difference between well-ordered-ness and political reality: 'The fact of reasonable pluralism is not an unfortunate condition of human life, as we might say of pluralism as such, allowing for doctrines that are not only irrational but mad and aggressive.' Ibid, p. 144.
14 Ibid., p. 355.
15 John Rawls, *The Law of Peoples with 'The Idea of Public Reason Revisited'* (Cambridge, MA: Harvard University Press, 1999), p. 75.
16 Ibid., pp. 85–8.
17 Ibid., pp. 121–3.
18 Ibid., pp. 124–8.
19 Ibid., p. 51.
20 Ibid., pp. 51–4.
21 Whether democratic peace concepts stand up to empirical evidence continues to be debated, usually through the employment of methodologically aware comparative studies. Some of these studies of democracy and war are taken up briefly in Chapter 8 here. As observed there, empirically based arguments undermining the democratic peace idea are substantially stronger.
22 The closest analogue, to my mind, is to G. W. F. Hegel's lectures on *The Philosophy of History*, trans. J. Sibree (New York: Dover, 1953), which see all humanity as going through a historical process that converges on the highest point of enlightenment exemplified in the Germany of his time. Oswald Spengler, *The Decline of the West*, trans. C. F. Atkinson (London: Allen & Unwin, 1926), is an oft-cited volume in a similar but less optimistic mould.
23 Suman Gupta, *Corporate Capitalism and Political Philosophy*, part 3.
24 E.g., G. A. Cohen, *Self-Ownership, Freedom and Equality* (Cambridge: Cambridge University Press, 1995); Alan Haworth, *Anti-Libertarianism: Markets, Philosophy and Myth* (London: Routledge, 1994).

5 *Habermas and Deliberative Democracy*

Habermas prefaces his critical reading of Rawls's liberal political system with these words: 'Because I admire this project, share its intentions, and regard its essential results as correct, the dissent I express here will remain within the bounds of a family quarrel.'[1] Habermas's critique of Rawls is more extensive, detailed and nuanced than the single-issue (boundaries) discussion in the previous chapter. It is also relatively mild; this generous acknowledgement is not merely a pleasantry. Much of the terminological composition of deliberative democracy, in which Habermas is undoubtedly the central (but far from sole) figure, owes something to Rawls. However, the differences are significant. Where Rawls uses equivalence of normative terms to present first principles from an imagined original position, Habermas's first principles derive from ideal communication situations. Rawls conceptualizes in terms of political models from simple to complex (I argued that he never quite attains to complex); Habermas extends his thinking primarily in relation to contending conceptualizations (like Rawls's) and possible applications to political reality (he comes to political realism quickly, but doesn't start from it). The insertion of political reality in Rawls's thinking is usually naïve, reductive, contradictory and retrospective; the appeal to political reality in Habermas's system is complex, contingent and responsive. Rawls moulds fragments of history to suit his purpose; Habermas is more sensitive to uses and misuses of history,[2] and generally cautious of them. They take quite different ideological directions. I should note that this brief comparison between Rawls and Habermas on methodological grounds is distinct from, but not unrelated to, the usual mode of distinguishing their positions. Both are usually regarded as engaged in the enterprise of extending and clarifying Kant's 'moral categorical imperative' (that laws are valid only insofar as there is consent about them among free and equal moral individuals), but with different emphases – Rawls by using conceptual models and focusing on procedure, Habermas by emphasizing the importance of discourse ethics. Kenneth Baynes has discussed this distinction, and the roots of both in Kant, in a useful fashion.[3]

On the whole, outlining the deliberative democracy position is a more demanding affair than outlining Rawls's liberal democracy, even with a predetermined focus on the boundary issue. Each conceptual step of deliberative democracy develops in terms of references to contending conceptual positions and immediate politically realistic apprehensions. Since taking account of all these is an unrealistic demand of a survey, I fall back on the somewhat simplistic and reductive presentation of the position in, so to say, quick strokes. This is still threaded around the boundary issue, and is detailed enough to reveal the problems that dog every conceptual step here too.

Rootedness in communicative theory and practice serves deliberative democracy well in that that is where the normative connotations of democracy and equivalent normative terms are located. The idea that it is in idealized communicative practice itself that fulfilment of democracy as an encompassing participative phenomenon – a *deep* fulfilment of democracy – is possible naturally sounds plausible. It may be expected that the processes in which the normative content of the term is revealed, are also the processes through which a practical elaboration of the term, with political intent and in close relation to that normative content, can be conducted. For Habermas, the notion of ideal communicative practice, whereby the normative connotations of democracy may become meaningful, is derivable from everyday communicative practice. Idealization involves directing communication as it is currently constituted more emphatically towards a facet of itself – rationality. In other words, the ideal communicative situation is one in which communication is rational or in which rational deliberation is possible. A great deal of Habermas's earlier work[4] is devoted to understanding what rational communication is, with particular attention to communication in the political sphere. This falls into two enterprises: that which deals with the constitutive *process* and *conduct* of rational communication (the unfolding of communicative action), and that which deals with the *environment* within which rational communication may occur (this is where the idea of the public sphere is located). Insofar as both devolve on deliberative democracy, these lead correspondingly: (a) to the identification of the conditions of rational communication or deliberation as first principles for democratic participation (not dissimilar to the first principles that are presented by Rawls from an original contract), and (b) to the consideration of the field with regard to which democracy can be conceptualized and from which democracy can emerge (i.e. the characterization of civil society and the institutional components of a constitutional democracy).

The identification of the conditions of rational communication or deliberation (as first principles for deep democracy) occupies many pages of scholarship and synthesis in Habermas, but is thereafter often reduced to straightforward prescriptions in Rawls's style. These prescriptions are: one, that such deliberation should be open as to participation and fully informed; two, that it would be free, in that no constraints would be imposed on participants (obviously apart from those that maintain this freedom), and in permitting all positions to be debated; three, all participants would be of equal status and have the same privileges in introducing, interjecting and interrogating positions in debate.[5] To these further conditions are sometimes adduced, such as willingness to arrive at consensus. When given a determinedly prescriptive turn, especially as in Joshua Cohen's essays on the subject, the distinction from Rawls's initial position is usually blurred.[6]

However, Habermas's conviction that the ideal conditions of rational communication can be derived or inferred from ordinary communication enables another mode of crystallizing rational communication. In this, the ideal conditions are not outlined as *prescriptions* to realize suitable deliberation, but as *means* to maximize benefits in any deliberative context.[7] Since rational communication is derivable from and returnable to ordinary communication, reference to real world debates is always useful. Insofar as rational deliberation is conducted for political purposes – to conceptualize and enable democracy – appeals to political reality to measure the efficacy and potential of rational political deliberation are a natural recourse. In different ways this is attempted in a sceptical fashion by Susan Stokes and Adam Przeworski in their examinations of real communication practices in politics – deliberative practices that occur in denotatively understood democracies. Stokes's studies of advocacy and influence in policy-making processes in democratic settings, and Przeworski's examinations of the costs of deliberation and election processes,[8] introduce debilitating discontinuities between ideal rational communication and real communication practices in so-called democracies. These discontinuities largely arise because the democracy that is conceptualized in ideal communicative situations is replete with normative connotations, whereas that which is examined in real communicative practice is denotatively given. More optimistic realist approaches to democracy based on rational communication attempt to *institute* the ideal conditions for such communication in an empirically examinable fashion, so as to observe their viability. In this mould are the reports of McCoy and Scully or David Ryfe,[9] wherein the results of setting up deliberative democratic constituencies and processes in specific organizations and forums are given. These naturally suffer from two limitations: they are necessarily with regard to simple constituencies and particular issues that have only a remote connection to the enormously complex and extensive field that the theorists of deliberative democracy address; and their prescriptive mode of instituting (however provisionally) such empirically examinable situations itself belies the deliberative process.

To a significant extent, the slippages between deliberative democratic conceptualization and communicative practices in existing democracies discerned by Przeworski, Stokes and others – and the implicit problems of trying to examine deliberative democracy through experimental empirical methods along the lines of McCoy and Scully or Ryfe – arise from boundary considerations. The harmonies and promises that are observed in the latter are unconvincing primarily because the self-imposed boundaries of observation and inference are too narrow, too rigidly formulated, to be politically relevant. The distortions of ideal rational deliberation that the former describe with reference to existing democratic contexts are obviously limited by that set of boundaries, essentially those of the liberal and denotatively democratic nation-state[10] (from a realist perspective, essentially oligarchies). In contemporary political practice distortions in real deliberation appear all the more formidable because they extend beyond state boundaries; as cosmopolitan democrats repeatedly observe, the reality of globalization and transnational/international exchanges, flows and balances are both outside and inside domestic domains.

Habermas and other theorists of deliberative democracy are, of course, fully aware of this. Habermas has written extensively both about the importance of the nation-state as the arena of democracy in practice, and of the particularly urgent need to rethink democracy because of the gradual dilution of nation-state solidarities by globalizing forces. For Habermas, the idea of democratic practice and the conception of nation-state have always gone together, and involved alignment 'according to the principles of an association of self-governing free and equal citizens', with: (i) a legal system that is individualized and shields private property from the state; (ii) territorially defined membership; (iii) cultural integration – through descent, language, history, etc. – which can be used for political mobilization; (iv) a democratic mode for the legitimation of political authority.[11] These conjoin democratic political processes with the everyday experiences and actions of citizens, or the *lifeworld* of the nation-state. Globalization, which for Habermas consists in the 'increasing scope of commercial, communicative, and exchange relations beyond national boundaries', affects the security of the rule of law within the administrative state, dilutes the sovereignty of the territorial state, reduces collective cultural solidarities and encourages the growth of cross-boundary networks, and undermines such democratic legitimacy as the denotatively understood liberal democratic nation-state currently has.[12] The task of rethinking democracy is therefore significantly a matter of politically realist responsiveness, and consists in:

> the transnational task of bringing global economic networks under political control, as an alternative to futile adaptations to the imperatives of locational competition. This project, of course, has to remain true to the subtle dynamics of the opening, and the renewed closure, of socially integrated lifeworlds. Moreover, it is a project that nation-states, paradoxically, can pursue from within their current scope of possibilities, but which they could realize only beyond the current limits.[13]

This emergent future is presented as a 'postnational constellation'.

There is therefore in Habermas's deliberative democracy a dual conceptual impulse, the two strands of which are given in a consecutive fashion. To begin with there is the impulse deriving from the first principle possibilities of ideal rational communication, and these later merge with the realist impulse of responding to globalization and the dilution of nation-state boundaries. There is a false note in linking the two impulses in this consecutive fashion that is little remarked: the first impulse, based on rational communication possibilities, flows from the understanding that these possibilities have not been realized and true democracy (normative connotations intact) is in the prospect of this conceptualization; the second impulse flows from the understanding that democracy was sufficiently realized when nation-state solidarities were strong (that denotative uses of democracy were apt), but this is regrettably not the case any longer and impels conceptualization. Habermas approaches democracy both as if it has never really been, and as if it has really been but is in danger of passing. There is no reconciling this contradiction in Habermas's approach; he simply wants it both ways. In deliberative democracy itself the two impulses however merge beautifully. Deliberative democracy is both drawn from first principles coeval with ideal rational communication which allow for a realization of truly participative politics, and is responsive to a postnational constellation or a transnational political order.

There is another somewhat problematic point worth making here. Habermas's response to the challenge to nation-state solidarities and the increasing porousness of their boundaries is not to do away with boundaries or reconceive different kinds of boundaries. His response is simply to expand the boundaries in much the same terms. Note how the words *opening* and *closure* are deployed in his description of the project of the postnational constellation, and the nature of the paradox in question. The postnational constellation is one which both hangs on doggedly to the concept of nation-state as necessary, and draws boundaries around a group of nation-states in terms of the same kinds of solidarity. Habermas's championing of the life-world and liberal self-determination (ultimately a matter of protecting property) commits him to a spirit of conservism (distinct from, but not unrelated to, conservatism) which always imposes boundaries that are ultimately analogous to nation-state boundaries, and always leaves him somewhat nostalgic about the nation-state itself as the repository of democratic practice:

> The self-referential concept of collective self-determination demarcates a logical space for democratically united citizens who are members of a particular political community. Even if such a community is grounded in the universalist principles of a democratic constitutional state, it still forms a collective identity, in the sense that it interprets and realizes these principles in the light of its own history and in the context of its particular form of life. The ethical-political self-understanding of citizens of a particular democratic life is missing in the inclusive community of world citizens.[14]

Put that way, the boundaries of deliberative democracy are first and foremost the nation-state as an association of self-governing citizens and above that an association of such nation-states. The idea of association allows for fluidities which are always sealed by appointed boundaries. This also sounds like the ideal of the European Union, which is precisely what Habermas is at[15] – but more of that soon.

Nevertheless the conceptualization of deliberative democracy with these dual impulses, and their implicit problems, leads to further clarifications which have inspired theoretical debate and extension – and indeed further problems. It is in the *institutionalization of procedures of communication* in line with the principles of rational communication outlined above, that Habermas sees the possibility of realizing a deliberative democratic practice:

> Now, democratic procedures are meant to institutionalize the forms of communication necessary for a rational will-formation. From this standpoint, at least, the institutional framework in which the legitimation process occurs today can be submitted to critical evaluation. With some institutional imagination, moreover, one can think of how existing parliamentary bodies might be supplemented by institutions that would allow affected clients and the legal public sphere to exert a stronger pressure for legitimation on the executive and judicial branches. The more difficult problem, however, is how to ensure the autonomy of the opinion- and will-formation that have already been institutionalized.[16]

The optimistic solution to the problem lies in the expectation that such institutionalization will enable not just the participation but also thereby the *concretization of solidarities of a democratic civil society* in a mutually strengthening fashion:

> The concept of deliberative politics acquires empirical relevance only when we take into account the multiplicity of forms of communication in which a common will is produced, that is, not just ethical self-clarification but also the balancing of interests and compromise, the purposive choice of means, moral justification, and legal consistency-testing. . . . 'Dialogical' and 'instrumental' politics can *interpenetrate* in the medium of deliberation if the corresponding forms of communication are sufficiently institutionalized. Everything depends on the conditions of communication and the procedures that lend the institutionalized opinion- and will-formation their legitimizing force. [This] model of democracy, which I would like to propose, relies precisely on those conditions of communication under which the political process can be presumed to produce rational results because it operates deliberatively at all levels.[17]

The interpenetration of procedural institutionalization and deliberatively participative *demos* is the heart of deliberative democracy, within postnational boundaries. Such pluralism as exists inside the postnational boundaries – such as the internalized nation-states, and the overlapping ethnic, cultural, migratory, etc., boundaries across them – can be managed deliberatively with such interpenetration in place, is the idea. The postnational constellation *contains* pluralism (as it contains nation-states) as such within demarcated boundaries and overarching homogeneities of democratic citizenship; the institutionalized conditions of communication interpenetrating with the deliberatively participative *demos* releases the pluralism therein.

The deliberative democratic idea of interpenetration of suitable institutions and participative *demos* has an interesting bearing on recent debates about civil society (often referred to by cosmopolitan and radical democrats, and in studies of democratization). In the 1980s and 1990s particularly the idea of civil society has attracted attention, as giving substance to that aspect of collective existence, interaction and action which is outside established corporate, state, interstate or transnational bodies. Civil society thus loosely amalgamates a range of formal and informal organizations, alignments and movements, which are seen to be crucial to the emergence or maintenance of democracy from *below*. Much theory (John Keane, Adam Seligman, Nicholas Deakin, Jean Cohen and Paul Hirst dwell on this[18]) has been devoted to finding a suitable compromise between the conceptual looseness and institutional clarification, the bottom-up enhancement and the institutional constraints, that should operate on civil society. Though, typically, theorizations of civil society threaten to dissolve even the postnational boundaries that Habermas refers to, the paradoxical circularity between its openness and its institutional containment (democratic, of course) actually confirms boundaries of citizenship in Habermasean terms. This paradoxical circularity is famously summarized by Michael Walzer: 'Only a democratic state can create a democratic civil society; only a democratic civil society can sustain a democratic state.'[19]

The essential outline of the conceptualization of deliberative democracy is now in place – the enumeration of a few further problems therein remains. Worth noting here, with the boundary issue in mind, is Michelman's argument that the whole construction of deliberative democracy is based on a regressive premise, which ultimately undermines it comprehensively; every conceptual step sees the regressive premise reinserted. This regressive premise has to do with boundaries, or with that aspect of it which passes for pluralism. The participative ideal of rational communicative practice, and the expectation that institutional arrangements for deliberative democracy will emerge from within that practice itself, is what Michelman focuses on. Insofar as Habermas deals with it, the management of pluralism becomes possible *after* the institutional provision (say, in the form of fundamental constitutional and legal tenets) that allows rational deliberation to occur is in place. Michelman objects that the very planning and instituting of such provision is impossible if the deliberative ideal and the condition of pluralism are assumed. Deliberate democracy makes it impossible for the conditions to emerge that make it possible (hence, regression):

> [According to deliberative democracy] epistemically-democratically construed, the rational derivability of fundamental laws from the very idea of a critically self-conscious, democratic discourse directed to universal reasonable agreement is a necessary condition of the rightness of politics. It is not, however, a sufficient condition, and what keeps it from being one is a circumstance of pluralism: we have not, as particular individuals and groups, sufficient reason to submit our political fates to what any given gang of savants may *say* are the true derivations of constitutional norms from the idea of democratic discourse. In these circumstances, nothing suffices for validity short of actual submissibility, at any time, of pending derivations to the critical and corrective rigors of *actual* democratic discourses.[20]

It is possible to accept that deliberative democracy will work anywhere once the conditions for its operation as described by Habermas are in place. But how can those conditions themselves be determined and obtained deliberatively and with universal participation? This intractable question arises particularly since at the moment of their being determined the conditions obviously don't exist. This is a difficult objection to get past. The only obvious answer seems to be that the realization of the conditions for fully fledged deliberative democracy cannot be required to be obtained through full participation and deliberation. But that in turn will inevitably detract from the legitimacy of whatever version of the required conditions is instituted.

In many ways, Michelman's regressive objection is analogous to Hume's sceptical argument about induction.[21] Just as the sceptical argument simply doesn't affect the practice of inductive reasoning, so it may be expected that Michelman's regressive argument may simply get drowned out in a gradually accruing and gathering deliberative practice that slowly comes to be regarded as universal in effect. This is perhaps possible. But there are political realist matters which, when brought to bear on deliberative democracy, suggest that Michelman's objection is more likely to be applicable than otherwise. As I have observed above, the conceptualization of deliberative democracy is threaded around other political philosophical reflections and in response to ongoing politically realistic contingencies. Habermas and other theorists of deliberative democracy have constantly sought to bring these formulations to bear on such matters of ongoing interest as the universal applicability of human rights or the prerogatives of a constitutional democracy for maintaining stability. The idea is that both the conviction in rational communication as the means to bringing about a true participative democracy, and the desire to preserve constitutional democracy as it has evolved so far in the face of globalizing changes, can be shown to be efficacious if contemporary and much debated problems can be resolved by drawing upon them. But such attempted resolutions of politically real problems often run into difficulties that are rooted in the contradictions underlying the conceptualization. And typically, the problems that prove to be most unwieldy are those that arise from boundary considerations, such as military intervention and immigration. Thus, Habermas's championing of human rights as universal principles that can be endorsed through rational deliberation in *all* contexts,[22] sits uneasily with Habermas's own attempts to come to rational evaluations of conflicts arising ostensibly from human rights violations, and concordant recommendations. This occurs notoriously, for instance, in Habermas's support for NATO intervention in the Kosovo War and the conduct of that military action. Zolo's analysis of this, which I summarized in Chapter 3 as an interrogation of cosmopolitan principles, can be reiterated here to question the deliberative democratic position too.[23] Similarly, while Habermas often analyses the positions that obtain with regard to immigration in the German context sensitively,[24] this is just as often based on majoritarian sympathies and a consuming Eurocentrism (with implicit cultural polarizations not too far off from Rawls's) that could all too easily be bent to less harmonious ends. It is not insignificant that insofar as democracy exists denotatively, Habermas thinks of it as Western constitutional democracy; he firmly believes that democracy and the nation-state and, for that matter, human rights and quite possibly rational thinking itself are uniquely European inventions (without any attempt to explore political histories and cultures elsewhere) that are universally effective; nation-state solidarities drawing on the lifeworld, including those based on kinship, ethnicity, traditional and territorial claims are important to his conceptual efforts and are always tactfully given space to play; as far as Habermas goes the ends of a postnational constellation are those that can be realized through the European Union; Habermas generally seems not to be aware of the imperialist power politics and economic vested interests that inform much of the West's relationship to the East (or the North's to the South) and vitiates the exercise of 'just wars' and 'crimes against humanities' tribunals; and his interest in the phenomenon of immigration is only to the extent that it affects the majority population of Europe in unwelcome ways. (In pointing these out I am not suggesting that what Habermas considers as universally effective are in fact not so; I am inclined to think they often are. The point is that Habermas's identification of the universal principle is often unashamedly and inadequately presented as a European claim, made primarily for Europe's interests.) Thus immigration is usually viewed by Habermas as a *problem* of non-European incumbents disturbing existing

European solidarities;[25] and the accommodation of non-European cultures within Europe is regarded as a matter of *toleration* (despite recognizing the paternalistic thrust of that term[26]). The import of these turns of theory in relation to context is seldom given much attention. Unsurprisingly, mild gestures towards Habermas's Eurocentrism are made in one of the few attempts, by Ilan Kapoor, to work out the connotations of Habermas's (and also Mouffe's) theory of democracy in Third World contexts, precisely because it doesn't self-evidently offer itself to that field:

> [It may be plausibly argued] that Habermas is ultimately drawing out what he believes are universal rational structures, thus distancing communicative reason from 'Western reason'; it remains, nonetheless, that Habermas's point of reference is Western, not non-Western, history. Had Habermas supplemented his views with historical analysis of non-Western societies, and had his concept of rationalization not so neatly coincided with Western historical development, perhaps doubts about his universalist arguments would be minimized.[27]

The above discussions of explanative conceptualizations of democracy from first principles, Rawls's liberal democracy or Habermas's (and others') deliberative democracy, clarify the scope of democratic theory with both national and international/transnational effect, and reveal the problems that revolve particularly around boundary considerations. More importantly, it appears that despite the different ideological bent of the two conceptual positions, the problems regarding boundaries and pluralism seep through in analogous and unresolved ways. There is also an overall similarity in the normative emphasis of both (which in fact chimes in with cosmopolitan democracy) such that the denotative and connotative aspects of democracy are obscured. The manner in which the linguistic ambiguities of democracy enter conceptual fields and impinge upon not just theory but also perceptions of the politically real is given an indicative turn in the most linguistically self-aware (and informed by discourse analysis) of conceptual positions in this field – radical democracy. Radical democratic concepts seek to write into themselves both an effective agenda for political thought, and a concordantly demonstrative and aware linguistic performance of themselves. The reference of these to the politically real in the international/transnational domain, or for that matter in domestic domains, is, I feel, tangential – but cannot be overlooked in this survey. The next chapter turns to them.

NOTES

1 Jürgen Habermas, 'Political Liberalism: A Debate with John Rawls', *The Inclusion of the Other: Studies in Political Theory*, trans. Ciaran Cronin (Cambridge: Polity, 1998/1st German edition 1996), p. 50.

2 Particularly evidenced in warnings about the misuse of history that Habermas issues in a responsive fashion – as in Jürgen Habermas, 'A Kind of Settling of Damages', *The New Conservatism*, trans. S. W. Nicholson (Cambridge: Polity, 1989).

3 Kenneth Baynes, *The Normative Grounds of Social Criticism: Kant, Rawls, Habermas* (Albany, NY: State University of New York Press, 1992) – a summary of the differences between Rawls and Habermas appears on pp. 4–8.

4 I am lumping together such detailed examinations of communication and the nuances of reason, and the connection of these to political legitimation and the public sphere, in Jürgen Habermas's *Legitimation Crisis*, trans. Thomas McCarthy (London: Heinemann, 1976); the two volumes of *The Theory of Communicative Action*, trans. Thomas McCarthy (Boston, MA: Beacon Press, 1984/1981 [1st vol.] and 1987/1981 [2nd vol.]); and *Structural Transformation of the Public Sphere*, trans. Thomas Burger (Cambridge, MA: MIT Press, 1989).

5 Jürgen Habermas, *Moral Consciousness and Communicative Action*, trans. C. Lenhardt and S. W. Nicholson (Cambridge, MA: MIT Press, 1990), pp. 88–9.

6 See Joshua Cohen, 'Deliberation and Democratic Legitimacy', in James Bohman and William Relig (eds.), *Deliberative Democracy: Essays on Reason and Politics* (Cambridge, MA: MIT Press, 1997) – especially his five features of deliberative democracy, pp. 72–3, and four procedural conditions, pp. 74–5. Also Joshua Cohen, 'Democracy and Liberty', in Jon Elster (ed.), *Deliberative Democracy* (Cambridge: Cambridge University Press, 1998).

7 The line taken in James D. Fearon, 'Deliberation as Discussion', in Elster (ed.), *Deliberative Democracy*, pp. 44–5.

8 In Susan C. Stokes's 'Pathologies of Deliberation', and Adam Przeworski's 'Deliberation and Ideological Domination', both in Elster (ed.), *Deliberative Democracy*; and in their contributions (and the other papers generally) in Adam Przeworski, Susan C. Stokes and Bernard Manin (eds), *Democracy, Accountability, and Representation* (Cambridge: Cambridge University Press, 1999).

9 Martha McCoy and Patrick L. Scully, 'Deliberative Dialogue to Expand Civic Engagement: What Kind of Talk Does Democracy Need?', *National Civic Review* 91: 2, Summer 2002, pp. 117–35; David Michael Ryfe, 'The Practice of Deliberative Democracy: A Study of 16 Deliberative Organizations', *Political Communication* 19: 3, July 2002, pp. 359–77.

10 I have avoided using the term 'nation-state' because in politically realist terms, of course, the conjoint homogeneity implied therein is a misconstruction – no imagined community of *a* nation (cf. Benedict Anderson, *Imaginary Communities: Reflections on the Origin and Spread of Nationalism* [London: Verso, 1983]) coincides with the accepted boundaries of *a* political state. But Habermas regards the formulation to be both tenable and crucial in the historical development of Western liberal democracy. The emphasis in Habermas should be taken with the clarification that is offered by Michael Walzer, *On Toleration* (New Haven, CT: Yale University Press, 1997): he maintains that 'nation-states' do not refer to a homogeneous composition in any sense (which rarely, if ever, obtains in reality) but mean only 'that a single dominant group organizes the common life in a way that reflects its own history and culture and, if things go as intended, carries the history forward and sustains the culture' (pp. 24–5).

11 Jürgen Habermas, 'The Postnational Constellation and the Future of Democracy', *The Postnational Constellation: Political Essays*, trans. Max Pensky (Cambridge: Polity, 2001), pp. 62–5.

12 Ibid., pp. 65–8.

13 Ibid., pp. 81–2.

14 Ibid., p. 107.

15 Habermas takes the European Union as his 'exemplary case' of a transnational constellation in ibid., p. 88.

16 Jürgen Habermas, 'Popular Sovereignty as Procedure', in Bohman and Relig (eds), *Deliberative Democracy*, pp. 56–7.

17 Jürgen Habermas, 'Three Models of Democracy', in *The Inclusion of the Other*, pp. 245–6. These points are also covered in Habermas's *Between Facts and Norms: Contributions to a Discourse Theory of Law and Democracy*, trans. William Relig (Cambridge, MA: MIT Press, 1996). This emphasis on the procedural as a mode of distinguishing deliberative democracy from other theoretical models is also made in an economical fashion in Amy Gutmann and Dennis Thompson, 'Why Deliberative Democracy is Different', *Social Philosophy and Policy* 17: 1, Winter 2000, pp. 161–79; and in Sayla Benhabib, 'Toward a Deliberative Model of Democratic Legitimacy', in Sayla Benhabib (ed.), *Democracy and Difference* (Princeton, NJ: Princeton University Press, 1996).

18 John Keane, *Democracy and Civil Society: On the Predicaments of European Socialism* (London: Verso, 1988), and John Keane, *Civil Society: Old Images, New Visions* (Cambridge: Polity, 1998); Adam A. Seligman, *The Idea of Civil Society* (New York: Free Press, 1992); Nicholas Deakin, *In Search of Civil Society* (Basingstoke: Palgrave, 2001); Jean Cohen, 'Interpreting the Notion of Civil Society', in Michael Walzer (ed.), *Toward a Global Civil Society* (Providence, RI: Berghahn, 1995), pp. 35–40; Paul Hirst, 'Democracy and Civil Society', in Paul Hirst and Sunil Khilnani (eds), *Reinventing Democracy* (Oxford: Blackwell, 1996), pp. 97–116.

19 Michael Walzer, 'The Concept of Civil Society', in Walzer (ed.), *Toward a Global Civil Society*, p. 24.

20 Frank I. Michelman, 'How Can the People Ever Make the Laws? A Critique of Deliberative Democracy', in Bohman and Relig (eds), *Deliberative Democracy*, pp. 164–5.

21 See David Hume, *A Treatise of Human Nature*, Book 2 (Glasgow: Fontana/Collins, 1962), parts III and IV. The induction paradox has exercised philosophers through most of the twentieth century. It has cropped up in Bertrand Russell, *The Problems of Philosophy* (Oxford: Oxford University Press, 1967/1912), pp. 33–8; has been allegedly resolved by Karl Popper's notion of falsifiability – see *Objective Knowledge* (Oxford: Clarendon, 1972); has been restated as the 'grue' problem by Nelson Goodman in *Fact, Fiction and Forecast* (Indianapolis, IN: Bobbs-Merrill, 1965/1955); has been laid at Ludwig Wittgenstein's doorstep by Saul Kripke, *Wittgenstein on Rules and Private Language* (Oxford: Blackwell, 1982); and has been satisfactorily dissolved in R. M. Sainsbury's *Paradoxes* (Cambridge: Cambridge University Press, 1995/1987).

22 See Jürgen Habermas, 'Remarks on Legitimation through Human Rights', *The Postnational Constellation*, pp. 113–29.

23 Danilo Zolo, *Invoking Humanity: War, Law and Global Order*, trans. Federico and Gordon Poole (London: Continuum, 2002/2000), pp. 78–82.

24 Jürgen Habermas's views on immigration appear in: 'Citizenship and National Identity', in *Between Facts and Norms*, trans. William Relig (Cambridge: Polity, 1990/1996); and 'Struggles for Recognition in the Democratic Constitutional State', trans. Shierry Weber Nicholsen, in Amy Gutmann (ed.), *Multiculturalism: Examining the Politics of Recognition* (Princeton, NJ: Princeton University Press, 1994).

25 This seemed to me the thrust of a lecture by Habermas that I attended at the Royal Institute of Philosophy, London, on 28 March 2003 – it was initially advertised with the title 'Religious Tolerance – Pacemaker for Cultural Rights', but I think the title was changed just before the lecture was delivered to something like 'Minorities and Cultural Rights'. What made it so was not so much the content of generalized statement that he circulated in advance (and which I have before me), as the manner in which the generalizations were elaborated in terms of specific examples and the loaded language it was couched in. Similar linguistic loadedness is also available in the section on 'Discourse between the West and other Cultures: Asiatic Values' in the essay 'Remarks on Legitimation through Human Rights', *The Postnational Constellation*, pp. 123–6.

26 Jürgen Habermas's section in Giovanna Barradori, *Philosophy in a Time of Terror: Dialogues with Jürgen Habermas and Jacques Derrida* (Chicago, IL: Chicago University Press, 2003), p. 41. On the various attitudes to the idea of toleration in pluralitic democracies see George L. Fletcher, 'The Case for Toleration', *Social Philosophy and Policy* 13: 1, Winter 1996, pp. 229–39. Habermas's use of 'toleration' (as indeed Rawls's) is paternalistic largely because it comes with an abstract normative weight; a more politically realist apprehension of the term is less so – as in Michael Walzer, *On Toleration* (New Haven, CT: Yale University Press, 1997), where he examines the connotations of the term, with a defensive temper, in specific regimes and nation-states.

27 Ilan Kapoor, 'Deliberative Democracy or Agonistic Pluralism? The Relevance of the Habermas–Mouffe Debate for Third World Politics', *Alternatives: Global, Local, Political* 27: 4, October–December 2002, p. 477.

6 *Radical Democracy*

Radical democracy is rooted in the context of the 1980s, and derives its explanative/visionary thrust from that context. At any rate, it is that decade of exacerbating disenchantment with communist regimes and centralized planned socialist economics, and qualified enchantment with (denotatively and connotatively) liberal democracy and global capitalism, and apprehension of a coming end to the Cold War, that its proponents continue to be associated with. The work of the main proponents, Ernesto Laclau and Chantal Mouffe, particularly *Hegemony and the Socialist Strategy* (1985), was controversially effective within a politically real domain, and made a leap from explanative to visionary analysis of democracy therein. But their work undertakes very little (only rather sweeping) direct engagement with historical and material processes; rather it offers a series of propositions and linguistic performances which are designed to be received within ideological divides of the time. This presents certain difficulties in revisiting radical democracy in a survey of the present sort. The politically realist methodology is apt to stall in the face of only loose explanative analysis with politically real and hypothetically plausible bases, few significant predictive attempts, prescriptive analysis with intractable practical consequences, and a number of visionary pronouncements. But even other kinds of surveys, employing more idealist, norm-led, predeterminedly sympathetic methodologies, find it difficult to come to grips with radical democracy. The key point that is constantly, and with not a little relief, recognized is that in initially formulating radical democracy the politically real is not so much engaged *with* as engaged *within*. It is tangentially available. But the relief of having something other than the linguistic pronouncement and performance of radical democracy to refer to, the relief of having at least a tangentially referable context to place it in, can only be short lived. The proponents of radical democracy deliberately resist and withdraw such referentiality, by focusing on the modus operandi of reference itself. Aligning themselves with postmodernist and deconstructionist analysis, every kind of reference is constantly drawn back on itself as a matter of examining reference itself; the real world is only given here as something that is ideologically constructed within discourses. Analysis here cannot move beyond the conditions of their enunciation, and of the discursive frames within which that occurs. Naturally neither can a real base be said to exist by the proponents of radical democracy, nor can prescriptions be offered in those terms, only a self-aware linguistic performance is possible. The formulation of radical democracy is such a performance.

Nevertheless, there are two sides to this tangentially available context. On the one hand, it is expressed in adherence to an emancipative socialist desire to embrace different sorts of primarily identity-based social movements – resistance to mainstream ideologies and institutions from those who feel marginalized on the basis of race, class, gender, sexuality, cultural belonging, and so on. *Radical democracy could be regarded as an attempt to bring all these together, or juxtapose all these together, with the emancipative socialist desire intact,* but at the same time by dislocating that desire from the usual association of such alignment with Marxist theory and practice. This is because, on the other hand, the tangentially referred context is also expressed in repudiating 'classical' Marxism (or revolutionary socialism). In the context of the 1980s this mainly meant a rejection of communist regimes with single-party states (tending towards corruption and dictatorships) operating increasingly unsuccessful and stagnant centrally planned economies. The rejection of these came with a wholesale rejection of the Marxist ideology which those states claimed, its entire conceptual structure and related formulations – class analysis, the concept of hegemony, the critique of capitalist economics based on the labour theory of value and extortion of surplus value, the cultivation of proletarian values, and the aspiration to bring about an egalitarian society through redistribution and communal ownership. So *radical democracy could be regarded as a mode of expressing the desire of socialist emancipation against the established Marxist conceptual and institutional structures with which emancipative desires were usually associated.* Since the link between communist regimes and Marxist analysis is as shaky as the link between normatively connoted democracy and denotatively understood liberal democracy, the kind of wholesale repudiation performed by radical democrats is always open to contestation – that is where the controversies about radical democracy have centred. In retrospect, therefore, radical democracy has come to be identified less with what it says about democracy, and more with the position it took regarding 'classical' Marxism. The two-fold positioning of radical democracy – marked by the two italicized sentences above – is often reduced primarily to identification with the latter position. It is essentially in the retrospectively lumped together post-Marxist fold that the radical democrats are discussed. Thus, in a recent book entitled 'Post-Marxism', Stuart Sim throws in Laclau and Mouffe's radical democracy, along with works in a similar socialists-questioning-Marxism vein from Rosa Luxemburg and Antonio Gramsci to Louis Althusser, Nikos Poulantzas, Barry Hindess, Slavoj Zizek and others, on the grounds that 'Post-Marxism is now a well-established theoretical position'.[1] An abrasive debate in the *New Left Review* between Laclau-Mouffe and Norman Geras about the post-Marxist pretensions of radical democracy (of which more below) marked the arena within which radical democracy was received in the late 1980s.

The above contextualization of radical democracy in the 1980s, however, has given inadequate attention to the analytical ground on which its two-fold positioning occurs. Apart from tangential real world alignments, post-modernist/deconstructionist discourse analysis provides the common denominator between radical democratic emancipative aspirations and repudiation of 'classical' Marxism. It is the assumption of the absolute constructedness of politics in discourse that enables both a critique of the rhetorical-ideological turns of the latter, and the embracing of the multifarious efforts of social movements within the former. In a typically sweeping fashion, Laclau and Mouffe dispensed with Marxist reductiveness (which tries to unify multiple emancipative struggles by imposing an overarching materialist conceptual structure, by drawing equivalences) and embraced radical democracy (which champions pluralism of different emancipative social movements, while maintaining difference) through linguistic awareness:

> We, thus, see that the logic of equivalence is a logic of the simplification of political space, while the logic of difference is a logic of its expansion of increasing complexity. Taking a comparative example from linguistics, we could say that the logic of difference tends to expand the syntagmatic pole of language, the number of positions that can enter into a relation of combination and hence continuity with one another; while the logic of equivalence expands the paradigmatic role – that is, the elements that can be substituted for one another – thereby reducing the number of positions which can possibly be combined.[2]

Irrespective of the structuralist Saussurean terms used here, difference is given deconstructive weight by its implementation against the homogenizing political discourse of Marxism.

The almost symbolic culmination of this bringing together of post-modern/deconstructive discourse analysis with a reiteration of a spirit of Marxism, shorn of all materialist economic and class analysis, occurred in the early 1990s with the publication of Jacques Derrida's *Specters of Marx* (1994).[3] It is worth briefly registering this moment to put the post-Marxist positioning of radical democracy into perspective, and understand its relevance now. *Specters of Marx* underlined the necessity of keeping the spirit of Marxism alive, in the midst of increasing convergence on principles of liberal democracy and capitalist production. Derrida critiqued the discourses surrounding this convergence (with a penetrating attack on its main prophet, Francis Fukuyama), and reiterated the need to redress injustices which continue to obtain in the world. He hoped that the radical potential of the deconstructive process, the undeconstructible universality of justice (oddly contradictory positions), and a renewal of the spirit of Marxism would enable that. Derrida took the *spirit* of Marxism seriously: a revitalized *spirit* of Marxism would have to be coeval with the plurality and shifting nature of 'realities' and the discourses they are approached by (somewhat flippantly, a *hauntology* was recommended rather than a Marxist ontology), and not the totalizing and monolithical and monological affair that Marxism had become. Derrida presented these ideas with typical stylistic panache, drawing as much on the self-reflexive and necessarily unstable quality of his own performative text as on the conventions of philosophical analysis and argument. What the responses to Derrida's text by liberal-left intellectuals of the time[4] showed was a remarkable consanguinity with this approach despite differences in details and agendas.

Derrida's seems to me a kind of end position for the post-Marxism that radical democracy fell in with in the 1980s. The manner in which discourse analysis enables a programme of radical democracy insofar as it alludes to democracy, and especially with regard to the international/transnational domain, is a somewhat different issue. This entails negotiating the boundaries within which democracy (denotatively) works, and boundaries across which radical democratic aspirations (entirely normatively connoted) should reach.

Laclau and Mouffe's reflections on the manner in which socialism deterred democracy (echoing that disconnect between socialism and democracy that Bobbio observed), and on how certain qualified socialist aspirations should continue to inform democratic aspirations, result in interesting implicit and explicit negotiations with boundaries. Like Zolo, Laclau and Mouffe in fact do not go as far as formulating a new reconceptualized democracy either; they capture the impulse as Zolo does, and recognize the subversiveness of democracy as Bobbio does, and transform both of these into a constant struggle with boundaries. This struggle itself, it is maintained, will gradually and in an ongoing (never to be concluded) and pluralistic fashion, characterize the emergence of a new kind of democracy – there can be no democracy as an end-product or conceptual final position, there can only be a constantly fought over and fluid *conceptual* process through which democracy will operate. In a sense, thus, while (like Zolo) not actually presenting a framework for democracy, they also do not suggest (here unlike Zolo) that such a framework is possible. The very struggle of enunciating the democratic aspiration with socialist fervour becomes the process that *is* a reconceptualized – or, in their terms, a radical – democracy.

To a significant extent, what Laclau and Mouffe do with the conceptual impulse, and *as* the conceptual process, is contained in their mode of expressing themselves. The terminology is important here, especially when it addresses the all-important boundary issues involved. At an explicit level, the field within which a subversive and pluralistic process like democracy can unfold is one that Laclau and Mouffe constantly struggle to express by evoking boundaries reminiscent of the nation-state and other kinds of societal enclosures. But this occurs only to immediately undermine them. It is in this spirit that they speak of 'society' and the operation of antagonisms within it, for instance:

> [Apropos] the identification of 'society' with an ensemble of *physically* existing agents who live within a given territory. If this criterion is accepted, it is obvious that antagonisms occur *among* those agents and are not external to them. But it does not necessarily follow, from the 'empirical' coexistence of the agents, that the relations among them should be shaped according to an objective and intelligible pattern. (The price of identifying 'society' with the referent would be to empty it of any rationally specifiable content.) . . . Antagonism as the negation of a given order is, quite simply, the limit of that order, and not the moment of a broader totality in relation to which the two poles of antagonism would constitute differential – i.e. objective – partial instances. . . . The limit of the social must be given within the social itself as something subverting it, destroying its ambition to constitute a full presence. Society never manages to be fully society, because everything in it is penetrated by its limits, which prevents it from constituting itself as an objective reality.[5]

And similarly, it is in this spirit that Mouffe speaks of 'political community':

> Politics is to a great extent about the rules of the *respublica* and its many possible interpretations; it is about the constitution of the political community, not something that takes place inside the political community, as some communitarians would have it. Political life concerns collective, public action; it aims at the construction of a 'we' in a context of diversity and conflict. But to construct a 'we' it must be distinguished from the 'them', and that means establishing a frontier, defining an 'enemy'. Therefore, while politics aims at constructing a political community and creating a unity, a fully inclusive political community and a final unity can never be realized since there will permanently be a 'constitutive outside', an exterior to the community that makes its existence possible. Antagonistic forces will never disappear and politics is characterized by conflict and division.[6]

It is the rhetorical tactic – the same in both quotations – that makes the point: the boundaries which are evoked by terms like 'society' or 'community' are negated without replacement. In other words, the terms are deployed with negative effect, to demonstrate that they have no substance and reference beyond a binary rationale of meaning: they are constructed with apparently objective effect, but only against a binary opposite that is not objective – not *there*, so to say. Boundaries are radically dispersed – or rather, they are caught in a linguistic gesture of metaphoric relativization ('we' and 'they'; 'inside' and 'outside'; part and whole). Laclau and Mouffe's evocation and dispersal of boundaries is a linguistic enactment, which allows theory to flow as a self-sustaining linguistic construction (and in linguistic terms, with a plausible air about it all). As such, it seems to draw in the normative content of democracy smoothly, to give it, ultimately, no more than evanescent linguistic substance.

Implicitly, and again with more of visionary rhetorical effect than applicable explanative or prescriptive analysis, boundaries are reinserted against boundaries in the radical democratic embracing of identity-based social movements. This becomes more evident as the post-Marxist moment passes, and the independent political asseveration of the conceptual process of radical democracy comes to the fore. Chantal Mouffe's contribution to the collection of essays *Radical Democracy* (1996), marking an attempt to present an agenda of radical democracy with much of the post-Marxist repudiation of 'classical' Marxism left behind, offers the following:

> A radical pluralist approach, informed as it is by a nonessentialist view of politics, acknowledges the impossibility of a fully realized democracy and of the total elimination of antagonisms. It views all forms of agreement as partial and provisional and as products of a given hegemony. Its objective is the creation of a chain of equivalence among the democratic demands found in a variety of groups – women, blacks, workers, gays, lesbians, environmentalists – around a radical democratic interpretation of the political principles of the liberal democratic regime. Such an interpretation emphasizes the numerous social relations where subordination exists and must be challenged if the principles of equality and liberty are to apply. This challenging should lead different groups struggling for a radicalization of democracy to recognize that they have a common concern; that is the establishment of a common political identity as 'radical democratic citizens'.[7]

This essay is surrounded by essays from representatives of those groups – Seyla Benhabib considering feminism, Amarpal Dhaliwal reflecting on racial minority rights, Jeffrey Escoffier pondering the cultural politics of homosexuality[8] – who see some degree of promise in radical democracy for universalizing their identity-based political positions. Repetitions and elaborations of these sentiments, without extending them to a sphere of application, have become staple since in Mouffe's writings. Since that progresses on the understanding that it is their very enunciation which exposes radical democracy in process, rather than any verifiable real world outcome or expectation – and since that enjoins a need to look closely at such enunciation – two more similar quotations can be productively examined here:

> The creation of political identities as radical democratic citizens depends . . . on the collective form of identification among the democratic demands found in a variety of movements; women, workers, black, gay, ecological, as well as in several other 'new social movements'. This is a conception of citizenship which, through a common identification with a radical democratic interpretation of the principles of liberty and equality, aims at constructing a 'we', a chain of equivalence among their demands so as to articulate them through a principle of democratic equivalence. For it is not a matter of establishing a mere alliance between given interests but actually modifying the very identity of these forces.[9]

And elsewhere:

> To be capable of thinking politics today, and understanding the nature of these new struggles and the diversity of social relations that the democratic revolution has yet to encompass, it is indispensable to develop a theory of the subject as a decentred, detotalized agent, a subject constructed at the point of the intersection of a multiplicity of subject positions between which there exists no a priori or necessary relation and whose articulation is the result of hegemonic practices. Consequently, no identity is ever definitely established, there always being a certain degree of openness and ambiguity in the way different subject positions are articulated.[10]

There are boundaries in there – the boundaries between a 'variety of groups' sustained by their memberships' sense of belonging to and advocating the cause of such groups. These are not coincidental with the explicitly interrogated boundaries of 'society' examined in *Hegemony and Socialist Strategy*; these are nevertheless institutionally or with civil prerogatives organized (such that they can be identified as 'social movements') boundaries. A couple of linguistic strategies are deployed to render the politically determined (and with determination) holding to these boundaries consistent with the endless dispersal and scattering of 'decentred, detotalized', unhegemonic pluralism that radical democracy claims. On the one hand, the effort to bring consistency rests in the idea of a 'chain of equivalence' between these to find 'common concern' and establish 'radical democratic citizenship'. There's an unresolvable paradox here: the latter terms suggest some notion of universal humanity and political coexistence underlying those boundaries, but its expression is constantly deferred by asserting the hegemonic anti-pluralistic tendency of any such idea. On the other hand, the effort to bring consistency also rests in the idea of 'a subject constructed at the point of the intersection of a multiplicity of subject positions', given as something to be aspired to for radical democracy. It is difficult to discern why this is regarded as an aspiration and not as simply a description of subjectivity as commonly understood now. This can only be an aspiration insofar as Mouffe is not stating the condition of subjectivity, but stating it to make it cohere with identity-based groups in social movements; this is an attempt not to understand subjectivity in itself, but to draw subjectivity as the link that holds the 'chain of equivalence' between different social movements together in radical democracy. But therein also lies the unresolvable paradox. If in the subject 'no identity is ever established' – or at least thought of as such – then what is the *raison d'être* of the various groups engaged in social movements? It seems pretty clear that any attempt to elaborate on the manner in which Mouffe presents boundary negotiations – from subjectivity to identity-based groups (in social movements) to the common concern of radical democratic citizens – simply do not cohere. They fail at the intersection of each level of enunciation.

This linguistics of equivalent normative terms, I have observed already, plays with interestingly obfuscative effect in studies of cosmopolitan, Rawlsian and deliberative conceptualizations of democracy, arguably with the possibility of becoming assimilated into a normatively homogenized democratic quest. This can be said about Laclau and Mouffe's performance of linguistic equivalence (post-Marxist) while reifying differences of identity through radical democracy too. It is clear from the many approbatory responses to radical democracy, and in the fact that it has passed through the portals of institutionally sanctioned political theory, that radical democratic enunciations are seen to hang together. This occurs, it seems to me, primarily because the 'chain of equivalence' that Mouffe mentions so frequently is not so much there to be established as performed on the surface of her texts. Equivalence between the different groups, and between all of them and uncertain subjectivity, and all the uncertain subjectivities and the common concern of radical democratic citizens, are, so to say, *performed* in their being put together in consecutive sentences and linguistically cross-linked. And this linguistic performance, and the self-announcement thereby of emerging and processive radical democracy, appears to be plausibly a *democratic* act because of the connotative content and minimum meaning that the term comes with in everyday usage. The linguistic performance that enunciatively includes all subjectivities and groupings and movements and humanity without any attempt to rationalize these terms is simply in the spirit of the uncompromising minimum meaning – the totality of *demos*. The moral approbation that this term connotatively embodies is already given through chains of equivalences – with pluralism, freedom, equality, rights, inclusion, etc. All that is necessary for Mouffe to do is simply perform a syntactically comprehensible exercise of linking these for radical democracy to be seen to be occurring, generally well-received and institutionally accepted. Mouffe's later texts also depend tangentially for their effect on the politically real context of our world and its exchanges (to which she refers so little, or only sweepingly), just as the post-Marxist effect of Laclau and Mouffe's *Hegemony and Socialist Strategy* depended on tangential reference within the 1980s. That their formulations are sustained by a self-referential discourse formation that simply chimes in with other conceptual positions regarding democracy, and ultimately the connotative presumptions regarding democracy, of our ethos is confirmed constantly in their later writings.[11]

There's another final twist to radical democracy's play on democracy in linguistic performance, to clarify which I return to the 1980s. I have mentioned already the abrasive debate between Laclau/Mouffe and Geras in the *New Left Review*, which in many ways concretized the post-Marxist status of radical democracy's emergence.[12] Though, in presenting his critical response to *Hegemony and Socialist Strategy*, Geras necessarily found himself pushed into the position of defending 'classical' Marxism (perceivably in pointing out the poverty of Laclau and Mouffe's account of the Marxist tradition), it was essentially the logical inconsistencies and rhetorical strategies therein that he addressed. He noted that the alternative radical politics presented by Laclau and Mouffe was as discursively constructed as all the essentialisms they denounced, and felt it demonstrated 'complete theoretical vacuity'.[13] This naturally hit home, and not only were Laclau and Mouffe drawn into an enraged reply, but also into a subtle shifting of terms which gave their performance of the radical democratic process a less post-Marxist turn. Asserting that:

> The radical instability and threat to identities posed by capitalist expansion necessarily leads to new forms of collective imaginary which reconstruct those threatened identities in a fundamentally new way. Our thesis is that egalitarian discourses and discourses of rights play a fundamental role in the reconstruction of collective identities,[14]

they maintained that this needs to be achieved within the framework of liberalism.[15] Geras naturally remained unconvinced, and rightly concerned about the future of 'socialist agency',[16] but missed an opportunity to interrogate what was meant by framework of liberalism. The framework of liberalism has remained the base on which radical democracy is enunciatively being built, and despite numerous other similar assertions the question of what that consists in remains open. It appears in the quotation from Mouffe's contribution to the edited book *Radical Democracy* referred to above:

> [radical democracy's] objective is the creation of a chain of equivalence among the democratic demands found in a variety of groups – women, blacks, workers, gays, lesbians, environmentalists – around a radical democratic interpretation of the political principles of the liberal democratic regime.[17]

There this is preceded by a useful clarification:

> The aim is not to create a completely different kind of society, but to use the symbolic resources of the liberal democratic tradition to struggle against relations of subordination not only in the economy but also linked to gender, race or sexual orientation, for example. . . . What we advocate is a type of 'radical liberal democracy' – we do not present it as a rejection of the liberal democratic regime or as the institution of a new political form of society.[18]

'Liberal democratic *regime*' is, it seems to me, clear enough here – it exists already, its democratic nature doesn't need questioning, it already provides the resources for radical democracy to be undertaken. Evidently, in the 'liberal democratic regime' democracy is instated yet again as legislative denotation. This brings us back full circle from the interrogation of 'social' in *Hegemony and Socialist Strategy*; all given nation-state-like boundaries may be interrogable, the boundaries between subjectivity and identity groups and radical democratic citizenship may stretch out suggestively from that interrogation, but only to be returned to the given boundaries of the 'liberal democratic regime'. In fact, it is the given boundaries of liberal democracy (denotatively understood) which enable the boundaries of various identity-based groups and their struggles. Yet again, the 'chain of equivalences' through which radical democracy performed itself on the stage of democracy's normative connotations and minimum meaning, is suavely, unquestioningly, unwaveringly switched into the existing denotative understanding of existing democratic regimes. The whimper in which the grand performance of radical democracy ends – or carries on – is no more than a ripple in the 'symbolic resources of the liberal democratic tradition'.

If the politically real international/transnational domain, and the politically realist methodology, have receded behind the cloud of discourse in this consideration of radical democracy, it makes a comeback in the next chapter on democratization studies. Interestingly, however, that too is drawn towards a similar direction.

NOTES

1 Stuart Sim, *Post-Marxism: An Intellectual History* (London: Routledge, 2000), p. 1.
2 Ernesto Laclau and Chantal Mouffe, *Hegemony and Socialist Strategy: Towards a Radical Democratic Politics*, 2nd ed. (London: Verso, 1985/2000), p. 130.
3 Jacques Derrida, *Specters of Marx: The State of the Debt, the Working of Mourning, and the New International*, trans. Peggy Kamuf (New York: Routledge, 1994).
4 Best available in Michael Sprinkler (ed.), *Ghostly Demarcations: A Symposium on Jacques Derrida's Specters of Marx* (London: Verso, 1999). In responding to *Specters of Marx* each essay in *Ghostly Demarcations* made its own summary of Derrida's contentions. Some wondered what the political nuances of Derrida's gesture in making this intervention are. This is what Terry Eagleton did in a dismissive fashion, and largely what Aijaz Ahmad and Tom Lewis attempted in a more considered but unconvinced fashion. Others, such

as Antonio Negri, Pierre Macherey and Warren Montag, summarized Derrida's arguments so as to incline them towards their own established ideological proclivities. Rastko Mocnik extended Derrida's observations to an interesting re-examination of the symbolic efficacy of the concept of commodity fetishism. Fredric Jameson provided an extensive and generally sympathetic examination of Derrida's text, taking into account both its performative and argumentative qualities, and clarifying what sort of actual slippages and possible accommodations are available therein with Marxist class-centred analysis. Werner Hamacher pondered the performative elements of Marx's presentation of the workings of capital with Derridean inspiration. Despite ideological and methodological differences, all of them engage with Derrida essentially in his own terms by assuming the primacy of discourse analysis and accepting uncritically that the economic considerations which underlay Marxist thinking are irrelevant.

5 Laclau and Mouffe, *Hegemony and Socialist Strategy*, pp. 126–7.

6 Chantal Mouffe, 'Democratic Citizenship and Political Community', in *The Return of the Political* (London: Verso, 1993), p. 69.

7 Chantal Mouffe, 'Radical Democracy or Liberal Democracy', in David Trend (ed.), *Radical Democracy: Identity, Citizenship, and the State* (New York: Routledge, 1996), p. 24.

8 Seyla Benhabib, 'From Identity Politics to Social Feminism', in ibid., pp. 27–41; Amarpal K. Dhaliwal, 'Can the Subaltern Vote?', in ibid., pp. 42–61; Jeffrey Escoffier, 'Culture Wars and Identity Politics', in ibid., pp. 165–78.

9 Mouffe, 'Democratic Citizenship and Political Community', *The Return of the Political*, p. 70.

10 Mouffe, 'Radical Democracy: Modern or Postmodern?', ibid., p. 12.

11 As in Ernesto Laclau, *Emancipation(s)* (London: Verso, 1996); Chantal Mouffe, *The Democratic Paradox* (London: Verso, 2000).

12 This consists of three exchanges in *New Left Review* (*NLR*): Norman Geras, 'Post-Marxism?', *NLR* 163 (May–June 1987), pp. 10–72; Ernesto Laclau and Chantal Mouffe, 'Post-Marxism Without Apologies', *NLR* 166 (November–December 1987), pp. 79–107; Norman Geras, 'Ex-Marxism Without Substance', *NLR* 169 (May–June 1988), pp. 34–61.

13 Geras, 'Post-Marxism?', p. 74.

14 Laclau and Mouffe, 'Post-Marxism without Apologies', p. 104.

15 Ibid., p. 105.

16 Geras, 'Ex-Marxism without Substance', p. 61.

17 See note 7.

18 Mouffe, 'Radical Democracy or Liberal Democracy?', p. 20.

7 Democratization Studies and Comparative Politics

Democratization studies – essentially, consideration of the emergence and consolidation of denotatively understood democratic legislative arrangements in different contexts, and processes underlying that – is by definition attentive to the notion of democracy across boundaries, or in the international/transnational domain. It involves attempts to discern where democracy could be said to be or not to be; where democracy could be thought of as emerging; whether democracy can be qualified by degrees or types (Western/Eastern, European/American, majoritarian/representative, associated with Rhine model or Anglo-American model capitalism) of being; what implications these conditions have within boundaries (nation-state, other administrative, communal, ethnic, etc.); and what effects and transactions these conditions enable or impel across boundaries. A distinction is possible between democratization studies and the comparative study of democracies, on the grounds that the former investigates processes of change and transition while the latter simply compares features between stable achieved democracies. Such a distinction, while apparently plausible, actually seldom holds to the field of research in question – they merge into each other constantly. Even studies which seem to accept that certain states are stable democracies within their boundaries, and proceed to examine them comparatively as if they are static and nonporous formations, do so with underlying notions of degrees of democracy (e.g. in terms of measures of participation, or institutional arrangements for democratic deliberation) and the in-process nature of democratic practice (thus, usually coming up with proposals and recommendations for strengthening processes of participation and building necessary infrastructures). These are effectively studies of democratization too, addressing many of the areas identified above as within that field, albeit with a stronger emphasis on internal democratization or comparative democratization within domestic domains. The entire area of empirically based research and thinking about democracy in denotative terms, especially since the 1960s, can be appropriately characterized as democratization studies. This cohesive field appears to me to be marked by shifting emphases and prerogatives: whereas previously the emphasis has been more on processes within closed domestic spaces, the emphasis has now moved squarely towards processes that cross or transcend boundaries. Given the growing interest in and evidence of global movements and political and economic influences and interdependence noted in previous chapters, the shift of emphasis is a natural one.

As such, there is a clear relation between the study of democratization and the methods of comparative politics. In the 1960s and 1970s democratization studies was often regarded as one of many branches within the authoritative reach of comparative politics. The comparative politics methodology has a salutary empirical grounding and empirically verifiable air about it, focused as it is on documentation of real world processes. It seems to allow democracy to be approached, unusually, with little regard for its normative connotations and minimum meaning. Interestingly, while in principle the relationship between comparative politics methodology and democratization studies persists, the fortunes of the former and the latter have diverged. Those who think about and use comparative politics methods self-consciously are increasingly defensive and cautious. Democratization studies, however, though still based primarily on comparative methods, have moved from strength to strength, and almost absorbed and reinvented comparative politics within its singular concerns as a separate field. Political discourse, particularly in the transnational/international domain, uses comparative measures and observations with unprecedented authority and verve now when democracy or democratization is the issue. In other areas of political discourse (for instance, developing strategies and policies for economic development, poverty alleviation, environment protection, etc.) such data is used more cautiously, pragmatically and strategically – until it is recruited to the analysis of democracy and democratization. In brief, it seems to me that now comparative politics is rightly a cautious and measured affair, deeply conscious of its limitations, except when it is used in democratization studies.

This divergence between attitudes to the comparative methodology in general and in relation to democratization studies in particular can perhaps be explained in terms of the shift in emphasis noted above. Democratization studies' changing emphasis from primarily discrete states or domestic domains juxtaposed against each other to cross-border and trans-border processes may well be responsible for the divergence. Quite possibly, this shift has meant that in democratization studies the comparative politics methodology has come to be used in more imaginative and thoughtful ways compared to more conventional use elsewhere – the former has interrogated and played with the nuances of *comparison* more effectively. There is some evidence of this, which I touch on later in this chapter. I suspect, however, that this divergence is more due to the insidious insertion of the normative connotations of democracy within the apparently denotatively focused understanding of democracy that the comparative methodology applies to.

Those who assume a larger view of comparative political research and its methodology, i.e. one not confined to democracy and democratization, do naturally register the complexities of that particular area. This larger view has of late increasingly come with circumspection and defensiveness which extends to the use of comparative data for examining democratization and globalization processes. In an edited volume devoted particularly to the many methodological pitfalls and consequent conceptual ambiguities of comparative politics, *Comparing Nations* (1994), for example, one finds interesting – and almost incidental – remarks on the space of democratization studies. In an essay there on the 'Use and Misuse of Statistics in Comparative Research' Mattei Dogan observes:

> The appropriate dose of quantified data depends on the kind of questions that you ask and the goals pursued by comparing. For instance, a reply to the question: Is the gap between poor and rich countries increasing? has to be based on solid statistical data, carefully analysed. By contrast, when Samuel Huntington asks: 'Will more countries become democratic?' the analytical reasoning becomes more important than the statistical evidence.[1]

It seems to me that the question attributed to Huntington deliberately gestures towards the heart of much democratization research since the 1960s, which often casually makes unwarranted inferences from statistical data. In a separate paper in the collection, Dogan reflects on the complexities of interpreting data showing that discontent with a given institutional system and particular functionary's practices is higher in pluralistic democracies than in definably other kinds of regimes.[2] Another work examining the many fallacies and possible strengths of the comparative politics methodology by B. Guy Peters also warns particularly about the difficulties of analysing 'homogenizing trends' like globalization and democratization:

> The common, homogenizing trends influencing so many of the world's governments will make comparative politics both more profitable, and more difficult. The common trends observable in the environment of politics can be conceptualized as providing common stimuli to which different countries will respond in their own particular way. On the other hand, the common nature of these trends is making comparison more difficult, given the diffusion of political styles and political practices.[3]

Worth noting here is not only the anxiety about increasing difficulty in identifying distinct spheres of political practice for comparison, but also the observation that interpretations of comparative data dictate political responses.

Those with a broad view of comparative politics often exhort caution about the manner in which comparative data *is* acquired and used in discussions of democracy (anxiously), and sometimes ponder how it *should be* collected and used (with uncertainty). Such circumspection comes with the perception that rough and ready denotative definitions of democracy (such as the formal existence of an elective multi-party system with concordant and operational institutions), which democratization studies often draw upon, cannot be convincing without greater conceptual clarification and thereby awareness of limitations. This implies laying out the conceptual bases, the rationale and implications, of such denotative presumptions. That in turn calls for a kind of theorization that few comparative researchers feel equipped to conduct, and few democratization researchers using comparative data have bothered to engage in. An interesting attempt to gesture to the kind of conceptual basis for democracy that someone with a broad view of comparative politics may feel comfortable with appeared in a book by Lawrence C. Mayer, published, not insignificantly, in 1989. In presenting a survey of the achievements and failed promises of comparative politics after the 1950s, he champions, in pragmatic comparative interests, Schumpeter's procedural definition of modern democracy (discussed in Chapter 2). Mayer's main argument is that comparative political science saw a methodological revolution in the 1950s by adopting a new purpose:

> This new purpose entailed the standard of being more comparative – that is, generalizing about more settings or systems using fewer variables – than configurative – describing the interaction of a wide variety of variables in a single system.[4]

A rejuvenation of empirical political science research was consequently anticipated, which has only materialized to a small and unsatisfactory extent. Mayer's survey of different areas in which this new purpose was exercised finds much to criticize in the achievements to that date, and considers ways forwards. One of these areas is that of 'industrial democracies'. The comparative study of industrial democracies, Mayer finds, is replete with poorly conceptualized criteria of comparison leading to questionable inferences. In particular he expresses doubts about the manner in which Rostow and others (I come to this soon) have pushed comparative data and observations towards prescriptive analysis. It is with a view to clarifying the kind of conceptual basis that can aptly be said to inform the collection and study of comparative data that he points to Schumpeter's second procedural definition of democracy.[5] By Mayer's argument, Schumpeter's definition is particularly amenable to the 1950s onwards revolution in comparative political science on four grounds: one, the emphasis on the competitive election procedure keeps confusions about values at bay; two, it has face validity and doesn't disturb commonly held assumptions about democracy; three, it is precise insofar as it minimizes ambiguities about selecting which contexts should be regarded as democratic and which shouldn't; and four, it allows for workable gradations to be made of degrees of democracy in administrative procedures.

The shortcomings of existing democratization research, it is suggested, arise from using inadequate definitions without being cognizant of an amenable conceptual framework for them – such as Schumpeter's.

The invocation of Schumpeter's definition to *clarify* the comparative position was perhaps misguided, but the intention remains noteworthy. Schumpeter's procedural definitions of democracy are both open to various problems and ambiguities that I have touched on in Chapter 2 – they are therefore as likely to confuse as clarify if pondered in this context. But to dismiss Mayer's gesture here on those grounds would be to miss the point. What attracts Mayer to Schumpeter's definition is that it derives from a given and reasonably well-conceptualized position which is amenable to the comparative researcher's work. It is not merely a quickly adopted denotative phrase, it gives conceptual content to that denotative turn by trying to lay out specific procedures which can be compared, and by deliberately (but not too jarringly) distancing the definition of democracy from normative connotations and the minimum meaning. This conceptual content both enables the comparative researcher's work, and helps him/her guard against unwarranted inferences and associations which an unconsidered formal definition is unlikely to resist. Irrespective of whether Mayer's choice of Schumpeter is a helpful one, it is certainly an indicative one. It expresses well the desire of those with a broad view of comparative politics to see more conceptual weight underlying the use of comparison in democratization studies, and misgivings about the manner in which comparison is often used in democratization studies.

There is good reason both for the desire and the misgivings: though comparative politics is closely related to democratization studies, the latter has habitually done something – indeed something that has made it a popular and brash area of comparative politics – which goes against the grain of careful comparative research. Either thoughtlessly or systematically, and certainly consistently, democratization studies tend to make normative inferences and present normatively loaded prescriptions from denotatively based comparative data and observations. Democratization studies, in its modern forms, works with tacit normative expectations of democracy while engaging with formations that are denoted as democratic on formal grounds. This always presents a risk of skewing the comparative exercise – both in the selection and in the interpretation of data and observations – in favour of advocacy for alignments which are denoted as democratic. Since democratization studies emerged from and continue primarily within geopolitical spaces that are denoted as formally democratic, some sort of complicity between the apparent objectivity of an empirical comparative exercise and the tacit advocacy of normative expectations can sometimes be reasonably suspected.

Rostow's and Lipset's work provide useful early instances of democratization studies using a comparative methodology. In W. W. Rostow's work in the area a comparative methodology is already accepted as well ensconced. He brings this together with a specific geopolitical perspective – his interest in this area was not generated simply by scholarly developments but also by his perception of post-Second World War threats to US dominance, or US democracy as he saw it, especially from Eurasia (read, the Soviet Union and Eastern European communist countries):

> Whatever the military situation might be, a Eurasia coalesced under totalitarian dictatorships would threaten the survival of democracy both elsewhere and in the United States. It is, therefore, equally in the American interest that the societies of Eurasia develop along lines broadly consistent with the nation's own ideology; for under modern conditions it is difficult to envisage the survival of a democratic American society as an island in a totalitarian era.[6]

The Cold War politics that encouraged both a presumptive division of the world into democratic and authoritarian set the tone for democratization studies. The characterization of the capitalist West as unambiguously *democratic*, and the lumping together of much of the rest of the world as implicitly *authoritarian*, is a kind of reductive and polarized geopolitical mapping that continues to resonate (albeit with certain necessary qualifications). Such reductive and polarized geopolitical mapping involves an assertion of the normative content of these terms *not* by trying to define them in any sense, but by creating a series of geopolitical associations. Instead of spending time sorting through the theoretical and practical connotations of this mode of thinking of democracy, Rostow thereby: (a) presents some places as both connotatively and denotatively democratic or autocratic, (b) *then* tries to flesh out democracy or autocracy by outlining the cultural, economic and political characteristics of those places, and (c) *finally* presents observations – and sometimes prescriptions – on how places that are both connotatively and denotatively autocratic have/can become like places that are both connotatively and denotatively democratic. Thereby a process of polarizing geopolitical perceptions is set in motion; the world is simply divided into good and bad. The altruistic air with which democratization studies address the authoritarian context is constantly imbued with the virtue of speaking from and on behalf of the good polity. Seymour Martin Lipset makes this switch between the denotative and connotative senses of democratization entirely explicit in his pioneering work in democratization studies, *Political Man* (1960): after identifying capitalist Western countries as embodying democracy in practice, he clarifies that what he means by democracy is 'the good society itself in operation'.[7]

For both Lipset and Rostow, the comparative exercise and inferences from it follow with slightly different analytical emphases. Lipset's comparative political surveys of stable democracies and unstable democracies/

dictatorships in primarily European and English-speaking countries on the one hand and Latin America on the other (but with occasional incursions into Asian countries) led influentially to the surmise that democratization is dependent on economic and social development along lines that have been tried and tested in the West. However, the surmise does not entail a rigid set of prescriptions. Indeed, Lipset's view is that democracy actually thrives on conflict or cleavage, when that is contextualized in different ways within: (a) an economic condition that provides basic stability, (b) a social composition that is accustomed to it, and (c) institutional structures that encourage these with stabilizing (rather than destabilizing) effect.[8] Much of Lipset's study therefore is an examination of stable democracies where these have been achieved, and some of it speculates on different ways in which such stable democracies can be emulated or reproduced – or *developed* elsewhere. Rostow's survey of different regimes in Asia, Africa and South America and the potential for democratization therein, comes up less with a developmental model than prescriptions for policy that can be implemented within any state formation with a sufficient will to do so. The idea therefore is that democracy can be deemed to exist in a political state at any level of development if suitable policies and institutions are in place. It is also averred that such a democracy will be successful if it restrains itself to a modernization programme (Rostow outlines six rules in this regard[9]) – modernization is regarded as more an aspect of democracy in practice than a precondition.

The essential outlines of Lipset's and Rostow's comparative political studies of democracy and democratization, both in terms of differences and similarities, appear to me to persist in much future attention to the field – despite more complex distinctions and more graded focal points being introduced. This is especially true for those studies that discerned and responded to a series of regime changes from the 1970s to the 1990s, in Europe (especially Eastern), South America and Africa, that were regarded as establishing democracy (with both denotative and connotative effect). These regime changes have been fashionably swept together as constituting a 'Third Wave' of democratizations by Samuel Huntington.[10] The terminology of democratization as taking place in waves has a somewhat different ring to the kind of categorizations of degrees of democracy and authoritarianism that Lipset and Rostow worked with. The *waves* metaphor conjures up a gradual convergence of different contexts, in different phases of intensity, towards a particular ideal of democratic organization and practice. That, in turn, suggests that the ideal position (in which the connotative and denotative can merge seamlessly) somehow precedes the realization of a democratic regime, and provides a measure for it, in a manner that is indifferent to particular geopolitical experiences. This however is not what actually occurs in most studies of so-called 'Third Wave' democratizations since they derive from the methodological and ideological conventions of earlier comparative political studies. These still depend on geopolitical mappings that are reductive and polarized: it turns out that the countries that ostensibly became democracies in the so-called First and Second Waves – the US and Western Europe – are taken as embodying the ideal position that Third Wave countries have to aspire to. It is seldom asked in this area whether the democratization process (as reaching towards coherence with normative connotations) could be regarded as complete in the contexts that are thus denoted as democratic; or whether it is possible that in some sense such contexts are gradually becoming less democratic by that measure. Researchers into Third Wave democratization rarely chose to go into the complexities of lifeworld that might interrogate their zonalized, with both connotative and denotative effect, view of the world.

Nevertheless, thereby democratization studies has become a carefully elaborated area of academic enquiry and several complex distinctions and graded focal points have been introduced therein beyond the initial efforts outlined so far. A great deal of close attention has been brought to bear on more coherently selected contexts and criteria. This has included studies particularly of the models of representative government (Lijphart[11]), elective practices (Katz[12]), processes of ideological and administrative functioning (Barnes, Kaase *et al.*[13]), in currently denoted democracies. Countries that have experienced regime change in a denotatively democratic direction have been compared and contrasted with particular explanatory factors in view. The degree to which primarily capitalist economic development has arguably impelled such change is examined in books by Rueschmeyer, Stephens and Stephens; Haggard and Kaufman; Larry Diamond; and Przeworksi, Alvarez, Cheibub and Limongi.[14] The role that leaders of different social movements and alignments play in pro-democratic transitions from authoritarian regimes was explored influentially in O'Donnell, Schmitter and Whitehead's work and that of Higley and Gunther.[15] How institutional and structural reform and change consolidate democracy is the thrust of Linz and Stepan's work and that of Hadenius.[16] The extent to which pro-democratic regime change is propelled by civil society and social movements (again with the normative associations examined in relation to deliberative democracy and radical democracy theorists), especially in South America, Eastern Europe and Asia, has received a prodigious amount of attention – in books by Haynes; Jelin and Hersberg; Quigley; Taylor; Escobar and Alvarez; Clark; Wiarda and Weinstein; Catarina Kinnvall and Kristina Jönsson,[17] and others. I have referred here only to a small number of authored and edited volumes. Each of these foci and emphases come with critiques of other approaches. Thus an emphasis on economic development and modernization is criticized for not being able to account for reasonably stable democratization of poor countries and the importance of the will of citizens and civil society. The notion that democratization is completed by institutional reform and construction is questioned for the degrees of anti-democratic manipulability in the latter that has often been manifested. Euphoric championing of social movements and civil society as agents of democratization has been countered by scepticism about their often hidden agendas and the character of their post-democratization incorporation into the establishment. And so on. Of particular interest in this study: there's also growing awareness that much of democratization studies have been conducted on a conservative basis with regard to boundaries.

The conservatism with regard to boundaries derives from the reductive and polarized origins of democratization studies from comparative politics and a Cold War world view. In most instances democratization is understood as something that pertains to and is confined within the boundaries of given political states (countries); democratization studies generally deal with democracy as a domestic matter. Even when international factors are necessarily brought into the analysis of democratization – in terms of the exertions of international pressure groups and regulatory bodies, the necessity of taking international economic flows or information flows into consideration, etc. – it is with the assumption that the establishment of a democratic regime is ultimately manifested within constituted political states. The international political view that is usually espoused in democratization studies is very close to the anarchic *realpolitik* view that Kenneth Waltz advocated,[18] with political states as the primary units working on the principle of self-interest. The thrust of the internationalist perspective of democratization studies lies more in its epistemological prerogatives (following the comparative politics methodology) than in understanding of the empirical field. The givenness of political state boundaries is simply a convenient circumstance, which dovetails into an inherited penchant for defining democracy through association with particular areas and to create polarities.

Some of this conservatism is beginning to be redressed in promising ways. To some extent this has been a matter of interrogating whether democratization as it is commonly understood is about the extension of democracy in a participatory sense, or whether it is more aptly the extension of Western/Northern hegemony under the guise of the rhetoric of democratization. In contemplating this question, there is scope here for sifting through the mixture of normative connotations and legislative denotations, and moving towards careful politically realist assessments of democracy in our world, particularly in the international/transnational domain. Amongst the many books that address the complexity of boundaries under the purview of democratization studies, the essays edited by Jochen Hippler are of interest. Almost all in this collection are directly devoted to demonstrating that the rhetoric of democratization has often been calculated for advocacy of Western/Northern hegemony in relevant Third World contexts.[19] On a somewhat different note, though I have objected to the normative deployments that occur in this area, it should be registered that the idea of civil society has been self-consciously recruited as something that impinges upon democratization and the practice of democracy in productive ways too. Democratization studies on the relationship between democracy and civil society have undermined the inherited conservatism, even while reifying the inherited switches between normative connotations and legislative denotations.

Cross- or trans-boundary processes are examined with the intention of going beyond the conservatism of democratization studies in Jean Grugel's edited volume, *Democracy without Borders*.[20] In the introductory chapter, the editor objects to precisely the kinds of conservatism, reductiveness and polarization, derived from Cold War world views, that have characterized this area, and offers the following realization:

> Democracy has . . . become 'globalized'. It is intimately tied up with pressures generated at the international level and the agency exercised by a number of transnationally active groups and organizations. To win international acceptance and success in the contemporary global order states must, it is generally assumed, create systems that can plausibly be called 'democratic'.
>
> The globalization of democracy takes on a particular form at the regional level: as struggles for democracy get underway in a particular region, authoritarian states in the region can find the costs of isolation too great a price to pay. It becomes difficult for them to use arguments that democracy is a foreign import when their immediate neighbours are trying, perhaps successfully, to introduce it. At the same time, civil society organizations imitate or learn from tactics from neighbouring countries or even further afield, and external agencies frequently apply 'recipes' or 'best practice' formulae that are regional in their assumptions and prescriptions.[21]

Despite the salutary intentions of this collection – self-consciously working against the limitations of conventional democratization studies – it nevertheless subscribes to those limitations itself. That this collection is itself, while protesting otherwise, in the mould of conservative democratization studies is evident within the above quotation. The reductive 'Third Wave' geopolitical mapping of traditional democratization studies is assumed wholesale, and this focus remains on Africa, South America, East and Central Europe. Within these the rhetoric of polarization (authoritarian versus democratic) continues to be applied, even though the excessive neatness of these as antonyms are pondered. Political state boundaries are implicitly maintained. These are held as being interactive (neighbours affect each other, civil societies within different boundaries influence each other) rather than porous, and the complicity of some political state interests with international pressure groups and organizations is overlooked by presenting the latter as simply transnational agents. Democracy, even though admittedly globalized, is still conveniently denotatively and connotatively given. The democratic credentials of so-called Western democracy are not opened to interrogation, and more specifically the democratic character of their international agendas is left unquestioned.

In a similar vein are also debates about the prospects of comparative studies in relation to democratization, not with reference to transitions and regime changes, but to transnational actors playing regulatory roles in an increasingly interconnected and interdependent world. Bruce Morrison's edited book, *Transnational Democracy in Critical and Comparative Perspective*,[22] is relevant here. Most of the papers in this either put in a plea for not losing sight of state-centred comparative studies of democracy in approaching this important and new field, while some content themselves with laying out a preliminary model of the actors involved and their interconnections from local to transnational level.[23] The main suggestion for the practice of comparative politics in this field, and therefore worthy of note, comes from David Beetham. While noting that democratic arrangements and criteria for measuring democracy that comparative politics usually accepts for nation-states need not be relevant to international formations (like the UN, World Bank, IMF, WTO, etc.), he suggests that some of these could nevertheless, and with modest ambitions, be applied to the latter. This could occur by taking 'some of the main international institutions we actually have, and explore what are the assumptions about membership, representation, accountability, and so on that are embedded in their existing practice'.[24] Though such an exercise is likely to extend the ambiguities and connotative/denotative confusions of democratization studies outside conservative state-centred lines, the displacement of denotative object involved may well entail a more rigorous reconsideration of the conceptual basis of democratization studies.

Democratization studies in relation to the comparative methodology is, however, the area where more imaginative rethinking about democracy may occur. To move towards a conclusion for these observations on democratization studies I would like to touch upon the recent work of Laurence Whitehead as opening up such a possibility. Though, in terms of examples, Whitehead's interest is primarily in South American and Asian countries, his introduction to terms like democracy and civil society registers all the complex nuances implicit therein, and his theorizations on international and transnational linkages are splendidly nuanced and complex, and generally less ideologically partisan than is usual. To a great extent this is due to the methodological ploy of organizing these complexities not by resorting to the reductions and polarizations that enable conventional comparative political study, but by using appropriately fluid and complex analogies. Instead of artifically *making* the area ideologically and methodologically amenable, the idea here is to illuminate it in all its complexity by defamiliarizing it – by consistently threading observations around an accommodative analogy that reveals it in an unfamiliar and therefore clarifying light. To this end,

Whitehead employs the analogy of theatre or dramatic performance to the playing out of democratization and democracy in practice. The chapter where Whitehead explains why 'the complex dynamics, shifting agendas, and multiple interactions that characterize all [democratic transition] processes can be integrated and brought into focus by the construction of an analogy with theatre and drama'[25] informs the present study to a significant extent.

It seems likely to me that such imaginative turns in democratization studies will in the future add to politically realist explanative analysis. And, very possibly, go beyond the constraints of politically realist analysis by rationally developing prescriptive analysis from that explanative base. By and large, as it stands, however, democratization studies is still primarily associated with ideologically partisan conservative patterns – which insert into our politically real world the kind of normatively loaded confusions and ambiguities that are seen to operate, in a variety of ways, in cosmopolitian democracy, Rawlsian liberal democracy, deliberative democracy, radical democracy. And yet, the comparative methodology, especially when applied with clearly defined denotative limitations, is also sometimes used to interrogate the formulations, descriptions, convictions and excesses of less empirically focused and more normatively led conceptual positions regarding democracy. In fact the attachment to the real world which the comparative methodology of democratization studies brings, however tenuously and conditionally, is often the most – sometimes only – effective way of questioning connotative/denotative switches and ambiguities about boundaries that characterize so many of the surveyed positions. Democratization studies often carry us into their own obfuscations, but also have a demonstrable capacity to return conceptualization to a careful consideration of the real world and political realism. Some instances of this are picked up in the next and final chapter of this part, where the articulation and mobilization of democracy in the context of real world processes is considered briefly – before moving on to the specific context of the invasion and occupation of Iraq in 2002–2004 in Part II.

NOTES

1 Mattei Dogan, 'Use and Misuse of Statistics in Comparative Research', in Mattei Dogan and Ali Kazancigil (eds), *Comparing Nations: Concepts of Strategies and Substance* (Oxford: Blackwell, 1994), p. 63.

2 Mattei Dogan, 'The Pendulum Between Theory and Substance', ibid., pp. 297–313.

3 B. Guy Peters, *Comparative Politics: Theory and Methods* (Basingstoke: Palgrave, 1998), p. 225.

4 Lawrence C. Mayer, *Redefining Comparative Politics: Promise Versus Performance* (Newbury Park, CA: Sage, 1989), p. 15.

5 Ibid., Ch. 4 – the advantages of the Schumpeterian definition are discussed in pp. 107–10.

6 W. W. Rostow, *The United States in the World Arena: A Study in Recent History* (New York: Harper & Row, 1960), p. 544.

7 Seymour Martin Lipset, *Political Man: The Social Bases of Politics* (New York: Doubleday, 1960), p. 439.
8 Ibid., Ch.1.
9 W. W. Rostow, *Politics and the Stages of Growth* (Cambridge: Cambridge University Press, 1971), pp. 300–1.
10 Samuel Huntington, *The Third Wave: Democratization in the Late Twentieth Century* (Norman, OK: University of Oklahoma Press, 1991).
11 Arend Lijphart, *Democracies: Patterns of Majoritarian and Consensus Government in Twenty-One Countries* (New Haven, CT: Yale University Press, 1984).
12 Richard S. Katz, *Democracy and Elections* (New York: Oxford University Press, 1997).
13 Samuel H. Barnes, Max Kaase *et al.*, *Political Action: Mass Participation in Five Western Democracies* (Beverly Hills, CA: Sage, 1979).
14 D. Rueschmeyer, E. Stephens and J. Stephens, *Capitalist Development and Democracy* (Cambridge: Polity, 1992); Samuel Haggard and Robert Kaufman, *Political Economy of Democratic Transitions* (Princeton, NJ: Princeton University Press, 1992); Larry Diamond, *Developing Democracy* (Baltimore, MD: Johns Hopkins University Press, 1999); Adam Przeworski, Michael Alvarez, J. A. Cheibub and Fernando Limongi, *Democracy and Development* (Cambridge: Cambridge University Press, 2000).
15 G. O'Donnell, P. C. Schmitter and L. Whitehead (eds), *Transitions from Authoritarian Rule* (Baltimore, MD: Johns Hopkins University Press, 1986); J. Higley and R. Gunther (eds), *Elites and Democratic Consolidation in Latin America and Southern Europe* (Cambridge: Cambridge University Press, 1992).
16 Juan J. Linz and Alfred Stepan, *Problems of Democratic Transition and Consolidation* (Baltimore, MD: Johns Hopkins University Press, 1996); Axel Hadenius, *Democracy and Development* (Cambridge: Cambridge University Press, 1992); Axel Hadenius, *Institutions and Democratic Citizenship* (Oxford: Oxford University Press, 2001).
17 Jeffrey Haynes, *Democracy and Civil Society in the Third World* (Cambridge: Polity, 1997); Elizabeth Jelin and Eric Hersberg (eds), *Constructing Democracy* (Boulder, CO: Westview, 1996); K. F. F. Quigley, *For Democracy's Sake* (Washington, DC: Woodrow Wilson Centre Press, 1997); Lucy Taylor, *Citizenship, Participation and Democracy* (Basingstoke, Macmillan, 1998); Arturo Escobar and Sonia Alvarez (eds), *The Making of Social Movements in Latin America* (Boulder, CO: Westview, 1992); John Clark, *Democratizing Development* (London: Earthscan, 1991); Howard Wiarda and James Weinstein, *Civil Society* (Boulder, CO: Westview, 2003); Catarina Kinnvall and Kristina Jönsson, *Globalization and Democratization in Asia* (London: Routledge, 2002).
18 Kenneth Waltz, *Theory of International Politics* (New York: McGraw Hill, 1979).
19 Jochen Hippler (ed.), *The Democratisation of Disempowerment: The Problem of Democracy in the Third World* (London: Pluto, 1995).
20 Jean Grugel (ed.), *Democracy Without Borders: Transnationalization and Conditionality in New Democracies* (London: Routledge, 1999).
21 Jean Grugel, 'Contextualizing Democratization', in ibid., pp. 19–20.
22 Bruce Morrison (ed.), *Transnational Democracy in Critical and Comparative Perspective: Democracy's Range Reconsidered* (Aldershot: Ashgate, 2003).
23 Bruce Morrison's (pp. 37–54) and Katherine Fierlbeck's (pp. 67–84) contributions emphasize the importance of historical understanding; Chadwick F. Alger's (pp. 87–105) charts out connections between NGOs, the UN and local authorities – all in ibid.
24 David Beetham, 'Fashioning Democracy at National and International Levels', ibid., p. 150.
25 Laurence Whitehead, *Democratization: Theory and Experience* (Oxford: Oxford University Press, 2002), p. 36 in Ch. 2.

8 *Democracy and the Real World*

In the above examinations of some of the most influential conceptual positions regarding democracy of our time – realist perspectives, cosmopolitan democracy, Rawlsian liberal democracy, deliberative democracy, radical democracy, comparative democratization studies – certain links and concurrent patterns are discerned. My focus has primarily been on attempts to embrace an international/transnational domain; it is evident that this focus is not so much a chosen delimitation as the central concern of conceptual efforts now. I presented the discernible links and patterns between these positions as playing around two themes in generally contradictory or obfuscating ways, and often with dangerous implications. Primarily, the tendency and implications of slipping in an unaware or irrational fashion between the connotative and denotative nuances of democracy is remarked. And, I noted the various ways in which boundaries are closed, crossed and opened, often simultaneously – with agonized irresolution, with worrying normative unilateral possibilities, with exclusionary implications masked as universalist inclusiveness, with humanitarian intentions that can be appropriated with ease to serve narrower ends, with radical rhetoric that shrouds approval of *status quo*, with pluralistic and multiculturalist aspirations that entail polarization and ideological hegemony, within linguistics performances, idealized and partisan locations, selective or skewed arrangements of real world observations, etc. There is therefore an overarching disposition to this conceptual field, it seems to me. Assertions, contestations and anxieties in the field converge around certain superseding loci, particularly:

1. a penchant for inserting decontextualized ethical norms into politics – wherein norms are associatively joined together on the basis of prevailing usage and expectations (and given denotative content wherever possible), rather than derived from historical and material analysis; and
2. the conviction that individual subjects/citizens, groups/communities of different sorts, international/transnational formations or alignments of various kinds, and humanity as a whole can be held apart and yet blurred into each other for a sought-after 'unified field theory', so to say, of politics – where and how this is done is more a matter of conceptual ease (and political exigency?) and less of observed and analytical veracity.

Though my own mode of analysis has revolved around the linguistic play and conceptual articulations involved in the above, these are *not* matters that refer only or even predominantly to the field of discursive construction and performance. These matters do not derive within discourse, are not simply communicatively and discursively constructed, are not enacted on the surface of texts and communications, do not impinge in ways that can be charted through discourse alone, and are certainly not resolvable in discursive gestures and processes. To my understanding, these are material matters, deriving from and referring to and articulated within and with effect on empirical reality. All conceptual positions, irrespective of claims to the contrary, have to do with the visceral and tangible experiences and exchanges of the real world, and their articulations are referential and contemplative and embedded therein, more perhaps as transitory illuminations than as impenetrable post-structuralist post-modernist ether. If the ambiguities and expectations of everyday usage have to be struggled against, and seep into and inform considered and rigorous conceptualizations of democracy, it is because the field of everyday usage is constituted in political claims, policies and actions, economic processes and dispossessions, and so on. The articulation of each conceptual position constantly draws upon and occurs in and returns to – explanatively, predictively, prescriptively, with visionary intent – the real world. The responsibility of theorists and researchers (broadly intellectuals, understood in different ways) is accorded and sometimes withheld on that understanding. So, the broad conceptual positions regarding democracy in the international/transnational domain discussed above are inextricably wound up in a complex relationship with perceived and examinable events and observations of the real world. The manner in which they relate to the understanding and consideration of, let's say, micro-levels of observations and documentations – subfields of political investigation – of real world processes must necessarily be a crucial element of such a survey, and such a study, as this one. The above observations on the broad conceptual positions regarding democracy in the international/transnational domain would be incomplete without juxtaposing them against and with regard to particularly focused and observable facets of that domain.

To that end this chapter is devoted to addressing some specific and much discussed facets of the current international/transnational domain, with particular attention to the manner in which democracy is articulated therein, and in which some of the conceptual positions outlined above appear. These pave the way for a detailed consideration of democracy in the international/transnational domain, with reference to the complex real world context of the invasion and occupation of Iraq, September 2002–June 2004. Existing investigations of three facets in particular of the current international/transnational domain, with a strong bearing on ideas of democracy, demand attention: existing arrangements for international/transnational governance and economic regulation; the disposition and processes of mass media; the perceived convergence of social movements (particularly on anti-globalization or anti-capitalism). These especially demand attention in view of the context I come to in Part II. That I focus on these here is not because these are the only aspects of the current world with a bearing on democracy. Nor is my consideration of these in any way extensive. My choice of these, and the limits of my discussion of these, is guided by the preceding and forthcoming strands of this study. The following is mainly a matter of registering the continuity between this and the next part, and giving this survey closure by indicating where research and thinking can be thought of as currently situated.

EXISTING ARRANGEMENTS FOR INTERNATIONAL/TRANSNATIONAL GOVERNANCE AND ECONOMIC REGULATION

As observed in Chapter 3, cosmopolitan democrats have focused primarily on the United Nations as the organization through which democratic governance in the transnational/international domain may be realized. Bobbio's discernment of a 'democratic inspiration' therein, and Held's, Archibugi's and others' sense of the potential therein, and indeed realist doubts about such optimistic views of the UN derive from readings of its current status. Thus both Bobbio and Zolo present their views in terms of differently nuanced readings of the evolution of international alignments from the Peace of Westphalia to the League of Nations to the UN. Without going into the complexity of that history, with regard to the UN's current status and its relation to concepts of democracy two points are important (and both are recruited in Bobbio's argument about the UN's 'democratic inspiration'). One, constitutionally and pragmatically, it appears to operate on the basis of a multilateral democracy of sovereign states principle. Thus, in the UN General Assembly, all member states, irrespective of domestic ideology or military and economic power, have an equal say in making resolutions which are equally binding on all. This could be thought of as an internationalist approach to democracy. Two, simultaneously, but with less functional effect, the UN champions a principle of liberal democracy which inclines it towards the promulgation of particular, at present domestically based, arrangements as extendable to a transnational level. Thus, the 1948 UN Universal Declaration of Human Rights includes Article 21, which not only endorses democracy's normative connotations ('1. Everyone has the right to take part in the government of his country, directly or through freely chosen representatives. 2. Everyone has the right to equal access to public service in his country'), but also gives it denotative content by accepting majoritarian processes ('3. The will of the people shall be the basis of the authority of government; this will shall be expressed in periodic and genuine elections which shall be by universal and equal suffrage and shall be held by secret vote or by equivalent free voting procedures'). This could be thought of as a transnationalist approach to democracy. At present these have only a sort of good-practice function in the UN, and multilateral agreement is the functional means of UN operations. The possibility of making liberal democratic principles functional in the UN, by placing the multilateral mechanism as subject to the constitutional enshrinement of liberal democratic norms/practices, gives cosmopolitan democrats hope. In recommending reforms in that direction, cosmopolitan democrats hope to overcome the kinds of anti-democratic unevenness that are instilled in the current multilateral mechanism in the UN – a matter that realists focus on particularly.

Realists point out against such hopes that neither the apparently universal and decontextual norms of liberal democracy as championed by the UN, nor the multilateral democracy that apparently operates in the UN, conform to their ostensible purposes in the real functioning or constitution of the UN. A close historical analysis of the evolution and functioning of the UN shows that it serves as a forum for controlled power politics to protect existing (state, or larger than state) vested interests. The normative connotations of democracy have been endlessly manipulated by states and alignments which have associated it with their denotatively democratic credentials to hide realist and narrower interests. Even the multilateral democratic mechanism, as currently functional in the UN, is *constitutionally* undermined to serve those interests. In view of these observations, the 'democratic inspiration' that is discerned in the UN is actually either due to the misdirections of political rhetoric or due to wishful thinking. The UN cannot be reformed to fulfil its potential because such potential isn't in it. Democracy in the transnational domain, if possible at all, must be sought elsewhere. International democracy may have some mileage by the rationalization of the multilateral mechanism, but that would need a reforming will and agency powerful enough to overcome existing vested interests, and it is difficult to see where that can emerge from yet.

Since the democracy deficit (in its own terms) of the multilateral mechanism as operative in the UN now is a matter on which cosmopolitans and realists – indeed all parties – agree, and since this has a particular bearing on some of the debates described in Part II, a brief registering of this situation is in order here.[1] Though the June 1945 UN Charter (amended 20 December 1971) recognizes the 'sovereign equality' of all members in Article 2.1, and in the procedures of the General Assembly (one member, one vote, and two-thirds majority decisions in Article 18), this is compromised immediately in the constitution and procedures of the UN Security Council. The identification of 5 of the 15 members therein as permanent in Article 23 (China, France, Russia, UK and US), and the veto votes that they have (Article 27.3), introduce an insurmountable obstruction to the principle of equitable multilateralism. The manner in which the remaining ten members are arrived at (according to Article 23, in terms of contribution and equitable geographical distribution, and more clearly defined in terms of geopolitical spread in Resolution 1991 A (XVIII) of 17 December 1963) does nothing to circumvent their joint comparative weakness in decision-making. This unevenness is replicated in that, while UNSC decisions are binding according to its determination on all UN members, these decisions require no ratification from and are not answerable to the General Assembly. The reasons for this unevenness are found in the history and persistence of military and economic factors from the midst of which the UN emerged and continues to exist – we need not go into these for this study.

However, the UN in itself is actually only a small part of existing international/transnational arrangements with democratic claims, and the space it occupies in current conceptual positions is arguably excessive. A series of transnational alliances and organizations, some regionally defined and some with wider and more dispersed global effectiveness, which incorporate particularly transnational economic and military regulatory and executive functions (and more generally impinge on governance in general), are more central to current debates about democracy in this field. These include such widely discussed formations as the G8 and the European Union, which combine economic, military and administrative possibilities (the latter with unprecedented regional effectiveness); economic regulation and investment bodies such as the World Bank, the World Trade Organization (WTO), the International Monetary Fund (IMF), the North American Free Trade Association (NAFTA), and so on; security-centred bodies such as the North Atlantic Treaty Organization (NATO). These have increasingly made strong claims of having an effective transnational character and fostering liberal democratic principles with both denotative/connotative effect. These have also increasingly come to be regarded as facets of an international establishment that systematically undermine the normative connotations of democracy (as in reality fostering global inequality, serving dominant economic and political interests, and extending unfreedom and repression in marginalized sectors). Clearly the fissures that work across the different conceptual positions about democracy in the international/transnational domain outlined above, cut into (impassioned) debates in this area too. The claims made on all sides work with similar kinds of normative assumptions about democracy and confusions about the denotative scope of democracy.

To some degree, checks on the excessive normativity and confusion about practice that occupies this entire area are provided by empirically based attempts to check claims with some sort of comparative perspective. Such attempts are notoriously open to generating their own confusions as I observed in the previous chapter; they are usually limited by the artificiality of their standards and the selectivity of their range, by their subservience to terms which seem to overstep those limits, by their being conducted within and for the benefit of partisan organizations (like states and corporations), and by the multiple ways in which they can be interpreted. Nevertheless these are often rigorous studies that question attractive ideas and claims about democracy in real world terms, and sometimes indicate currently predominant observations. Two such areas of empirical observation (as disposed now), which have a bearing on democratic claims implicit in current transnational economic and military arrangements, are worth taking note of: one, addressing the effects of global capital mobility and (especially conditional) foreign investment; and two, addressing evidence relating to the democratic peace concept (that is so crucially centred in Rawls's formulations, so implicit generally in the normative expectations of most current conceptual positions, and so aggressively used in real world political rhetoric).

A plethora of empirically based observation and research attests that the transnational economic regulation, policy recommendations and aid that is provided by the World Bank, WTO, IMF, NAFTA, etc., on the basis of extending democratic norms (such as freedom, choice and equality) through facilitating trade and market liberalization, have demonstrably undermined those norms. Joseph Stiglitz's revelations on the manner in which the World Bank and the IMF followed ideologically led doctrines of trade liberalization that were contrary to the enrichment of developing countries;[2] Amy Chua's examination of South East Asian, African, Post-Communist Russian and African contexts to conclude that 'the global spread of free market democracy has . . . been a principal, aggravating cause of ethnic instability and violence throughout the non-Western world';[3] Richard Peet's similarly broad-ranging study of the disenfranchisements caused and ideological manoeuvrings of IMF, World Bank and WTO operations[4] – are but three studies with a wide scope of comparative observations, which coalesce with numerous more regionally focused and event-specific studies in the area. Generally, insofar as these consider notions of democracy, they test its normative connotations by directing them against the agencies and processes through which democracy is claimed to be instilled and consolidated; equally, in doing so, those normative connotations are also asserted. Thus, Chua ultimately locates the problem of exacerbation of Third World conflicts due to free market democracy in its formalization as (and denotative equivalence with) majoritarian politics – because such democratization increases the political presence and power of indigenous minorities in ways that disturb stability in developing countries. And she suggests ways of making 'democracy mean more than majority rule'[5] which chime in with the views of cosmopolitan and deliberative democrats. So, while valuably clarifying the conceptual confusions regarding democracy and manipulations wrought through such confusions, these also – as far as the single issue of democracy goes – don't go much beyond that, except in looking hopefully to existing conceptual prescriptions and visions. Ambiguities of current conceptual positions are actually more effectively, but rarely, examined when clear characterizations of what are *denoted* as democratic are adopted to conduct empirical studies of economic arrangements. The clearest measures of democracy (denotatively understood) are still, of course, those pertaining to political processes and institutions within states – within what are commonly *called* liberal democracies. Several studies have found evidence that policies and actions by transnational economic organizations such as those named above have a contradictory or counter-intuitive relationship to denotatively democratic arrangements. Thus, applying an economic legal perspective to the conditionality (especially in insisting on privatization) that has systematically attached to IMF aid to developing countries (but deliberately unevenly not to developed countries) through the 1980s and 1990s, Daniel Kalderimis finds that it is:

> . . . not conducive to healthy democracy. Issues that would usually be at the centre of democratic debate are simply removed from the table. A country reliant on the IMF is bound to follow certain paths in relation to many of the most pressing issues concerning the population: taxes, foreign investment, social welfare, land distribution, privatization. This means that, no matter which party is in power, the agenda on important points is fixed. This leads to elections being trivialized through candidates campaigning not on serious policy differences but on minor or personality issues.[6]

An extended empirical study on foreign direct investment and economic growth in denotably democratic countries leads Indra de Soysa to believe that it is not so much the formal elective mechanism and increased participatory possibilities that lead to growth, as the institutional facilitation of contestation.[7] De Soysa sees both as aspects of democracy denotatively understood (she draws her conceptual model from Dahl's 'polyarchy'), and uses rigorously defined and limited measures of participation (election rolls) and contestation to provide an empirical basis for inferences. Using public opinion polls as indicators of democratic consent, Carl B. Hamilton finds that disapprobation of WTO's, IMF's, and World Bank's policies, objectives and achievements are not clear cut even in developing countries, and are often received with approval.[8] These and such empirical studies are of course severely limited by their self-imposed methodological restrictions in denoting democracy; but it is precisely that which places them as effective foils to valuable, but equally limited, empiricist studies led by normative presumptions about democracy. Nor do these lend themselves easily to ideological advocacy, and their precise place in conceptualization is far from clear. But, it seems to me that realist conceptualization may rest vitally on questioning the complexities, presumptions and findings of such studies.

In a somewhat different direction, similar empirically based comparative studies are also interrogating the conceptual associations made between democracy and peace – cheerfully claimed with transnational effect by the

UN, NATO, EU, etc., and by denotatively liberal democracies like the US and the UK. Here, it seems to me, the stronger observations and analyses are given by those who do not find evidence for such an assumption. Especially noteworthy here is Errol Henderson's study of democratic peace theories. Addressing himself particularly to the observation that post-Second World War there have been no conflicts between denotatively democratic states, he finds both existing dyadic peace and monadic peace propositions to be problematic in relation to empirical evidence. His analysis instead leads him to a different contention:

> . . . a combination of factors including bipolarity, nuclear deterrence, alliance aggregation, and trade links contributed to the formation of an international security regime among the major-power democracies and their minor-power democratic allies. It was this international regime – more than joint democracy – that allowed for postwar joint democratic stability.[9]

Another sustained examination of the democratic peace theory, this time based on public opinion research as an indicator of empirically measurable democratic perspectives (with many warnings about the limitations of this), comes from Philip P. Everts. With various measures of public responses to the Gulf War of 1990–1991, the Yugoslav Conflict and the Kosovo War at hand, Everts decides that 'democracies are sensitive to the stimulating effects of a successful war as long as the human costs remain limited and are kept out of sight',[10] and that in different ways perceptions of justice, domestic interest and security/risks can all be managed to gain democratic legitimacy for war from a democratic public opinion point of view. These perceptions drawn from public opinion research have been confirmed in such analysis of pro-war public opinion polling as is available for conflicts after 11 September 2001.[11] Careful empirically based analysis lending credence to the democratic peace theory has more or less tapered away after 11 September: support for this generally appears now in accepting democratic peace as a given proposition before proceeding to extend its scope and application.[12]

Before moving on to considerations of democracy and the mass media, a final and obvious observation about existing arrangements for transnational/international governance. There is now universal acceptance that at a formal level existing international/transnational arrangements are either aligned or skewed in favour of, or operate in a manner that is conditional to, the domination of the US as the single post-Cold War superpower. The manner in which US economic and military power impinges upon, and determines or manipulates or occasionally defies the operation of, formal international/transnational arrangements has been prolifically documented from a plethora of perspectives and methodologies – so numerous and familiar is this literature that it doesn't need elaboration here. Many of the obfuscations in conceptualizing democracy highlighted in this part, and aspired to or assumed in existing formal arrangements in the international/transnational domain, are often explicitly linked with the extension of US domination and imperial ambitions. Thus, the political framework of decontextualized and universalized normative connotations of democracy are increasingly read as being means used for the covert imperial extension of US power; and the switching of those normative connotations with the US's self-proclaimed denotatively democratic status the means of that covert extension. It is also observed that this perception – quite possibly, this reality – is increasingly generating, at various levels from states to regional alliances to civil society, anxiety if not outright hostility, towards the US. Continuing and effective multilateralism in international/transnational organizations may be regarded as at least a formal registering of the imbalance of power and influence that the US represents. There is some evidence that in the only formally balanced multilateral forum in the UN, the General Assembly, the distance between US policy and the preferences of the rest of the world had been consistently growing between 1991 and 2001,[13] and that this might be the case too in the wake of the invasion and occupation of Iraq in 2002–2004.

THE DISPOSITION AND PROCESSES OF MASS MEDIA

The enormous amount of research undertaken in recent years on the mass media in relation to the theory and practice of democracy[14] attests to the importance of this area. The main thrust of this research is to reconcile the connotations of democracy with the often determinative role that mass media play in politics: especially in mediating perceptions and participations across nation-state boundaries, and given that media corporations often operate as transnational entities. Established approaches to the relationship between media and democracy have continued to be revisited. These often maintain that mass media can enable normative weight (consistent with the connotations of democracy) to be given to the functioning of democracies (denotatively understood), by providing information and analysis in an objective and fair fashion in the public interest. Much research addresses the impediments to public interest media functioning, primarily partisan ideological interventions (often tacit and shrouded ones) by those who control and own media provision and services – the state and/or private corporations. Research into partisan manoeuvring of the media by state–corporation nexuses generally follows the powerful analytical apparatus put in place by Noam Chomsky and Edward Herman.[15] Chomsky's view of the media's propagandist function does not point to straightforward advocacy through images and slogans but to the implications of selectivity and presentation of information and images, and the sources they derive from and attributions of authority they come with. Thus it is not so much a centralist propaganda programme that is discerned, as a complex interplay of environment and media to converge on certain ideological presumptions. In documenting and theorizing this sophisticated propaganda model of mass media, Chomsky usually appeals to distortions from the normative connotations of democracy.[16] Similar appeals to the normative connotations of democracy and demonstrations of the undemocratic propagandist functioning of the mass media have continued to appear persuasively and particularly with regard to the US's allegedly pro-democracy and anti-terrorist wars after 11 September 2001.[17] Less politically responsive, and more theoretically engaged approaches to the nuances of democracy in the context of mass media in the international/transnational domain, now usually maintain that the above stated conviction in public interest media is questionable and idealistic.[18]

One direction taken in responses to the perceived inadequacy of public interest mass media as a pragmatic mode of protecting democracy (connotatively and denotatively understood) is to gesture towards possible alternatives. In this spirit James Curran proposes a remodelling of media provision around a number of nodes representing different sectors: private enterprise, social market, civic, professional and public service.[19] He still places public service at the core of the model, but the formal and distinct incorporation of other sectors purportedly enables wider participation and representation, and moreover comes with increased transparency of interests, and embraces information flows and divergent perspectives/debates across a range of boundaries (therefore is attuned to a dynamic international/transnational domain). In a similar direction, but with a different emphasis, are reflections on the possibilities of democratic participation and representation arising from new media and information technology. Increased speed and variety of information flows, and the facilitation of simultaneous communication and group interactions, across boundaries through new media and information communication technologies are naturally of interest. These have already had a demonstrable impact on democratic theory and practice, both by their effect on democratic processes (denotatively understood), and by opening up possibilities of invigorating democracy (connotatively understood). These are receiving[20] and will continue to receive attention. Of particular interest within this broad area has been the use of new media and communication technologies in protests and activism on an international scale, often addressing transnational arrangements.[21] I discuss the nuances of such activism and protests below; the point to be noted here is that these claim, and are often regarded as revitalizing, democracy (with connotative implications intact) in ways that are outside processes that are formally denoted as democratic. To a crucial degree, the international reach of such activism, and therefore the creation of a perceivably democratic anti-establishment sphere, with visible gestures and activities, has flourished through the co-opting of new media and communication technologies.

Another direction taken by responses to the perceived inadequacies of public service mass media focuses on the understanding of democracy itself. Such responses attempt to take on board some of the recent conceptualizations of democracy that extend to the international/transnational domain. Thus, for example, Jostein Gripsrud brings Habermas's notion of the public sphere and envisioning of deliberative democracy to bear on media culture,[22] and Elizabeth Jacka argues the need to embrace radical democracy to conceptualize the place of mass media in politics[23] (along the lines of John Hartley's work on the role of television[24]). Such attempts however often replicate the debates and ambiguities that have occupied the broader conceptual field. Jacka's championing of radical democracy for media studies is a case in point: it was published with a rejoinder from Nicholas Garnham,[25] which effectively presented a debate that was analogous in many ways to the macro-level exchange between Laclau/Mouffe and Geras.

THE PERCEIVED CONVERGENCE OF SOCIAL MOVEMENTS

Propelled primarily by a series of well-coordinated, quantitatively significant, visible and effective protests staged at meetings of transnational economic and military alignments such as the World Bank, IMF, WTO, NAFTA, and G8 (and especially after the protests in Seattle in December 1999 during a WTO meeting), a substantial body of literature has engaged with 'social movements'.[26] These are generally characterized as 'anti-globalization' or 'anti-capitalist' movements, and explorations of these have been driven by several perceptions.

First, it appeared that the visible manifestation and increasing frequency of such gestures are merely the tip of the iceberg. These are symptoms or surface manifestations of a larger and deeper phenomenon. These represent the convergence of: a range of identity-based or local-issue-based activities and gestures (addressing poverty, localized oppressions, culture-specific disaffections, the operations of corporations/states on specific ecosystems, etc.) within the global South or East; left and right oriented marginal political factions with specific agendas (ending Third World debt and mistreatment of migrants, protecting the environment or animal rights, extending Christian charity, etc.) in the global North or West; and locally as well as transnationally active NGOs. The scale of the phenomenon merits attention, because behind such moments of convergence lie an enormous variety of protest activities dispersed among those interest groups in a large number of locations.

Second, these moments of convergence present an opportunity to announce some degree of commonality of objective and purpose in them, or perhaps to generate such commonality of purpose amongst them. These very divergent interests can be presented as aligned in a specific direction through the adoption of an inclusive terminology (a political linguistic performance suggestive of universal interest and purpose). This is encapsulated in the term *movement*, especially when appended to 'anti-capitalist' or 'anti-globalization' – negatives of terms that already claim or aspire to embrace a wide variety of ideological and material diversities. Phrases like 'globalization from below' and 'movement of movements' come with a similar rationale.

Third, though the impetus of conceptualization are the moments of convergence of diverse interests, the fact still remains that these are momentary convergences involving provisional pacts that retain their diverse and fragmentary character at all times. To retain the promise of the convergence (already given shape through the linguistic performance of unity and purpose), and yet at the same time not disturb the diversity of interest groups entering provisional pacts, is a tricky business. This involves something more than linguistic performance; it involves an empirical exercise in mapping this field in a manner which seems to make diversity and convergence coherent and continuous. Here the sociological metaphor of the field is more useful than the political metaphor of movement.[27] Mapping this field may involve disposing different kinds of interests into a finite number of structurally related categories (such as identity-based, issue-based and region-based), or presenting the different interests as aligned with a finite number of ideological positions (radical, liberal, moderate), or presenting the diverse kinds of protests and activities involved as falling into a limited number of types (direct action against transnational/state/corporate entities, reform of existing state and transnational entities, NGO-based facilitations, enabling communal autonomy). Such reductive categorizations introduce a conceptually neat middle ground which can be diversified and converged as necessary.

Fourth, the conceptualization of balance between convergence and divergence in social movements is necessarily a kind of mirror image of that which such social movements seem to oppose, and in fact a great deal of transfer or co-opting of the normative assumptions made by globalization and democracy theorists is unproblematically possible. As observed in previous chapters, normative connotations are often conflated with denotative applications in problematic ways in relation to *existing* processes and organizations. In much research and theorization of social movements the normative connotations of democracy are inflected with denotative effect for such movements apparently *against* existing processes and organizations that are already denoted as democratic. This has the interesting consequence of social movements entering into some sort of competition of democratic virtue with establishment organizations and alignments in the same connotative/denotative terms; opponents of globalization claim the same kind of democratic legitimacy (of embracing diversity and convergences) that agents of globalization claim. Held and McGrew are therefore understandably able to see little contradiction between the promise of cosmopolitanism through globalization processes and the promise of anti-globalization movements.[28]

Just as the radical democratic views of Chantal Mouffe are compatible with existing liberal democracies (while making much of social movements), so those examining social movements find that their autocephalous and decentred character is not designed to challenge the established order beyond a point (direct action, therefore, does not come with governing ambition; anarchism in social movements is conditional to the superstructural domainance of the current globalized capitalist order). Rarely, when a concerted programme of superstructural change is recommended while optimistically embracing what is characterized as the 'anti-capitalist movement'/'anti-globalization movement'/social movements – implying transnational and international regime change, asserting the importance of universalization, and transformation of economic processes towards socialist ends – these are viewed with unease. Callinacos's *An Anti-Capitalist Manifesto* (2003) is a good example of such an optimistic turn.[29]

Fifth, and finally, combining ideas of superstructural change with existing understandings of social movements causes unease because that recalls the protean materialist critiques and transformative agendas rooted in Marxism. Some activists involved in the so-called social movements, and particularly most social movements researchers and analysts, are most anxious to distance themselves from the international communist and working-class movements of the past. To seek a position outside the universalist, totalist, solidarist, materialist, class- and labour-analysis-based discourse of Marxism's many political agendas, while taking possession of the anti-establishment, egalitarian, radical, empowering edge of Marxist discourse, is the primary common ground that most social movements research and analysis share (in common with cosmopolitan, radical, deliberative democrats). To a great extent, social movements are conceptualized as both replacing and shattering that which was born as a working-class movement against the exploitations of industrial, agrarian and colonial capitalism and with universal human interests at stake. Analogous to Geras's scepticism about the claims of radical democracy, those who are sceptical of the claims of social movements activists (sometimes, for many activists are still explicitly Marxists of some variety) and researchers/analysts (almost invariably) find themselves looking back to the working-class movement to come to grips with the phenomenon of the convergence of global social movements.[30]

With that admittedly sweeping overview (any overview would necessarily be so for a field which defines itself as not amenable to overviews), and more to the point of the current study, it is useful to consider some of the ways in which democracy is articulated in relation to social movements. Attempts to conceptualize and participate in social movements, with a sense of possessing a convergent direction, usually come with an instinctive rather than rationalized attribution of democratic legitimacy. Such attributions naturally fall in with the given normative connotations of the term in ordinary usage (the global scope and diversity of interests encapsulated in social movements seem to justify it) and resist the established denotative attributions of the term. In resisting established denotative attributions, social movements also denotatively attribute themselves as democratic. Thereby, through social movements, and against most formal institutions of governance and economic regulation, democracy is extended to the international/transnational domain too. Importantly, though, this hasn't yet enabled rationalization of the implications and practice of democracy. Thus, in inaugurating an influential series, 'A Movement of Movements',[31] in *New Left Review*, Naomi Klein fleetingly observes: 'The fight against globalization has morphed into a struggle against corporatization, for some, against capitalism itself. It has also become a fight for democracy.'[32] This effectively notes the claim *as* a claim, and subtly leaves it as a secondary consideration. A more explicit noting and assumption of the claim while deferring consideration of its rationale and content appears in Callinacos's *An Anti-Capitalist Manifesto*, which self-consciously tries to synthesize and develop arguments made by Pierre Bordieu, Noam Chomsky, Walden Bello, Naomi Klein, Antonio Negri, Michael Hardt, and others. After examining varieties of anti-capitalism, he identifies democracy (along with justice, efficiency, and sustainability) as one of the key values, and expands in the following words:

> But what would that involve more concretely? Three themes emerge from the critical literature – the need to revitalize existing liberal democracy, with its passive atomized electorates and politicians obsessed with keeping the favour of the corporate media empires and maintaining a steady flow of business donations; the demand for the democratization of the economy; and a preference for the decentralization of power. Not much thought has yet gone into how these and other aspirations might be realized institutionally.[33]

Callinacos therefore decides to postpone consideration of this till further debates have taken place, and focus on the economic content of the anti-capitalist agenda, which is presumptively aligned with its democratic aspirations. There is a subtle evasive manoeuvre in there. Callinacos effectively predisposes two of three democratic concerns as economic matters anyway – in the first of which, he gives a rather laboured economic turn to understanding the malaise of liberal democracy (as denoted now) to avoid having to clarify that revitalizing it effectively also means retaining the essential structures of liberal democracy as it is denotatively ascribed now. The particular cause of discontent with liberal democracy noted thus (donations) is easily rectified legislatively without disturbing the superstructure and its problems particularly. What I think Callinacos is saying, by implication, is that much of the so-called anti-capitalist movement literature does not want to rock the boat of liberal democracy (denotatively ascribed) too much. In fact elsewhere Callinacos goes on to recommend measures as part of that agenda that would mean radical transformation of liberal democracy as it is understood now, perhaps its erasure in any prevailing denotatively ascribable sense. Such measures include removal of immigration controls and extension of universal citizenship rights, and defence of public service and renationalization of private industries. Callinacos, it seems to me, is recommending the dissolution of liberal democracy as it exists now under the guise of going along with the larger desire in social movements to retain it in a modified normatively appealing form, or just retaining it wholesale while passing on the normative buck to social movements themselves. The brusque way in which he announces that not much thought has gone into how these aspirations may be institutionally realized also sounds suspect; the previous chapters show that revitalizing liberal democracy in institutional terms has been considered variously and substantially, and indeed some of those involved in social movements theory and practice have also presented concrete proposals.

Speaking both as an activist (new 'anarchist') and an academic (anthropologist) observer of social movements, David Graeber, for instance, argues that the kind of centralist 'party' notion of democracy with a correct theoretical analysis that Callinacos seems to be waiting for (and arguably this study is seeking) is unnecessary and counterproductive. An alternative mode of democratic practice which undermines the establishment majoritarian democracy has already emerged in direct action through social movements, and is centred on consensus. He delineates its operation as follows:

> The basic idea of the consensus process is that, rather than voting, you try to come up with proposals acceptable to every one – or, at least, not highly objectionable to anyone: first state the proposal, then ask for concerns and try to address them. Often, at this point, people in the group will propose 'friendly' amendments to add to the original proposal, or otherwise alter it, to ensure concerns are addressed. Then, finally, when you call for consensus, you ask if anyone wishes to 'block' or 'stand aside'. Standing aside is just saying, 'I would not myself be willing to take part in this action, but I would not stop anyone else from doing it'. Blocking is a way of saying 'I think this violates the fundamental principles or purposes of being in a group'. It functions as a veto; anyone can kill a proposal completely by blocking it – although there are ways to challenge whether a block is genuinely principled.[34]

To a great extent the viability of this democratic process has to be taken on trust, for it is given as issuing with the authority of an activist and academic who can play witness to the integrity of it in action. The main problem here though is that this process of consensual democracy may plausibly operate in a pre-selected group of essentially ideologically aligned members, but it is difficult to see how it can be institutionalized in a sphere which incorporates wide ideological divergences and even incommensurable differences (which is the sphere in which majoritarian democracy is denotatively institutionalized). To see this kind of consensual operation as an alternative to voting practices in complex domestic and international domains is misplaced. Decentralization of institutional operation to limited self-selected ideologically aligned groups is obviously a necessary corollary of this to enable its extension to complex domains, as is the need to hold such groups in discrete communities (but then by whom and how will the interpenetrations and exchanges between these communities be coordinated?), and the exclusion, for instance, of unprincipled individuals and individualists who find it difficult to align with any group (what should be done with them? should they be left out of the democratic process? would the process then be democratic?). The brief outline of how activists are organized in a hierarchy of groups by Graeber does little to answer those questions. Also at issue here is what principles are at stake, especially since important measures like 'blocking' will be checked by its principled nature. Of this Graeber gives little indication, but a paper by Amory Starr, which follows a similar ideological register and frame of references as Graeber's, develops this point in a noteworthy direction. This contextualizes itself in the frame of developing local sustainable production and concordant political strategies to maintain autonomy, such that the stranglehold of multinational corporations (and the transnational establishment that enables them) is undermined. This, and more so Starr's book,[35] provides valuable empirically based documentation of the laudable productive and resistance activities in local communities in underdeveloped and exploited contexts (in South America, Africa and Asia) – but nevertheless, Starr's derivation of a political philosophy of democracy and discernment of a democratic practice with transnational/international effect remains problematic in all the ways charted in previous chapters. In commenting on these local autonomous movements, Starr infers that the terms of self-determination and delinking with which they work,

> Denote the importance of putting action before ideology, as well as outright rejection of reformed versions of capitalism, the state, ideology, or any other intermediaries separating social problems from direct action in the space of everyday life. Further, and perhaps most importantly, autonomous movements assert that communities can find solutions to their problems within their own cultural traditions and collective talents. Unlike the New Left, contemporary autonomous movements reject the seizure of power as a strategy as surely as they reject the elusive politics of mass struggle; instead they work towards a 'revolution of everyday life'.[36]

'Outright rejection' of capitalism, state, without touching their power presents, it seems to me, an insurmountable paradox: capitalism and state do not quell from the exercise of repressive power that attacks such local enterprise and its political strategies and taps/saps its resources. Withdrawing ideology from the ken of autonomous social movements, confining them to limited cultural traditions, thrusting on them the upbeat rhetoric of 'revolution in everyday life' appear to form an effective formula for leaving alone the superstructure that makes their condition intolerable and their sustainability impossible beyond a point. This becomes transparent when Starr elucidates the superstructural arrangement. This amounts to a conflation of the normative connotations of democracy with the existing arrangements that are denoted as democratic (liberal state and international institutions), with a patrician conviction in the essentially altruistic nature of the latter:

> Supporting communities in their demands for sovereignty and autonomy defends spaces ruled by *alternative* epistemologies, values and economic systems. Through a federalist system, autonomous communities could engage in dialogue about common concerns, drawing on the strength of many knowledge and social systems. Positioning the (large) secular nation-state as the only political unit limits our ability to solve problems. In local autonomous zones, people could establish justice around issues of race, class, gender, and sexuality without waiting for laws, rulings, and enforcement funding from either the liberal state or the bought-and-paid-for international institutions.[37] [My emphasis]

The use of the word 'alternative' there, I think, says it all. The centre will hold in Starr's vision – with the secular liberal federal nation-state and international institutions – and this centre will remain for some reason passive, or for some reason will altruistically champion local efforts, with the added advantage of being relieved of their responsibility of protecting public interest and redistribution, which can all be devolved. Only religious conviction in the normative efficacy of democratic practice can explain the belief that largely impoverished autonomous zones give a hoot about equality of members irrespective of race, class, gender and sexuality; and only extreme ignorance of the local contexts that are in selective ways documented well can explain the conviction that they will not reify but ameliorate injustices on the grounds of race, class, gender and sexuality purely on their autonomous initiatives.

Social movements as understood and theorized now come with very mixed possibilities, and only momentary convergences.

To conclude this survey of conceptualizations of democracy in the international/transnational domain, a couple of final observations. There is a prevailing perception that the issue of democracy in the international/transnational domain has acquired particular urgency since the terrorist attacks in the USA on 11 September 2001. This is true in some obvious senses: in the manner in which the specificity and significance of the 11 September 2001 attacks have been focalized in the media and in academic discourse; and in the manner in which democracy has come to be evoked in political rhetoric and for military actions with effect on the international domain. Derrida's assessment of the perceived significance of the 11 September attacks comprehends what was at stake in a useful (though typically oriented toward discourse at the expense of materialist analysis) fashion:

> What is therefore threatened? Not only a great number of forces, powers, or 'things' that depend, even for the most determined adversaries of the United States, on the order that is more or less assured by this superpower; it is also, *more radically still* (and I would underscore this point), the system of interpretation, the axiomatic, logic, rhetoric, concepts, and evaluations that are supposed to allow one to *comprehend* and to explain precisely something like 'September 11'.[38]

The politically realist methodology rebels against the overestimation of discourse here, if not against the overestimation of the US's centrality in prevailing discourse. But with the recognition that for Derrida material reality and discourse are inextricable, discourse is material, the thrust of this is all too evident in at least one direction. Discourse analysts have taken particular note of the turn in political rhetoric that 11 September allowed, and the all too material implications of that turn since. Sandra Silberstein's analysis of Bush's post-11 September speeches to discern how a strategic polarity was constructed with 'Western democracy, "our very way of life" ' at the normatively justified end 'through words',[39] has been followed by a host of discourse analyses attesting to the continuity and consolidation of the process.[40] Analysis of post-11 September public perceptions of democracy shows that the term is seen to validate the contrary pulls of both protectionism (denotatively democratic states closing in for their security) and humanitarianism (normatively connoted democracy enjoining transnational pacifism) now.[41] The concentration of academic attention on 11 September and conflicts thereafter, and the claims of liberal democracy therein, speaks for itself. This study is undertaken with a post-11 September 2001 sense of urgency.

Finally, if the politically realist methodology of this study has led me to disagree and pick faults with (more often than approve of) the prevailing conceptual field, this is as much because I think there is reason to be sceptical of the dominant disposition of this field, as because of the inherently fractious nature of the issues it encompasses. In writing this, I find that I am uncertain of and inclined to disagree with formulations about democracy that I have proposed recently myself, both with regard to transformative socialist democracy within nation-states and in stating democratic principles which could be adopted in international politics.[42] Those were, simply, unrealistic.

NOTES

1 For all UN documents cited in this paragraph I have referred to the published versions in Hans von Mangoldt and Volker Rittberger (eds), *The United Nations and Its Predecessors Vol. 1* (Oxford: Oxford University Press, 1997), and referred to Bruno Suma (ed.) *The Charter of the United Nations: A Commentary* (Oxford: Oxford University Press, 1994).

2 Joseph Stiglitz, *Globalization and Its Discontents* (New York: W. W. Norton, 2003).

3 Amy Chua, *World on Fire: How Exporting Free Market Democracy Breeds Ethnic Hatred and Global Instability* (London: William Heinemann, 2003), p. 187.

4 Richard Peet, with assistants, *Unholy Trinity: The IMF, World Bank and WTO* (London: Zed/Kuala Lumpur: SIRD/Johannesburg: Wits University Press, 2003).

5 Chua, *World on Fire*, p. 274.

6 Daniel Kalderimis, 'IMF Conditionality as Investment Regulation: A Theoretical Analysis', *Social and Legal Studies* 13: 1, March 2004, p. 122.

7 Indra de Soysa, *Foreign Direct Investment, Democracy, and Development: Assessing Contours, Correlates, and Concomitants of Globalization* (London: Routledge, 2003).

8 Carl B. Hamilton, 'Globalization and Democracy', in Robert C. Baldwin and L. Alan Winters (eds), *Challenges to Globalization: Analyzing the Economics* (Chicago, IL: University of Chicago, 2004), pp. 63–91.

9 Errol A. Henderson, *Democracy and War: The End of an Illusion?* (Boulder, CO: Lynne Rienner, 2002), p. 125.

10 Philip P. Everts, *Democracy and Military Force* (Basingstoke: Palgrave, 2002), p. 194.

11 See, e.g., Murray Goot, 'Introduction: World Opinion Surveys and the War in Iraq', *International Journal of Public Opinion Research* 16: 3, Autumn 2004, pp. 239–68; Chaim Kaufmann, 'Threat Inflation and the Failure of the Marketplace of Ideas: The Selling of the Iraq War', *International Security* 29: 1, Summer 2004, pp. 5–48.

12 See, e.g., Karen Raler and William R. Thompson, 'The Democratic Peace and a Sequential, Reciprocal, Causal Arrow Hypothesis', *Comparative Political Studies* 37: 8, October 2004, pp. 879–908; David J. Galbreath, 'Democratization and Inter-State War: Why Reform Does Not Encourage Conflict', *Politics* 24: 3, September 2004, pp. 206–14.

13 Erik Voeten, 'Resisting the Lonely Superpower: Responses of States in the United Nations to U.S. Dominance', *The Journal of Politics* 66: 3, August 2004, pp. 729–54. This paper examines UN General Assembly voting, representing choices made by 154 states, between 1991 and 2001 to confirm that 'U.S. hegemony has elicited almost universal resistance' (p. 747).

14 Since 2001, the following books chart the area from different directions: C. Edwin Baker, *Media, Markets and Democracy* (New York: Cambridge University Press, 2001); Monroe E. Price, Beaton Rozumilowicz and Stefaan G. Verhulst (eds), *Media Reform* (London: Routledge, 2002); James Curran, *Media and Power* (London: Routledge, 2002); Herbert Gans, *Democracy and the News* (Oxford: Oxford University Press, 2003).

15 Edward S. Herman, *The Real Terror Network* (Boston, MA: South End, 1982); Noam Chomsky and Edward S. Herman, *Manufacturing Consent* (New York: Pantheon, 1988); Noam Chomsky, *Necessary Illusions* (London: Pluto, 1989); Noam Chomsky, *Deterring Democracy* (London: Verso, 1991).

16 Thus democracy is used with rhetorical effect to introduce the undemocratic character of current mass media operations in Noam Chomsky, *Media Control: Spectacular Achievements of Propaganda* (New York: Seven Stories, 1991/2000), p.10, as follows:

> One conception of democracy has it that a democratic society is one in which the public has the means to participate in some meaningful way in the management of their own affairs and the means of information are open and free.
>
> An alternative conception of democracy is that the public must be barred from managing of their own affairs and the means of information must be kept narrowly and rigidly controlled.

17 Stephen Hess and Marvin Kalb (eds), *The Media and the War on Terrorism* (Washington, DC: Brookings Institution Press, 2003); Sheldon Rampton and John Stauber, *Weapons of Mass Deception: The Uses of Propaganda in Bush's War on Iraq* (London: Robinson, 2003).

18 The arguments against the normative democratic expectations of public service mass media are laid out succinctly in Doris Graber, 'The Media and Democracy: Beyond the Myths and Stereotypes', *Annual Review of Political Science* Vol. 6, 2003, pp. 139–60.

19 James Curran, 'Rethinking Media and Democracy', in James Curran and Michael Gurevitch (eds), *Mass Media and Society* (London: Arnold, 1991/2000), pp. 142–8.

20 Ziauddin Sardar and Jerome R. Ravetz, *Cyberfutures: Culture and Politics in the Information Superhighway* (London: Pluto, 1996); Diana Saco, *Cybering Democracy* (Minneapolis, MN: University of Minnesota Press, 2002); Henry Jenkins and David Thorburn (eds), *Democracy and New Media* (Cambridge, MA: MIT, 2003).

21 Peter Van Aelst and Stefaan Walgrave, 'New Media, New Movements? The Role of the Internet in Shaping the "Anti-Globalization" Movement', *Information, Communication and Society* 5: 4, 2002, pp. 465–93; W. Lance Bennett, 'New Media Power: The Internet and Global Activism', in Nick Couldry and James Curran (eds), *Contesting Media Power* (Lanham, MD: Rowman and Littlefield, 2003).

22 Jostein Gripsrud, *Understanding Media Culture* (London: Arnold, 2002 [1st edition 1999]), Ch. 8.

23 Elizabeth Jacka, ' "Democracy as Defeat": The Importance of Arguments for Public Service Broadcasting', *Television and New Media* 4: 2, May 2003, pp. 177–91.

24 John Hartley, *Uses of Television* (London: Routledge, 1999).

25 Nicholas Garnham, 'A Response to Elizabeth Jacka's "Democracy as Defeat" ', *Television and New Media* 4: 2, May 2003, pp. 193–200.

26 Significant book-length studies include: Margaret E. Keck and Kathryn Sikkink, *Activists Beyond Borders* (Ithaca, NY: Cornell University Press, 1998); Donatella Della Porta and Mario Diani, *Social Movements* (Oxford: Blackwell, 1999); Robin Cohen and Sirin Rai (eds), *Global Social Movements* (London: Athlone, 2000); Veronika Bennholdt-Thomsen, Nick Fraaclas and Claudia Von Werlhof (eds), *There Is an Alternative* (London: Zed, 2001); Tim Jordan, *Activism! Direct Action, Hacktivism and the Future of Society* (London: Reaktion Books, 2002); Walden Bello, *Deglobalisation* (London: Zed, 2002); John Holloway, *Change the World Without Taking Power* (London: Pluto, 2002); J. Smith and H. Johnstone (eds), *Globalization and Resistance* (New York: Rowan and Littlefield, 2002); Feargal Cochrane, Rosaleen Duffy and John Selby (eds), *Global Governance, Conflict and Resistance* (Basingstoke: Palgrave-Macmillan, 2003); William F. Fisher and Thomas Pooniah (eds), *Another World is Possible* (London: Zed, 2003); Michael Hardt and Antonio Negri, *Multitude* (Harmondsworth: Penguin, 2004); *We Are Everywhere* (London: Verso, 2004).

27 This point is discussed at some length in Nick Crossley, 'Global Anti-Corporate Struggle: A Preliminary Analysis', *British Journal of Sociology* 53: 4, December 2002, p. 674.

28 David Held and Anthony McGrew, *Globalization/Anti-Globalization* (Cambridge: Polity, 2002), p. 131.

29 Alex Callinacos, *An Anti-Capitalist Manifesto* (Cambridge: Polity, 2003).

30 A good example of this is James Heartfield's essay 'Postmodern Desertions: Capitalism and Anti-Capitalism', *Interventions* 5: 2, pp. 271–89. Noting that the so-called

anti-capitalist movement was the preserve of an elite, and that there are disturbing implications in the role that NGOs play in such a movement, and that indigenism and direct action entails, Heartfield historically traces the manner in which the current preoccupation with social movements emerged to fill an ideological vacuum left by the declining influence of organized labour.

31 Most are collected in Tom Mertes (ed.), *A Movement of Movements: Is Another World Possible?* (London: Verso, 2004).

32 Naomi Klein, 'Reclaiming the Commons', *New Left Review* Vol. 9, May/June 2001, p. 83.

33 Callinacos, *An Anti-Capitalist Manifesto*, p. 111.

34 David Graeber, 'The New Anarchists' (in the 'A Movement of Movements', series, 5), *New Left Review* Vol. 13, January/February 2002, p. 71.

35 Amory Starr, *Naming the Enemy* (London: Zed, 2000).

36 Amory Starr, 'Anti-Globalization: The Global Fight for Local Autonomy', *New Political Science* 25: 1, 2003, p. 29.

37 Ibid., p. 41.

38 Giovanna Barradori, *Philosophy in a Time of Terror: Dialogues with Jürgen Habermas and Jacques Derrida* (Chicago, IL: University of Chicago Press, 2003), p. 93.

39 Sandra Silberstein, *War of Words: Language, Politics and 9/11* (London: Routledge, 2002), p. xii.

40 See particularly the special issue of *Discourse and Society* 15: 2–3, 2004, entitled 'Interpreting Tragedy: The Language of 11 September 2001'; and the special issue of *The International Journal of Public Opinion Research* 16: 3, Autumn 2004, entitled 'Public Opinion and the War in Iraq'.

41 Jane Mummery and Debbie Rodan, 'Discourses of Democracy in the Aftermath of 9/11 and Other Events: Protectivism versus Humanitarianism', *Continuum* 17: 4, December 2003, pp. 433–43. This makes inferences from letters to the editor of the newspaper, *The Australian*, written in the period of debates following 11 September 2001.

42 Suman Gupta, *Marxism, History and Intellectuals: Toward a Reconceptualized Transformative Socialism* (Madison, NJ: Fairleigh Dickinson University Press, 2000), Ch. 6; Suman Gupta, *The Replication of Violence* (London: Pluto, 2002), pp. 82–4.

Part II

9 *The Context*

In this part I examine a particular context with a view to determining to what degree and in what manner the conceptualizations of democracy in an international and transnational domain discussed in Part I may relate to politically real considerations. The context in question is that of the US- and UK-led build-up towards military action in and subsequent occupation of Iraq between September 2002 and June 2004.

This context is, of course, already an area of intense scrutiny and research (I have mentioned a few of the relevant publications at the end of Chapter 1). In addressing this area I do not contribute to the lines of investigative reportage, intervention and advocacy which are already amply in the public sphere. My interest in this context is guided here entirely by a desire to apply the politically realist methodology to the idea of democracy in international and transnational politics – by *using* this context as a case study. This necessitates a somewhat different mode of synthesizing, organizing and disposing the available documentation of this context from that which is found elsewhere at present. This also entails a focus on areas of documentation regarding this context that haven't received adequate attention so far. I clarify the distinctive features of my treatment of this context further below, by outlining some initial conditions which should be borne in mind when reading this part.

The initial conditions (methodological and clarificatory) with which this part is and should be approached are as follows.

First, to present the context of the US–UK-led build-up towards military action in and the subsequent occupation of Iraq between September 2002 and June 2004 as *a* context is necessarily reductive: it is only so insofar as certain events within that period are highlighted as being such that they cut across and impinge upon a wide variety of contexts. The particularities of the debates leading up to the invasion of Iraq by a US–UK coalition, the manner in which that was conducted and responded to, the repercussions it had on existing international arrangements, the different indeterminacies that resulted from it, etc. – these have the coherence of *a* context since they were highlighted accordingly. I use *highlighted* advisedly, because these concerns emerged through an enormously complex and extended network of exchanges, signals, messages and responses and counter-messages, that implicated a great many contextual considerations (cultural and historical accruals) which are not explicitly *in* this context. These exchanges took different forms: public statements and gestures by public figures, dossiers, debates and resolutions in a range of international and domestic organizations, newspaper and television reports and analyses, protest marches and other acts of dissent, guided and not-well-guided missiles and bombs, showers of pamphlets, aid packages and humanitarian gestures, silences, and so on. Seen in this fashion, as a network of exchanges, the highlighted events of this context were implicated, as I have just said, in a series of histories and political domains that are not examined here. The central event here, the military action in Iraq to remove the Saddam Hussain regime, was itself a climax of intertwined histories and their conjunctions: Iraq's colonial history from the mandate period, the history of the Ba'ath Party before and under Hussain, the particular relationship of Iraq to the US, the Iraqi state's relationship with its internal population and neighbouring countries (Iran, Kuwait, Jordan, Turkey). But beyond that also: the position of the US in the world since the Second World War, particularly since the Cold War, and even more particularly since 11 September 2001 and the military action in Afghanistan; the position of the UK in Europe and in relation to the US, and with regard to her former colonies . . . this kind of intermeshing and interpenetration of cultures and histories can carry on indefinitely. The task of giving the context (as it is characterized here) in question shape for the purposes of this study – or of disposing it so as to make it amenable to a consideration of democracy in the international/transnational domain – could become an unmanageable one, unless pragmatically delimited. In the following chapters I assume a pragmatic reductive position, with a narrow focus on the period in question (i.e., without teasing out all the historical and cultural accruals involved) and on the processes of highlighting that occurred therein.

Second, the characterization of the context as highlights within a network of exchanges comes with certain ancillary considerations. To a significant extent the context is characterized not only by *what* is highlighted, but *how and with what particular presumptions* highlighting occurs. Crucially, this relates to current presumptions about public-ness (underlying public statements and gestures and protests and actions), and about the mass media (mediating/moulding what is of international or local interest).[1] There is a particular emphasis on both in this part; the documentation here draws largely on public statements and records, and mass media reports and analyses. Further, highlights in the network of exchanges that characterize this context emerged in a continuous sequence, in a contingent and hasty fashion, and with immediate effects and *ad hoc* inferences (this is generally true for such contexts). In presenting the context in question I would like to be cognizant of its process of emergence and immediate effects. This justifies to some extent my decision not to tease out the historical and cultural accrual within the context in question; let me reiterate that a pragmatically reductive approach is adopted here. Also worth noting here: the process of highlighting in a network of exchanges doesn't necessarily exclude all the contexts that are implied but not explicit within it, and may allow pathways to a large number of them. These pathways are always potentially open and can be gestured towards – their possibilities lurk in a weighty fashion at all times – and picked up wherever necessary.

The third initial condition relates to the matter of the documentation that this part depends on, given the first two conditions. The focus on highlighted moments in a given network of exchanges inevitably means that the kind of documentation I draw upon – mainly public statements and records, and mass media reports and analyses – provides information that is in the public domain already. Nothing new is reported here, no revelations are offered, everything is based on information which is publicly available. However, there are matters of emphasis in the bringing up of certain documented facts or events below. Some of these documented facts or events had received sustained attention in the mass media and other public fora when they emerged. The documentation referred to in Chapters 10 and 11 (dossiers and related discussions, and UNSC debates) are such; in covering this still familiar territory here I am motivated by a desire to prolong and give a retrospective turn to the interest which was generated when they emerged. The documentation referred to in Chapter 12 (protest rallies) had received sporadic and transient attention in the mass media and public statements and documents; my evocation of these here has something of an archival zeal about it. The documentation brought up in Chapter 13 (Iraq reconstruction and CPA control) was largely available in a fragmentary fashion in the mainstream media and more continuously placed in special interest sections (such as business and finance) of mass media and other public outlets; in presenting these I hope to dislocate this material from closed or fragmentary discursive zones and bring it to a more central discursive space. Altogether, these areas of documentation are raised here so that they can be synthesized and disposed in a manner that is suitable for this study . . . which leads to the next condition.

The fourth condition is with regard to the manner in which the documentation in question is synthesized and disposed for the purposes, and bearing in mind the theme (democracy in international/transnational politics) of this study. Here, the context in question is presented as formed of several distinct narrative strands according to which the documentation is arranged. I think of the narrative strands as 'stories', not unrelated to 'news stories', only joined up and stretched out beyond the immediate consumer-oriented immediacy of newsworthiness. My use of 'stories' here is also linked to constructed narratives associated with literature; in synthesizing and disposing the documentation to render the context in question amenable as a case study for this book, I am effectively indulging in narrative construction (but these aren't fiction). There are, in fact, four such 'stories' which respectively form the substance of the following four chapters. As mentioned already, the first 'story' (Chapter 10) has to do with dossiers and the justification for military intervention in Iraq; the second 'story' (Chapter 11) with UN Security Council debates; the third (Chapter 12) with protest marches and other gestures of protest; and the fourth (Chapter 13) with reconstruction contracts and the CPA. There are actually many linked and overlapping but distinctly threaded 'stories' which I am able to discern in the material regarding this context that I have collected (for instance, I do not take up the 'stories' of oil, of private agencies providing security and defence services, of anti-terrorism legislation and rhetoric, of the conduct of military action in Iraq). The four I have chosen here seem to me of particular interest for this study for several reasons. The most important reason is that these four 'stories' appear to me to be those where the conceptualizations and applications of democracy in the international/transnational domain were negotiated and tested most explicitly for this context. The manner in which the four 'stories' intertwine with each other, and occasionally appear to refuse to link up with and even contradict each other, is particularly revealing for this study. These 'stories' allow for a consideration of almost the whole gamut of abstractions and generalities that has been covered in Part I. The process of highlighting through networks of exchange in terms of which these 'stories' unravel has the further advantage of enabling self-reflection on that process itself (thus tying in with condition two above). Finally, these 'stories' also have the kind of varied interests of documentation that I have touched on in the previous paragraph. Together, these four 'stories' give a reasonably comprehensive and yet self-contained view of the context in question.

The fifth and final initial condition with which I approach this part allows an ongoing emphasis on the purposes and theme of this study. The relationship of the four 'stories' to conceptualizations and applications of democracy in the international/transnational domain is specifically drawn out in each of the four following chapters. Each chapter lays out its 'story' in a pragmatic and convenient manner, to lead to and enable a brief 'Inferences and Observations' section at the end. The 'Inferences and Observations' sections reflect on the 'stories' that have just been presented with a view to immediately picking up their links with the generalities and abstractions discussed in Part I. In other words, these sections provide an immediate threading together of the latter with politically real considerations highlighted through the chosen context (this case study). These links are pondered and synthesized in the conclusion, Chapter 14, Iraq-Invasion-Democracy.

With these initial conditions in mind the four 'stories' follow.

NOTES

1 Insofar as such presumptions go, the connotations of my use of the term *highlighting* (with simile effect) may be regarded as being akin to the kind of propagandist selectivity and conformity that Noam Chomsky, Edward Herman, Michael Parenti and others have documented so extensively in the 1980s. Looking back on this exercise in 1988, Chomsky summarized the findings as revealing a conservative 'state–corporate nexus' in the operations of the so-called democratic Western mass media – which serves a propaganda function for established power (in 'Democracy and the Media', *Necessary Illusions: Thought Control in Democratic Societies* [London: Pluto, 1989]). My use of the presumptions that operate in mass media *highlighting* is however not confined to the specific ideological inclination and contexts that Chomsky addresses. That is germane to the context I address, but my intention in using the term *highlighting* is to gesture towards that selectivity and ideological tilting that occurs in all mass media, in all contexts (albeit with different effects), in a general sense. To that extent, the idea of *highlighting*, with its presumptions, could be thought of as an almost unavoidably technical aspect of mass media processes. As such the idea is familiar to all students of the mass media, and is recognizable, for instance, in the simile of 'framing' used in a more neutral fashion also in the 1980s (and often thereafter) by David Altheide in *Media Power* (Beverley Hills, CA: Sage, 1985). I hope that the visual associations of a term like *highlighting* – as indeed *framing* – will render my intention here self-evident.

10 *Dossiers and the Justification for Military Intervention in Iraq*

THE FIRST STORY

In September 2002, two dossiers were released, making, in different ways, the case for military intervention in Iraq. As the briefest of backgrounds to these, the following could be noted. Iraq had ended cooperation on 31 October 1998 with the weapons inspections regime of the United Nations Special Commission to Oversee the Destruction of Iraq's Weapons of Mass Destruction (UNSCOM) that had existed since the ceasefire agreement of 3 March 1991 at the end of the First Gulf War ('Operation Desert Storm', starting 16–17 January 1991). This was followed by a bombing campaign by the US and the UK to destroy Iraq's nuclear, chemical and biological weapons ('Operation Desert Fox', 16–19 December 1998); and that in turn by United Nations Security Council (UNSC) Resolution 1284 creating the UN Monitoring, Verification and Inspection Commission (UNMOVIC) to replace UNSCOM, which Iraq rejected. Iraq's weapons capacities had not been inspected since 1998. Throughout this period economic sanctions imposed by UNSC Resolution 661 on 6 August 1990 had remained in place, which had been somewhat relaxed by the 'Food for Oil' programme introduced through UNSC Resolution 986 of 14 April 1995. In the interim the terrorist attacks of 11 September 2001 in the US had taken place, followed by a NATO (primarily UK)–US-led military action without UNSC sanction, but also without overt opposition therein (analogous in some ways to the recent NATO intervention in Kosovo, 24 March–10 June 1999), against Taliban-governed Afghanistan (7 October–mid-December 2001, but hostilities ongoing thereafter). Since then the US, with staunch support from the UK, has conducted what it regards as a 'war on terrorism' on several fronts (in terms of internal security arrangements, control of financial mechanisms, intensification of intelligence, threats against alleged 'terror states', etc.). Starting particularly from early 2002, both US and UK heads of state, George W. Bush and Tony Blair, had maintained with increasing vehemence the need to reinstate weapons inspections in Iraq or (preferably) militarily intervene if the Iraqi government continued not to comply with UN resolutions. On 7 September 2002, Blair and Bush met in Camp David,

Maryland, and jointly reiterated their determination to prove that Saddam Hussein's regime was harbouring 'Weapons of Mass Destruction' (WMD) and act accordingly.

Both the dossiers mentioned above were meant to strengthen the case for military intervention rather than just reinstatement of weapons inspections in that they suggested that the Iraqi state had already developed and were in possession of significant quantities of WMD that were an imminent threat to world stability. Both were received amidst wide publicity, with the media bringing them to public attention in a world that was already fully cognizant (mostly apprehensively) of US–UK-driven moves towards military action in Iraq.

The first was released on 9 September 2002 by the International Institute for Strategic Studies (IISS), a primarily US- and UK-based international think tank which doesn't receive direct government funding (it is funded through a range of other sources including corporate and individual sponsors) and could therefore be regarded as independent (it does pride itself however for the high level of contact it maintains with different governments, and especially its connections with highly placed US officials). It was entitled *Iraq's Weapons of Mass Destruction: A Net Assessment* (called the *strategic dossier* in short),[1] and its release was marked by three press conferences – in Washington, Brussels and London (a significant selection of locations). The dossier presented itself as a systematic and cautious analysis of evidence prior to 1991, and in 1998 and since, speculating on the possible missile, chemical and biological weapon holdings of Iraq in 2002. The conclusions were presented as speculative enough not to be seen to endorse military intervention, but suggestive enough to make military action appear plausible. In the event, the media reception of the dossier *highlighted* not so much its substantive content as its summarized conclusions; and the dossier was presented (characteristic of such official reports from 'think tanks') to encourage such highlighting: with constant summaries and bullet points, and with an overarching executive summary/press statement by John Chipman, the Director of IISS, which was read out at the press conferences (Chipman did so in London). The ambiguous suggestiveness of the document, not quite an endorsement of military intervention but near enough to be perceived as one, was summarized with admirable dexterity in the last lines of the press statement: 'This Strategic Dossier does not attempt to make a case either way, as to whether Saddam Hussain's WMD arsenal is a *casus belli per se*. Wait and the threat will grow, strike and the threat may be used.' Though the cautiously phrased dossier was received in the media as both favouring and discouraging military action, the connotations of the glib last phrase quoted above is worth pausing on. Its rhetorical intent is reasonably clear. The *threat* can only grow or be used; despite the speculative tone of the findings, the summary and its one catch-phrase condensation didn't dwell on the possibility that there was no real threat.

Its tendency, if not its substantive content, did prove useful; it carved a path towards more categorically phrased dossiers to come. More immediately, it was followed by rituals of commiseration and resolution-making to mark the first anniversary of 11 September 2001, and some public statements from Bush and Blair.[2] Bush made a couple of statements on 11 September 2002, neither of which explicitly referred to Iraq, but both of which looked forward to a continuing 'war on terrorism' – presenting the prospect in now familiar terms as a war of abstractions (democracy/freedom v. fanaticism/dictatorship), and as both a glorious mission and a grim duty. Characteristically, his address at the Pentagon at 10:05 a.m. warned all terrorists that: 'A greater force is amassed against them. They are opposed by freedom loving people in many lands.' And his Remarks to the Nation from Elis Island, New York, at 9:01 p.m. included the following resolution:

> This nation has defeated tyrants, liberated death camps, raised the lamp of liberty to every captive land. We have no intention of ignoring or appeasing history's latest gang of fanatics trying to murder their way to power. They are discovering, as others before them, the resolve of a great country and a great democracy. In the ruins of two towers, under a flag unfurled at the Pentagon, at the funerals of the lost, we have made a sacred promise, to ourselves and to the world: We will not relent until justice is done and our nation is secure. What our enemies have begun, we will finish.

Blair's speech to the Trades Union Congress (TUC) in Blackpool on 10 September 2002 was clearly addressed to a more sceptical audience, and perhaps one less given to grandiose abstractions. It was at any rate, and in keeping with the role Blair was to assume in coming months, more geared to making a specific case against Saddam Hussain – briefly:

> Because I say to you in all earnestness; if we do not deal with the threat from this international outlaw and his barbaric regime, it may not erupt and engulf us this month or next; perhaps not even this year or the next. But it will at some point. And I do not want it on my conscience that we knew the threat, saw it coming and did nothing.
>
> I know this is not what some people want to hear. But I ask you only this: to listen to the case I will be developing over the coming weeks and reflect on it.

Such statements should be contextualized firmly in terms of specific audience. The Pentagon as a particular locale and the nation as a general domain for Bush are significantly different from the TUC as Blair's audience. The traditional relationship between British trade unions and the Labour Party had been under strain since its advent to power under Blair, amidst prevailing perceptions that in government Labour was adhering to Thatcherite policies of privatization, deregulation and employment insecurity. In September 2002 a standoff over pay was brewing between the Fire Brigades Union (FBU) under trade union boss Andrew Gilchrist and the government. The FBU magazine for September 2002 had made a not unpopular equation between the government's foreign policy financial commitments and domestic budgeting: 'Gordon Brown, the Chancellor, believes it will cost the government at least £4,500 million to begin a war with Iraq . . . so a mere £280 million for our pay claim can easily be afforded. It is a question of politics, what is the most important, an adventure with George Bush or a decent Fire service?'[3] A firefighters' strike was called on 13 November, but fizzled out within a few months. Other unions (social services, higher education teachers, nurses, etc.) were also expressing deep dissatisfactions. Compared to the TUC, the Pentagon was a positively friendly environment, and the US as a 'nation' a sufficiently inchoate entity. In fact, the US in September 2002 was in the midst of growing domestic disaffections too: the economy appeared to be faltering (the government announced in September that the poverty rate had increased a little to 11.7 per cent, and the median household income had fallen 2.2 per cent; analysts observed that the industrial production had fallen by 0.3 per cent in August where it was expected to rise by 0.2 per cent, and that the unemployment rate had gone up to 5.9 per cent in the second quarter of 2002); there was widespread concern about corporate corruption in accounting practices following a series of scandals beginning with the collapse of ENRON (to which Bush and senior Republicans had been connected, and as a result of which Bush had signed an Anti-Corruption Bill on 30 July 2002); and a series of child abuse and paedophilia scandals connected to the Roman Catholic Church in the US was gathering momentum.

It is in this context that on 20 September 2002, Bush asked Congress for authority to use force against Iraq if necessary, and presented to the House of Representatives and the Senate a 35-page document on *The National Security Strategy of the United States of America.*[4] In the preface to this, Bush stated that, 'the United States will use this moment of opportunity to extend the benefits of freedom across the globe. We will actively work to bring the hope of democracy, development, free markets, and free trade to every corner of the world' (p. 4), and declared that, 'We are ultimately fighting for democratic values and our way of life.' A case was made here for pre-emptive military action against 'rogue states' where necessary.

Bush's case against Iraq in public statements until this point was based largely on assertions of the threat it posed, placed within a general rhetoric about the US's security and world mission. By 16 September 2002, in an attempt to stem the US–UK drive towards military action, the Iraqi government had accepted unconditional UN weapons inspections in Iraq, offered its full cooperation to returning UNMOVIC inspectors with assurances that

Iraq had no WMD. A more closely argued case for military action – with an academic-legal turn – appeared however soon afterwards in the 55-page dossier produced by the British government with the assistance of its Joint Intelligence Committee on 24 September 2002, *Iraq's Weapons of Mass Destruction: The Assessment of the British Government.*[5] This is more interesting than the IISS one because of its content, its status as a public document directly from the state, and because of the prolonged controversies that followed. Where the IISS dossier had been cautious and studiedly equivocal, this offered a series of categorical statements; as Blair put it in his preface, 'The threat posed to international peace and security, when WMD are in the hands of a brutal and aggressive regime like Saddam's, is real' (p. 7). The case, as that sentence indicates, is two-fold: first, that there is sufficient evidence that Iraq does possess and will obtain further WMD; and second, that the dangerous moral character of the Iraqi regime is unalterable and unquestionable. The first part of the case was made by reference to what appear to be well-quantified facts; the two most familiar, and quickly highlighted (staying highlighted thereafter) were the claim that 'Uranium has been sought from Africa that has no civil nuclear application in Iraq', and that 'The Iraqi military are able to deploy [missiles and biological/chemical weapons] within 45 minutes of a decision to do so' (Ch. 3). The second part of the case (Part 3 of the dossier) was made by arguing that the Iraqi regime was responsible for gross human rights violations, for its totalitarian conduct of government internally, and for aspiring to become a dominant regional power externally (points that Blair had made before, in that TUC address of 10 September, for instance). The dossier was prepared with a view to mass consumption: again bullet-pointed summaries were constantly provided; boxed clarifications and anecdotal evidence were inserted; and pictures were thrown in to break up the text. The claims of the imminence and reality of the threat of Iraq's alleged WMDs (especially such as the two mentioned above) were picked up and highlighted immediately in a variety of ways. The *Telegraph* reported on 25 September 2002 that a Mori poll showed that the dossier had failed to make the case for military action in the UK, with 48 per cent saying that it should not follow against 30 per cent saying it should. The *Guardian* reported that the dossier failed to convince world leaders – citing particularly France, Germany and Russia – who felt it did no more than justify further UN weapons inspections. Editorials in most British newspapers – conservative, liberal or labour oriented – expressed scepticism about the aggressive stance of the UK–US even with the case made in the dossier.

In the UK on 25 September 2002, after a nine-hour-long parliamentary debate on Iraq, 53 Labour Members of Parliament, joined by MPs from the Liberal Democrat, Scottish National and Plaid Cymru parties, staged a backbench rebellion against the government's position on Iraq. But, as far as Parliament went, this was short-lived. As the US and UK got down to intensive lobbying to get the UNSC to adopt a tough new resolution on Iraq (eventually unanimously voted as Resolution 1441 on 8 November 2002), the Labour Party's National Executive Council voted at the party's annual conference to reject a resolution that would have tied the use of military action on the part of UK to UNSC sanction. Meanwhile, some of the quantified 'facts' cited in the dossier passed into public statement: in his State of Union address of 28 January 2003, for instance, Bush quoted the dossier to reiterate the claim that Saddam Hussain 'recently sought significant quantities of uranium from Africa'. However, before going into the curious afterlife of the UK September 2002 dossier, it is necessary to take account of other dossiers to come.

By 10 October 2002, the US Congress adopted a resolution authorizing the use of unilateral 'pre-emptive' military action in Iraq at the behest of the President as and when he considered it necessary (296 for, 133 against) and on 11 October a similar resolution was voted by Senate (77 to 23). On 8 November the UNSC unanimously approved Resolution 1441, which set a deadline of 8 December for the Iraqi government to produce a complete listing of its weapons holding to facilitate the resumption of weapons inspections. Inspections were resumed on 27 November (under the supervision of UNMOVIC, led by Hans Blix, and the International Atomic Energy Agency [IAEA], led by Mohamed El-Baradei). On 2 December 2002 the Foreign and Commonwealth Office of the British government issued another dossier, *Saddam Hussein: Crimes and Human Rights Abuses. A Report of the Human Cost of Saddam's Policies* (23 pages),[6] to bolster the moral case for military action. The introduction made it clear that it was based on the testimony of Iraqi exiles, UN *rappoteurs*, human rights organizations and intelligence material. It was divided into several sections, dealing with torture, treatment of women, prison conditions, summary and arbitrary killings, persecution of Kurds and the Shia community, harassment of opposition, and conduct during the Kuwait invasion. In style again, much like the 24 September dossier, it was presented for general consumption – with coloured and boxed special interest stories and clarifications, text constructed largely of categorical statements and broken by pictures, explanatory appendices (one detailing torture methods). In the event this was received as a transparent propagandist effort which added little to public perceptions and the debate about whether military action was necessary or whether weapons inspections was sufficient. An Amnesty spokesperson was reported as saying that 'human rights should not be used as an excuse to go to war'. In an article of 25 September 2002 Amnesty's Secretary General Irene Kahn had already written: 'The human rights situation in Iraq is being invoked with unusual frequency by some Western political leaders to justify military action. This selective attention to human rights is nothing but a cold and calculated manipulation of the work of human rights activists.'[7] This dossier seemed to be no more than concrete evidence of this, and was quickly forgotten.

On 7 December 2002 in keeping with the deadline set in UNSC Resolution 1441, the Iraqi government's dossier was delivered to the UNSC. The manner in which this dossier was highlighted in the mass media had little to do with its contents. The key feature that stuck out about this was its length: scarcely any news item about it failed to mention that it was 12,159 pages long (in 43 volumes, 6 folders and 12 CD-Roms). Its length was widely regarded as a stalling tactic against the inevitability of military action. The reaction of the US and UK governments was dismissive: while promises were made that this would be scrutinized carefully by intelligence and experts, Jack Straw (UK Foreign Secretary) bluntly declared it a 'blatant lie', Blair was reportedly 'pretty sceptical', and Colin Powell described it as 'troublesome'. The only other aspect of this apparently carefully put together and comprehensive listing of weapons holdings and capabilities that attracted any media attention was its mode of delivery. It was delivered in Cyprus on 7 December, from where it was first handed to the US government instead of being circulated among members of the UNSC. The US government then distributed photocopies of the dossier to the other four permanent members of the UNSC – UK, China, France and Russia – and the ten non-permanent council members only received 'sanitized' versions of the dossier. This mode of distribution was apparently to control material in the dossier which could contravene weapons non-proliferation agreements. In the letter listing contents which was attached to the dossier, signed by Iraqi Minister for Foreign Affairs Najl Sabri, the possibility that this document may not be consistent with the weapons non-proliferation regime was mentioned.

Between 8 December 2002 and 3 February 2003, the date of the release of the next and final dossier on Iraq by the British government, a great many developments took place with regard to UNSC debates, UNMOVIC and IAEA weapons inspections in Iraq, and US–UK lobbying for support for military action which I come to in the next chapter. The 3 February dossier was entitled *Iraq – Its Infrastructure of Concealment, Deception and Intimidation.*[8] At 19 pages this was the shortest of the dossiers, and was divided into three parts: the first detailing Iraq's security organization, the second Iraq's intelligence network, and the third the effects of all this on the Iraqi people. This was presented in short statemental sentences – more in the style of a report than (as the other British dossiers were) a document of advocacy. Broadly two kinds of statements were made: apparently factual ('this is the case'), and apparently observational/inferential ('this is the result'). Two of both kinds were highlighted, each designed to make an unstated but self-evident point. The first part of the document tried to substantiate the statement that Iraqi intelligence outnumbered weapons inspectors by 200 to 1 (thus implying that this was the odds of weapons inspections being a viable solution to the threat posed by Iraq), and the second, with which the document ended, observed, 'The overall effect of the systems of control and intimidation is that every Iraqi is suspicious of all expect the closest family' (thus tangentially reiterating the moral case against the non-democratic or dictatorial Iraqi regime). It appeared first on the British government website as being based on up-to-date intelligence sources, and was initially given as authored by Whitehall officials P. Hanill, J. Pratt, A. Blackshaw and M. Khan. Since this appeared at a crucial moment in UNSC deliberations, its claims were reported widely. On 5 February, in an address to UNSC where Colin Powell detailed evidence provided by US intelligence suggesting that Iraq was in possession of WMD, he referred to the dossier with approbation: 'I would call my colleagues' attention to the fine paper that the United Kingdom distributed . . . which describes in exquisite detail Iraq's deception activities.'[9]

Until this point the usefulness of the exchange of dossiers (particularly the British ones) might have been questioned occasionally, but their integrity hadn't been questioned. As such, until this point the mode of highlighting through which these were sieved through the mass media and public statements followed a coherent logic of advocacy for a possibly justifiable position. From 6 February 2003, the logic of highlighting of especially two of the British dossiers (24 September 2002 and 3 February 2003) changed to a quite different track. We may think of this as a kind of afterlife of the dossiers, withdrawn from one kind of contingent discourse and inserted into another kind, and one that has a particular bearing on ideas of democracy. The curious afterlife of the two British dossiers began with the 3 February one.

On 6 February 2003 UK television's Channel 4 news broadcast an exposure of plagiarism in the 3 February dossier. Attention was drawn to this by a politics lecturer at Cambridge University, Glen Rangwala, who stated in the programme that in the 19-page dossier much of pages 6 to 16 had been copied directly (including grammatical and typographical errors) from a paper by a doctoral student, Ibrahim al-Marashi, at the Centre for Non-Proliferation Studies in Monterey, California, which was published in the journal *Middle East International* in September 2001. It was soon further revealed that other parts of the dossier had drawn upon unacknowledged sources in the public domain, particularly papers by Sean Boyne in 1997 and Ken Gause in November 2003 which appeared in *Jane's Intelligence Review*. The 3 February dossier, in other words, was not only largely plagiarized but could be regarded as mendacious in trying to pass off dated information in the public domain as originating from up-to-date intelligence sources. Further revelations followed: it appeared that the four named authors of the dossier had appeared as a mistake (their names were quickly removed from the government website), and that two of them – Alison Blackshaw and Murtaza Khan – actually worked in the Prime Minister's press office, under the supervision of the Downing Street Director of Communications (well known in the country as the chief of Labour Party's 'spin doctors'), Alistair Campbell. On 8 February 2003, Blair's office admitted 'serious errors' in the delivery of the dossier and apologized for them.

A more complicated turn in the afterlife of dossiers took place with regard to the 24 September 2002 dossier in late May. By this time, an extensive search for WMD by US and UK forces in vanquished Iraq had failed to come up with evidence of their existence, and had already cast serious doubts about the credibility of the British dossiers and public statements based on US–UK intelligence that had been used to justify the military action. The BBC *Today* programme's defence correspondent Andrew Gilligan made a series of reports (29 May 2003) for *Today* and *5 Live* programmes wherein he quoted an unnamed source ('mole' was the catchier media term) in the British intelligence services who revealed that the dossier was made 'sexier' before it was released – for instance, by putting in the claim that Iraq could launch weapons in 45 minutes without firm intelligence backing. It was suggested that the dossier, which was initially drafted by British intelligence as early as 5 September 2002, was then handed over to the Prime Minister's office and redrafted, possibly under the supervision of Campbell and Blair (indeed the 45 minutes claim had been inserted some time after 5 September). Gilligan wrote a piece in the *Mail on Sunday* reiterating the allegation on 1 June 2003; Campbell complained to the BBC's director of news, Richard Sambrook, on 6 June, and refuted the allegations in a news briefing; the BBC stood by Gilligan and an acrimonious exchange between the Prime Minister's office and the BBC followed. The Commons Foreign Affairs Select Committee questioned all parties to resolve the dispute, and there was widespread speculation in the media about the identity of the 'mole'. Meanwhile, the *Independent* published a piece on 12 June 2003 reporting that six items in the 24 September 2002 dossier had been lifted from reports, some of which were up to 21 months old – from a January 2001 briefing paper by William Cohen, former US Defense Secretary; a February 2001 statement by CIA Director George Tenet for a senate intelligence committee; an unclassified CIA report to Congress covering the period 1 July–31 December 2000; and from the 5 September 2002 IISS dossier. This bit of information, however, whirled away into oblivion as, on 10 July 2003, *The Times*, the *Guardian* and the *Financial Times* revealed the identity of the 'mole': David Kelly, Ministry of Defence biological weapons expert. It was later revealed that quite possibly the government had engineered the 'outing of the mole', and Campbell's diaries were quoted in reports suggesting his and possibly Blair's direct involvement. Kelly was subsequently examined by the Commons Foreign Affairs Committee (15 July) and then the Ministry of Defence's Intelligence and Security Committee (16 July), and soon after, on 18 July 2003, Thames Valley police found Kelly's corpse near his home. It was announced that Kelly had taken his life in a state of depression following interrogations. On 18 July the Prime Minister's spokesman announced an independent judicial inquiry into the circumstances of Kelly's death, led by Lord Hutton, law lord and former chief justice of Northern Ireland. The Hutton inquiry took evidence from all parties, including Blair, Campbell,

Defence Secretary Geoff Hoon, BBC executives and other relevant persons, which was copiously covered in newspapers and television and radio broadcasts. Significantly, in the course of this Brian Jones (a senior colleague of Kelly's in the Defence Intelligence Staff [DIS]) testified that he had formally complained about the September 2002 dossier and the manner in which it presented intelligence reports. In his report of 28 January 2004, much to the surprise of all media persons and analysts, Lord Hutton cleared the government and denounced the BBC for being primarily responsible for events leading up to Kelly's death. The BBC director resigned the next day, and the mass media started picking on the 'unanswered questions' arising from the Hutton inquiry, particularly with regard to the inaccuracies (the 45 minutes claim, the claim that Saddam Hussein had tried to obtain uranium from Africa) in the 24 September 2002 dossier.

Claims made in the 24 September 2002 dossier and reiterated in public statements by Bush and others in the US were also under the spotlight. By July 2003 key instigators of military action in Iraq like Vice President Dick Cheney (his speech of 24 July 2003 at the American Enterprise Institute was a case in point), Secretary of Defense Donald Rumsfeld (who was notoriously questioned about this by Senator Mark Pryor at a Senate Armed Services Committee on 10 July 2003), and Deputy Secretary of Defence Paul Wolfowitz found themselves having to defend the claims they had made to justify military action. In particular, the US mass media was rife with discussions of the 'yellowcake' story. Briefly, this referred to assertions about Iraqi attempts to obtain uranium from Africa made in the September 2002 dossier, and repeated by Bush in the January 2003 State of Union address. It had emerged that these assertions were based on fraudulent documents suggesting that Iraq had obtained 'yellowcake' (uranium oxide) from Niger. The CIA had apparently investigated the story and established its lack of credibility by February 2002, had informed the British government of this shortly after the publication of the September 2002 dossier, and CIA Director George Tenet had personally requested the removal of the claim from Bush's State of Union address of January 2003 before it was delivered.

The continuing failure to discover WMD in Iraq finally came to a head in 2004. The Iraq Survey Group, led by David Kay (who had been convinced of the need for military action in Iraq), was given the task of finding them. In an interim report of 2 October 2003 he had still seemed hopeful: 'We have not yet found stocks of weapons, but we are not yet at the point where we can say definitively either that such weapon stocks do not exist or that they existed before the war and our only task is to find where they have gone.'[10] In January 2004 he resigned from his position, and appeared before the Senate Armed Services Commission on 29 January to declare that he didn't believe that there were WMD in Iraq: 'It turns out we were all wrong, probably, in my judgment, and that is most disturbing,' he stated, and 'I believe that the effort that has been directed to this point has been sufficiently intense that it is highly unlikely that there were large stockpiles of deployed militarized chemical and biological weapons there.' He also expressed scepticism about the intelligence on which military action was conducted:

> SENATOR JOHN MCCAIN: Do you believe that those who'd provided false intelligence estimates ought to be held accountable?
> DR DAVID KAY: Absolutely.
> SENATOR JOHN MCCAIN: Do you believe that we need an independent outside investigation?
> DR DAVID KAY: I must say my personal view, and it's purely personal, is that in this case you will finally determine that it is going to take an outside inquiry both to do it and to give yourself and the American people the confidence that you have done it.[11]

As a result, after some hesitation, on 1 February 2004 Bush announced that an independent inquiry into US intelligence on Iraq WMD would take place, and on the next day Blair announced that one would take place in the UK too. Doubts were expressed about the remit of both inquiries. On 6 February 2004 former UK DIS employee, Brian Jones (who had testified in the Hutton inquiry), published an article in the *Independent*, in which he stated: 'In my view the expert intelligence analysis of the DIS were overruled in the preparation of the dossier in September 2002 resulting in a presentation that was misleading about Iraq's capabilities.'[12] He also maintained that the Prime Minister's preface (which was drafted by Campbell) had translated 'a probability into a certainty'.

The story rolls on, but this is probably a sufficient account of this aspect of the context in question.

INFERENCES AND OBSERVATIONS

Before moving on to UNSC debates leading up to the military action in Iraq, some immediate observations on the significance of the above details to this study. The question that is relevant here is: what sorts of presumptions about democracy are implicit in the above network of highlighted events, and how do they impinge upon the international/transnational domain? Obviously, the normative connotations of democracy are deployed in several reasonably precise ways in this 'story', and with obviously larger than domestic effect. However, one of the first characteristics of this 'story' that leaps to mind is how *little* some of the expected presumptions and associations worked. In almost every current conceptual position, the idea of democracy is associated with economic development and Western capitalism. As observed in Part I, studies of democratization have been significantly invested in economic development; cosmopolitan and deliberative democrats associate the expansion of global capitalism with the need to extend democracy; Rawlsian liberalism normatively rationalizes the capitalist state towards well-ordered and just democracy; radical democrats see democracy as conditional to liberal conditions and unrealizable in socialist planned economies; theorists of social movements claim to be democratic in opposition to the hegemony of a denotatively democratic capitalist order; and so on. Each of these conceptual positions has its popularly reduced equivalences, constantly reiterated in the media, in everyday conversation, in political rhetoric. At the level of politically real exchanges where the above 'story' is located, a divorce of the idea of democracy from any political economic content has been, I feel, rare for most of the twentieth century. However, such a divorce seemed to be in place and little remarked on in the exchanges described above.

The fact that in the above story political economy seems not to have played a substantial part could be regarded as symptomatic of larger politically realist considerations. It could be argued (and has been by neo-liberals and those who champion the primary importance of the market mechanism), for instance, that political democracy and economic considerations in fact only meet in a disjunctive fashion – and actually are best kept apart. Where political democracy, such arguments go, is most strongly asserted, it tends to undermine free market operations.[13] Arguably then, since the claims of democracy were being aggressively asserted in the above exchanges, it was expedient not to reveal how these would operate in political economic terms. From a different, and more plausible, direction much the same point can be made more forcefully. By this other argument, the association of high principles like democracy, human rights and free markets are actually red herrings to distract attention from the operations of economic vested interests which are contrary to those. According to Chomsky: 'In the current phase of intellectual corruption, it must be stressed that, like democracy and human rights, the economic doctrines preached by the rulers are instruments of power, intended for others, so that they can be more efficiently robbed and exploited.'[14] It has been widely suspected that the invasion of Iraq was largely motivated by US and UK economic interests: the desire to control Iraqi oil resources, to boost the US economy by providing investment opportunities in rebuilding Iraqi infrastructures after the 'war' was done, to provide a testing ground for immense defence expenditure and utility for increasingly privatized military and affiliated services, etc. These undermined the high principle of democracy in question so blatantly, that in championing the latter it was prudent not to draw attention to the political economic considerations at work. At the same time, it was not prudent to focus too intensively on Iraq's economic woes before the invasion either, since these were arguably the product of economic sanctions that had been in place since 1991. The exchange of dossiers and affiliated debates described above, by this account, was actually a screen that was meant to hide normatively unpalatable and essentially imperialistic political economic considerations. Arguably, the whole dossier business was a subterfuge to draw attention away from the *real* issue of political economic interests. After Bush presented that *National Security Strategy of the USA* paper on 20 September 2002, in which a determination to promote 'democracy, development, free markets, and free trade to every corner of the world' was expressed, very little of free markets and free trade figured in this story.

It seems to me likely that there is a great deal of truth in that last argument, and indeed in another 'story' which I take up below (Chapter 13 on reconstructing Iraq and the Coalition Provisional Authority) political economic considerations in relation to democracy figure more substantially. Despite these somewhat anticipative reservations, however, I think it would be a mistake to simply dismiss the claims for democracy that are contained in the above story.

Shorn of political economic considerations, however cynically, the exchanges detailed above operated primarily in terms of switches between the denotation and connotations of democracy, embedded in a moral discourse. Claims made in the name of democracy, and scepticism about those who made those claims, and attempts to ward off or substantiate such scepticism, operated in a public arena which actually showed not so much sharp divergences of ideological approach as extraordinary unanimity in accepting the moral discourse. Couched in general terms, the following could be thought of as the main claims and presumptions regarding democracy in an international/transnational domain that emerged therein:

- *Claim 1*: Representatives of (essentially majoritarian) governments of political democracies (so denoted) can act in the name of democracy (with normative connotations) in the international/transnational domain. The legitimacy that is accorded them by dint of an elective system within the domestic precincts of their political states can extend outside those precincts to other political states. This is asserted most emphatically by maintaining that such governments are thereby authorized to act with international effect (with domestic consent) to defend the democracy within – a threat to the democracy within is the prime justification for acting outside in the name of democracy.
- *Claim 2*: Claim 1, that action outside the domestic domain can be justified on the basis of democratic legitimacy from within, replicates itself in increasingly comprehensive ways as having moral legitimacy with transnational effect. First, it is asseverated that such domestic democratic legitimacy is coeval with the recognition of threatening external forces as undemocratic and illegitimate. If democratic legitimacy (even though domestic) is given for an aggressive act against external agencies, that is because those external agencies are recognized as being undemocratic and illegitimate. (This kind of polarization is reminiscent particularly of

Rawls's argument, and democratic peace theories generally). Second, and twisted in with that, it therefore follows that a domestic, democratic decision is ultimately based on some universally applicable moral idea of democracy; it is not a contextually determined and contingent decision, it has a universal moral perspective which has transnational legitimacy. Thus, domestic democratic legitimacy is also legitimacy that can be extended to extrinsic transformation – which could be manifested as a claim for championing world democracy, for carrying democracy from within outside (every extrinsic intervention to defend domestic democracy is by the same argument a step towards extending democracy outside). Third, and twisted in with both the above, the polarization of democratic inside and undemocratic outside is supported by associational and increasingly abstract moral claims which extend that polarization in all directions (freedom against oppression; love against hate; reason against madness; truth against falsehood; trust against suspicion; human rights against abuses; equality against inequality; consensus against tyranny, and so on).

- *Claim 3*: The only grounds on which Claims 1 and 2 can be countered are of moral self-contradictions embodied in the agents of democracy (democratically elected leaders of domestic domains). The only way in which this extension of moral claims with domestic democratic legitimacy to the international/transnational domain can be questioned is by using the same moral terms against the agents of such democratic claims: by showing that they are contradicting themselves. The issue is not so much what the effects of such actions in the external domain are, but the good faith with which such actions are undertaken as adhering to the universal normative connotations of democracy and of associated terms.

Such claims, as I have observed above, are tacit but coherently appropriable from the formulations offered by cosmopolitan and deliberative democrats. In the highlighted events of the above story, such claims are unquestioningly adopted with politically real effects.

The importance of domestic democratic legitimation in the US and the UK of the military action in Iraq is noteworthy. The only sanction that Bush and Blair received for their decision to conduct this was from the parliamentary bodies of their countries. To a significant extent the network of exchanges (involving dossiers) that is described above was conducted to secure such parliamentary and domestic sanction, and to that extent, the moral discourse of the dossiers indubitably worked. Despite all the scepticism about informational details, the obvious transparency of the unspoken political economic intentions, the general awareness of the theatricality of public performances involved, at some fundamental level the moral discourse of the exchange, with explicitly spelt out violence, received the domestic parliamentary legitimation that was sought. And however manipulated the select members of such parliamentary bodies may have been to secure this sanction, it is undeniable that they did represent in a majoritarian fashion a democratic electorate, and responded to what they regarded as the pulse of their electorate. To that extent, the dossiers did their job.

As far as the dossiers making the case for invasion go, both their immediate success and their curious afterlife were predicated on such claims as the three stated in a generalized form above. In giving the generalized claims above, I have drawn a kind of logical thread through them. In fact, the dossiers did not make such a logically coherent case in the network of exchanges in question; they primarily worked through a process of selective and rhetorically potent highlighting. It was not the logic of the argument that was being offered or received (that might have been tricky since the logic is, as seen in Part I, questionable); the logic was implicit, or more precisely presumptive, and the highlighting largely followed a pattern of commonly accepted foregone moral conclusions (such as dictatorship is bad, democracy is good, human rights must be respected, democracies shouldn't be threatened, everyone should be free, etc.). On the other hand, the dossiers eventually also undermined the initial legitimation they had helped secure through a process of highlighting too, and one that also followed a similar pattern of commonly accepted foregone moral conclusions (truth is good, in democracies people are free to choose because they know the truth, dictators will lie and democrats shouldn't, etc.). The pertinacity and moral fervour with which the latter process continues to unfold speaks for itself.

The network of exchanges described above – with the vehement swings and shifts therein – depended on an unquestioned and tacit moral discourse which enjoys widespread consensus. This deep moral discourse distracts attention from the logical aspect of the claims made for democracy; and it works through a process of highlighting that deliberately circumvents rational analysis of such claims. My contention in Part I is that these claims are not given rational attention even where political rationalization is undertaken; current conceptual positions are developed by accepting such claims as given and fitting them into their formulations. That such claims operate powerfully, and without interrogation, in the public sphere is, therefore, hardly surprising. The domestic democratic legitimacy which extends itself to the international/transnational domain is based on this deep and unquestioning moral discourse. This is no more than stating the obvious, but I wish to emphasize the *degree* to which this is proved to be effective and unquestioned, despite appearances of vociferous differences, in the above-described network of exchanges. This deep moral discourse builds on the deep normative content that William Connolly discerned (discussed in Part I) in certain terms in political discourse.

The moral discourse that operated in the above story was not only operational *within* distinctively defined domestic precincts that extend democratic legitimacy with aggressive extrinsic effect. Each level of the network of exchanges here – public speeches by Bush, Blair and others; the dossiers themselves; the highlighted news and analyses that were conveyed in the mass media; etc. – was addressed not simply to a domestic domain but to the international/transnational domain too. The means of publicity and consumption in place are irrevocably designed for this, and each step has the calculation of its international/transnational reach and effect in view while being taken. It is difficult to determine to what extent that makes the international/transnational domain itself generally characterizable as partaking of the deep moral discourse that informed domestic opinions in the US, UK and rest of Europe. Arguably, there is wide international (perhaps transnational) consensus in that deep moral discourse. Equally, it is possible that the process of highlighting allows for the specific contexts which accept that moral discourse to dominate, or to repress the presence of other less compliant contexts, so as to confer an apparently universal character to that discourse.[15]

Finally, in the network of exchanges of this 'story', the idea of democracy also operates on the presumption that its normative content is concretized in democratic political institutions. The optimistic notion that democracy can be embodied and ensured through institutional formations is best exemplified – and extended – in the work of cosmopolitan democrats, where the increasing reach of democracy is given essentially as a matter of domestic, regional and transnational institutional adjustment. Moral consent is given in terms of institutional sanction, or withheld as a matter of institutional incoherence. In the above story, every expression of a position with relation to the operation of democracy in domestic or international/transnational domains occurred with reference to the institutional status of that position. So the entire network of exchanges revolved around ambiguities of parliamentary, UN, NATO, EU, etc., sanctions; the legality or illegality of the military action; official commissions and enquiries to determine degrees of misconduct or soundness of conduct, etc. It is evident that the mode of drawing upon institutional prerogatives is far from consistent. There have been dramatic shifts in the mode of reference to institutional prerogatives; indeed, so unsteady has this been that arguably the *raison d'être* of each of the institutions in question has been undermined. It had been averred at one moment that the UNSC has to be obeyed and at the next that it can be disregarded; often the legal position looked exceedingly dubious and then suddenly it became immaterial; at several points parliamentary sanction seemed doubtful but only to turn out to be the opposite; governments seemed to be on the verge of being discredited by enquiries and investigative commissions but nevertheless came through all the stronger. Despite the undermining of institutional prerogatives that seemed to occur in the above network of exchanges, it is observable – and this is the point – that every move in the network of exchanges took place *with reference to* democratic institutional prerogatives. Every accusation and counter-accusation, every evasion and assertion, was translated onto some institutional procedure and prerogative, but not therefore in a way that consolidated the rational functioning of the institutions in question (quite the contrary). In terms of the above network of exchanges, it is arguable that democratic institutional prerogatives served not so much to protect or embody the rational unfolding of democratic process, as to be evoked to give legitimacy to a domestic decision with extrinsic effect after the fact. Democratic institutionality in the sphere of international and transnational affairs serves more a symbolic function than a rational democratic function.

This brings this study to another highlighted network of exchanges, another story, which is pertinent to this context: to do with the role of the UN in conflict resolution.

NOTES

All web pages referred to here were downloaded within the period September 2002 and June 2004.

1 International Institute of Strategic Studies (IISS), *Iraq's Weapons of Mass Destruction: A Net Assessment* (London: IISS, 2002) – this can be purchased through the website www.iiss.org/.

2 Quotations from speeches, interviews and statements by George W. Bush are mostly from transcripts placed on www.whitehouse.gov/news/. Quotations from Tony Blair's speeches, interviews and statements are largely from www.number-10.gov.uk/. Other government websites have been used here to access statements by these and other US and UK government figures, such as www.fco.gov.uk/; www.labour.org.uk/speeches; www.dod.gov/speeches/; www.state.gov/, as have newspaper reports (these are referred to in-text).

3 Albie Lythgow, 'Politics and the Pay Rise', *FBU Magazine*, Kingston upon Thames, Surrey, September 2002, p. 4.

4 *The National Security Strategy* dossier of 17 September 2002, downloaded from www.whitehouse.gov/nsc/nssall.html.

5 Joint Intelligence Committee (JIC), *Iraq's Weapons of Mass Destruction: The Assessment of the British Government*, 24 September 2002, downloaded from www.ukonline.gov.uk/featurenews/iraqdossier.pdf.

6 Foreign and Commonwealth Office, *Saddam Hussain: Crimes and Human Rights Abuses. A Report of the Human Cost of Saddam's Policies*, December 2002, downloaded from www.fco.gov.uk/Files/kfile/iraqdossier.pdf.

7 Irene Kahn, 'Iraq II: Who Cares About the People?', *International Herald Tribune*, 25 September 2002.

8 *Iraq – Its Infrastructure of Concealment, Deception and Intimidation*, January 2003 downloaded from www.number-10.gov.uk/files/pdf/Iraq.pdf#.

9 Records of the 4701st UNSC meeting (downloaded from www.un.org/Depts/dhl/resguide/scact2003.htm), S/PV.4701, 5 February 2003, p. 6.

10 David Kay, 'Statement on the Interim Progress Report on the Activities of the Iraq Survey Group (ISG) before the House Permanent Select Committee on Intelligence, The House Committee on Appropriations, Subcommittee on Defense, and the Senate Select Committee on Intelligence', 2 October 2003, downloaded from www.cia.gov/cia/public_affairs/speeches/2003/.

11 I have quoted this from the transcript of David Kay's Testimony to the Senate Armed Services Committee of 28 January 2004, downloaded from homepage.ntlworld.com/jksonc/docs/davidkay-sasc-20040128.html.

12 Brian Jones, 'There was a lack of substantive evidence. There was intelligence we could not see.' *Independent*, 4 February 2004, p. 6.

13 The argument that parliamentary democracy and market freedom operate against each other was made emphatically by F. A. Hayek, in 'Economic Freedom and Representative Government' (1973), *Economic Freedom* (Oxford: Basil Blackwell, 1991). It has been reiterated intermittently since, e.g. Arthur Seldon, *The Dilemma of Democracy: The Political Economics of Over-Government* (London: Institute of Economic Affairs, 1998).

14 Noam Chomsky, 'Democracy and the Market', in *Year 501: The Conquest Continues* (London: Verso, 1993), p. 100.

15 This refers to the well-documented unevenness of media access in the world and the domination of Western mass media at an international level.

11 *UN Security Council Debates*

THE SECOND STORY

The UNSC decided to reconvene the weapons inspection regime in Iraq through the setting up of UNMOVIC and using the agency of IAEA by Resolution 1284 on 17 December 1999. In the course of 2000 Dr Hans Blix was appointed Chairman of UNMOVIC, and from then till September 2002 the UNMOVIC College of Commissioners held ten sessions, and ten quarterly reports were presented to the UNSC.[1] Increasing military movement by US and UK forces in the Gulf region, and 'fighting talk' by Bush and Blair, gradually led to Iraq's decision to allow the unconditional return of the inspection regime (letter from Foreign Minister of Iraq to the General-Secretary of UN, 16 September 2002, S/2002/1034).[2] Throughout this period the UNSC resolved to continue the oil-for-food programme passed by Resolution 986, 14 April 1995, ostensibly to alleviate the suffering of the Iraqi people caused by economic sanctions imposed through Resolution 678 of 29 November 1990.

To grasp the nuances of the network of exchanges and highlighting involving UNSC debates leading up to the invasion of Iraq, particularly in the context of this study, it is necessary to bear in mind the outline of UN procedures given in Chapter 8. Of particular interest here are: the principle of multilateral democracy that the UN seems to accept, at least in the General Assembly; the undermining of that principle by the prerogatives and procedures of the UNSC; and the championing of normatively connoted democracy with a denotative turn in the UN's Human Rights declaration. Also relevant here are debates on the history, current position and future possibilities of the UN by cosmopolitan democrats and political realists discussed in Chapters 2, 3 and 8 of Part I.

Onwards with the story: in September 2002, as Iraq was confirming her willingness to cooperate with returning UN inspectors, Bush and Blair issued statements clarifying that they would accept UNSC prerogatives only insofar as these were agreeable to them. In other words, it was made clear that they were not seeking so much to implement the agenda of the UN as seeking the UN's sanction for *their* agenda (or a convergence of the UN's multilateral and their unilateral agendas). This meant that they didn't present the case for action in Iraq simply as a matter of upholding the principles of the UN, but more importantly as a matter of upholding their own principles through the UN. Implicitly, and interestingly, this brought to the fore a clash between commitment to the principle of multilateral democracy of states as embodied in the UN and the primarily ethical claim to the principle of democracy that is allegedly embodied in US and UK parliamentary states. This is implicit in the wording of the following quotation from Blair's speech to the Trades Union Congress in Blackpool of 10 September 2002:

> I believe it is right to deal with Saddam through the United Nations. After all, it is the will of the UN he is flouting. He, not me or George Bush, is in breach of UN Resolutions. If the challenge to us is to work with the UN, we will respond to it.
>
> But if we do so, then the challenge to all in the UN is this: the UN must be the way to resolve the threat from Saddam, not avoid it. . . .
>
> And let it be clear that should the will of the UN be ignored, action will follow. Diplomacy is vital. And when dealing with dictators – and none in the world is worse than Saddam – diplomacy has to be backed by the certain knowledge in the dictator's mind that behind the diplomacy is the possibility of force being used.[3]

The distance introduced between the UN and US–UK is worth noting. It is not taken for granted that the UN represents the right mode of ratification for use of force; that that may be so is generously, but conditionally, conceded by Blair. Working with the UN is regarded as a 'challenge', and their doing so is equally a 'challenge' to other UN members. Blair argues for action in Iraq on the grounds of Saddam Hussain's dictatorial behaviour (to which he is presumably opposed as the voice of liberal democracy) – a ground that in itself has no recognizable place in the multilateral democracy of the UN, or, such as it is, of the UNSC. These manoeuvres and clashes of principles of democracy are, if anything, more clearly demonstrated in Bush's address to the UN General Assembly on 12 September 2002. Here, after detailing the allegedly illegal weapons holdings of Iraq, Bush moved on to the following remarks:

> My nation will work with the UN Security Council to meet our common challenge. If Iraq's regime defies us again, the world must move deliberately, decisively to hold Iraq to account. We will work with the UN Security Council for the necessary resolutions. But the purposes of the United States should not be doubted. The Security Council resolutions will be enforced – the just demands of peace and security will be met – or action will be unavoidable. And a regime that has lost its legitimacy will also lose its power. . . .
>
> If we meet our responsibilities . . . the people of Iraq can shake off their captivity. They can one day join a democratic Afghanistan

> and a democratic Palestine, inspiring reforms throughout the Muslim world. These nations can show by their example that honest government, and respect for women, and the great Islamic tradition of learning can triumph in the Middle East and beyond. And we will show that the promise of the United Nations can be fulfilled in our time.

Like Blair, Bush promises to work with the UN but only insofar as that serves the purpose of the US. Apparently Bush's understanding of the aim of intervening in Iraq is, not unlike Blair's, for the sake of an ideological mission: to spread democracy in the 'Muslim world'. The tension between the multilateralism embodied in UN and the unilateral resolve of the US's professed ideological mission are clear, and deliberately played with by Bush as much as Blair. The tension could be played up and played on because, for both Bush and Blair, the two claims of democratic justification were equally poised: moral missionary democratic unilateralism may cancel out the principle of multilateral democracy, or supersede it.

Following Bush's expression of a desire to secure the 'necessary resolutions', US–UK set about drafting a tough new resolution to table at the UNSC. The various stages of the drafting of this resolution, the hard negotiations that surrounded the process, the many closed-door discussions and bargains that were struck in this connection, the calculations behind the different steps of the process were detailed in the mass media at great length. These formed as much of the day-to-day political debate in, say, the UK as the appearance of dossiers did. It is not my intention to outline all matters pertaining to UNSC debates here. To keep the focus of this study clearly on its subject, and indeed to delimit the contextual detail that needs to be kept in sight, I deal in this story primarily with publicly conducted UNSC debates, minutes and accounts of which are available in the public domain.

In view of possible unilateral action on the part of UK–US and the coming tabling of the draft resolution, the Non-Aligned Movement, chaired at the time by South Africa, requested (S/2002/1132) an open debate on 16 and 17 October 2002. This was the first of several open debates prior to military action in Iraq. In addition to representatives of the 15 UNSC members of the time (the five permanent members, Mexico, Ireland, Bulgaria, Syria, Norway, Singapore, Colombia, Cameroon, Guinea, Mauritius) the meeting was also attended by representatives of the Secretary-General, the UN member country involved in the dispute (Iraq), 48 other UN member countries not part of the UNSC (including Denmark for the European Union), and permanent observers for the League of Arab States, Palestine and Organization of the Islamic Conference (S/PV.4625, Resumptions 1, 2 and 3). Several points of interest from the perspective of this study emerged in this discussion:

- There was, naturally, general consensus on the undesirability of war, the importance of the UNSC as the appointed international body for the resolution of conflicts through a multilateral mechanism, the need for UNSC resolutions to be implemented, and the necessity for a UNSC coordinated inspections regime to be in place in Iraq. However, there was also some recognition of the unevenness of the operation of multilateralism in the UNSC. This took the form of concerns expressed by some representatives that all elected members' views were not being given adequate weight (in the light of reports that secret meetings had been held among the permanent UNSC members). The point was succinctly made by Dumisani S. Kumalo of South Africa: 'We believe that these elected members have their own special role to play in the Council's deliberations, because they bring credibility and balance to decision-making within the Council. We are therefore concerned if elected members are excluded from consultations on the most pressing issues before the Council. This can only lead to the erosion of the authority and legitimacy of the Security Council as a whole' (p. 5, Resumption 1); and by Stafford Neil of Jamaica: 'We must also register our concern at aspects of the decision-making process in the Council, especially with respect to the role of the elected members and the pre-eminence of the members with the veto power. Our view is that the full involvement of the elected members of the Council at all levels of the decision-making process is vital for giving legitimacy and authority to the Council's decisions' (p. 22, Resumption 2), and echoed by Bruno Rodrique Parrilla of Cuba and a few others. These are, explicitly, pleas to maintain as much of multilateral democratic legitimacy as possible. One significant interpretation of the wider import of such perceptions of unevenness was given by Jean-David Levitte of France: 'What is at stake in the ongoing negotiations is fundamental: even beyond Iraq, we are talking about the future of the international order, relations between North and South, and notably, our relationship with the Arab world. An action of uncertain legitimacy, one that does not enjoy the support of the international community, would not be understood and could gravely affect these relations' (p. 14, Resumption 3).
- The unevenness of the multilateral mechanism of the UNSC was particularly noted in accusations of the perception of double standards. It was observed by several (particularly Middle Eastern representatives) that similar flouting of UNSC resolutions had been evidenced from Israel, but no debate and action on the part of UNSC along the lines of the present one had followed. Israel, it was observed, definitely had weapons of mass destruction that it was prepared to use but no equivalent moves towards disarming Israel had been permitted. The point was particularly made by representatives of Algeria, Egypt, Jordan, the League of Arab States, Indonesia, Malaysia, Lebanon, Djibouti, Palestine, Saudi Arabia, Organization of Islamic Conference, Qatar and Syria. Unsurprisingly,

> none other than these representatives of dominant Islamic constituencies made significant reference to the issue of double standards being demonstrated with regard to Israel and Iraq. The raising of Israel's position on UNSC resolutions however did take a revealing (especially for this study) turn when Yehuda Lancry, representing Israel, chose to address the charge of double standards, in the following words: 'Is there a double standard, as certain Member States have alleged? There is a simple test. Take two States, one is a dictatorship and serial violator of Council resolutions and human rights that is dedicated to the acquisition of chemical, biological and nuclear weapons and fighting for regional domination; the other is a democracy upholding the principles of the rule of law and freedom of speech, a people whose survival has been tested for decades but who are still committed to peace, both for themselves and for future generations in the Middle East' (p. 3, Resumption 3). A retort to this followed in Mikhail Wehbe's statement representing Syria: 'What is truly strange about the Israeli logic is the talk about democracy while Israel is practising various kinds of murder and destruction in the occupied Arab territories. Is there a new concept called the democracy of occupation? Or is there a new logic regarding democratic occupation?' (p. 7, Resumption 3). That in turn led to a bitter exchange between them at the end of the debate, with each accusing the other of not possessing the moral status to claim democratic credibility. What was exposed on the floor of the UNSC, in fact, was that when the principle of multilateral democracy could not be defended some claim of allegiance to a morally loaded principle of majoritarian/representative democracy came into play (Israel deployed it precisely for that purpose). In brief, it was clear that the principle of multilateral democracy ensconced in the UN and the principle of majoritarian/representative democracy derived from certain domestic constitutions were being deployed in the field of international politics with contrary and opposing effect.

Incidentally, a stark demonstration of both the unevenness of UN multilateral democracy and of double standards, occurred a couple of months after this debate. On 22 November 2002 UN worker Iain Hook was fatally shot by an Israeli sniper in Jenin, and on 6 December 2002 it was reported that in an operation in the Gaza refugee camp the Israeli army killed ten people, including two UN school workers. Tensions between the UN and Israel mounted. UN workers had complained about the brutality of Israeli military operations in Palestine already, and on 4 December 2002 64 UN workers signed an unprecedented petition asking for the Israeli government to be held to account for these crimes. The Israeli government retorted with counter-accusations against UN aid workers of shielding terrorists. On 20 December 2002, Syria, on behalf of the Group of Arab States, tabled a draft resolution for voting at the 4681st meeting of the UNSC, which condemned the killing of UN employees by Israeli forces and destruction of UN property in occupied Palestinian territory. Following a familiar pattern of failed resolutions regarding Israel at the UNSC,[4] this resolution failed to be adopted despite 12 members voting for it because the US used its veto against it (Bulgaria and Cameroon abstained). John Negroponte, representing the US, explained in his statement that he voted against it because the US felt such a resolution endangered efforts to establish a roadmap to peace (see Press Release SC/7620).

As a result of the deliberations of 16 and 17 October, and following a prolonged period of discussion on the precise wording of the resolution (all the power politics implicit in which was gleefully reported in the mass media), on 8 November 2002 Resolution 1441 was unanimously adopted by the UNSC (see Press Release SC/7564). Briefly, it set up the conditions for an enhanced UNMOVIC and IAEA weapons inspections regime in Iraq, and demanded a complete declaration of all weapons holdings from the Iraqi government. Most crucially, no time limit was set for the weapons inspections to be completed, or for the demonstration of non-compliance with the resolution. It could be assumed that the weapons inspections would carry on till the business of disarming Iraq was achieved or confirmed; that being the case and with the absence of a time limit, the only time-bound statement that remained in the resolution was the expectation of 'immediate, unconditional, and unrestricted access' to inspectors being given by Iraq. The combination of no time limit being set on inspections along with the expectation of 'immediate' compliance with inspectors turned out to be a double-sided weapon. On the one hand, it seemed to allow the inspections process all the time necessary; on the other hand, 'immediacy' in Iraq's compliance allowed for the process to be subverted at any time. The vagueness of what 'immediate' constitutes was the substance of many debates to come over the following months. On the one hand, weapons inspectors were allocated all the responsibility needed; on the other hand, the mechanism to withdraw that responsibility and blame Iraq for it was also inserted.

In retrospective, it appears that this ambiguity in Resolution 1441 allowed all members to justify their positions in different ways. Those who didn't wish military intervention in Iraq could say that this was an endorsement of the UN inspections regime and contained no automatic condition for such action to be initiated (no 'automaticity' was the term in use in statements following the adoption of this resolution). To those in this position (explicitly France, China, Russian Federation, Syria, Ireland, Mexico, Singapore, Guinea, Cameroon, Norway and Mauritius) the lack of 'automaticity' suggested a postponement of hostilities until another resolution to that effect was adopted. John Negroponte of the US however interpreted the lack of 'automaticity' somewhat differently: 'If the Security Council failed to act decisively in the event of further Iraqi violation, the resolution did not constrain any Member State from acting to defend itself against the threat posed by that country, or to enforce relevant United Nations resolutions and protect world peace and security' (p. 8). Jeremy Greenstock of the UK saw the lack of 'automaticity' as indicating that further breach of Iraq's disarmament obligations would bring the matter back for discussion in the UNSC – 'But if Iraq chooses defiance and concealment, rejecting the final opportunity it has been given by the Council . . ., the United Kingdom – together, we trust, with other members of the Council – will ensure that the task of disarmament required by the resolutions is completed' (p. 9). That 'together, we trust' speaks volumes. Martin Belinga-Eboutou for Cameroon described the text of Resolution 1441 as 'a truly compromise text, without a victory for any side' (p. 11).

Resolution 1441 had stipulated that the first UNMOVIC and IAEA reports to the UNSC would be due 60 days after inspections were resumed. By 17 November 2002 UNMOVIC inspectors had appeared in Iraq to resume weapons inspections for the first time since 1998, which meant that the first inspections reports to the UNSC were due for 27 January 2003. As I have noted in the previous chapter, Iraq presented its dossier disclosing weapons holdings in accordance with Resolution 1441 on 7 December 2002.

The build-up to the first reports of UNMOVIC and the UAEA and the immediate aftermath saw an intensification of debates and differences, with attendant highlighting of rhetoric, which is pertinent to this study. The move towards a second UNSC resolution authorizing military action in Iraq was being aired by the US and UK well before the first reports were presented. It was evident that Blix and other UNMOVIC inspectors were under intense pressure from the US and UK to come up with results – or at least statements – that would tilt UN opinion in their favour. Meanwhile, in the public domain, both the US and UK had emphatically shifted the rhetoric of war away from the question of disarmament and threats from WMD, and towards a democratizing mission for the larger welfare of humanity. However, this shift of rhetoric couldn't hide the fact that significant rifts were opening up between governments even within Western Europe (which themselves have traditionally been aligned to this ethical rhetoric of democracy). This meant that the rhetoric of the democratizing mission was realigned to another sphere of the political discourse of democracy, that of 'old and new' democracies. This two-pronged shift in the debate – towards the ethical weight of a democratizing mission oriented towards the understanding and support of new democracies – characterized this phase of developments.

Thus, in Tony Blair's speech at the Foreign Office conference of 7 January 2003, while affirming that he regarded the US as a 'force for good; they have liberal and democratic traditions of which any nation can be proud', and that he sought a central position in Europe for the UK, he also had the following proselytizing sentiments to express in the context of the situation pertaining to Iraq:

> But reaching out to the Muslim world also means engaging with how those countries move towards greater democratic stability, liberty and human rights. It means building pathways of understanding between Islam and other religious faiths. This seems an odd thing for a politician to say – but then I am used to clerics offering me advice. But we need to engage with mainstream Islam at a theological as well as political level. Inter-faith dialogue is one important part of greater understanding. . . .
>
> In the end, all these things come back to one basic theme. The values we stand for: freedom, human rights, the rule of law, democracy, are all universal values. Given a chance, the world over, people want them. But they have to be pursued alongside another value: justice, the belief in opportunity for all. Without justice, the values I describe can be portrayed as 'Western values'; globalization becomes a battering ram for Western commerce and culture; the order we want is seen by much of the world as 'their' order, not 'ours'.

He appeared to be oblivious to the contradiction of that last sentence: *we want* juxtaposed against *theirs/ours*, already reflected in the comprehensive reduction of the *Muslim world* as implicitly lacking, therefore in need of, *our universal values*. Irrespective of these rousing sentiments, it became clear between 21 and 23 January (as the 27 January deadline for weapons inspectors' reports came closer) that the rift in Europe was widening. France had indicated that it would use its veto against any premature push towards a second resolution from the UNSC. In a joint press conference of 21 January celebrating the fortieth anniversary of their postwar friendship treaty in Paris, Chancellor Gerhard Schroeder and President Jacques Chirac pledged to intensify cooperation against a US-led war in Iraq. This was supported by Russia and China, both with veto powers in the UNSC. Some impolite name-calling between France and UK–US followed. At the same time NATO ambassadors announced that, mainly at the instance of France and Germany, the US's request that NATO should undertake advance military planning, particularly with a view to protecting Turkey (the only NATO member in the neighbourhood of Iraq), had been rejected. It was also becoming clear that such government-level support as was available within Europe, apart from the UK, was from the conservative governments of the comparatively late democracies Spain, Italy and Portugal, and the recently 'democratized' Eastern Bloc governments of Hungary, Czech Republic, Poland and Bulgaria. Bush, Powell and Rumsfeld all reportedly expressed irritation (particularly with France and Germany), dismissing them as 'old Europe', and sought to embrace the support of European 'new democracies'. Bush and Rumsfeld reportedly did this in their usual pugnacious fashion; Powell in a slightly more politic fashion, carefully mixing up the ethical democratizing mission attitude with thoughts about old and new democracies on the eve of the presentation of the UN weapons inspectors' reports to the UNSC. In a speech at the World Economic Forum at Davos, Switzerland, on 26 January 2003, Powell had the following to say to, and in, Europe:

> New democracies created with high hopes can founder if ordinary citizens do not see direct improvements in their lives. Transitions can be chaotic and wrenching. Democratic systems take time to develop and deliver. Meanwhile, autocrats will sing sirens' songs of stability, consumption will squander a nation's treasury, extremists will feed on frustrations and fear, populists will pander and make fake promises of fairness.
>
> By helping strengthen civil society, independent media, democratic institutions and the rule of law, we can build confidence among citizens to stay on the difficult course of reform. And governments striving to do right must have good reason to count on other members of the world community to help them through the rough times to the point where democracy and development are stable and self-sustaining.

In passing he also noted that 'Multilateralism cannot become an excuse for inaction' – but by this time Powell's views on this issue were public already. After France and Germany's joint statement on 21 January, Powell had reportedly given an interview on the same day, indicating both his irritation with France and stating that he did not think UN inspections in Iraq will work (reported in the *San Francisco Chronicle* on 22 January 2003).

It was in this environment that Hans Blix, on behalf of UNMOVIC, and El-Baradei, on behalf of IAEA, presented their reports at the UNSC on 27 January 2003 (S/PV.4692). This did little to sway either the war-seekers or the war-opposers in Europe. In fact the inspectors' reports played along the lines of ambiguity already noted in the wording of Resolution 1441. Blix reported on the issues about weapons holdings regarding which UNMOVIC sought evidence and clarified that no conclusion could be drawn regarding these yet. It emerged that what they were about was not so much *ascertaining the presence of WMD* with a view to destroying them, as asking Iraq to *prove that it did not have any*. This fine and rather crucial distinction appeared as a clarification of the nature of Iraq's cooperation. Blix made a distinction between cooperation in 'substance and process' (p. 4), and stated that in process 'Iraq has cooperated rather well' but expressed doubts about Iraq's cooperation in substance (on the supposition that Iraq must have documents detailing destruction of suspected WMD which it had not produced). Both Blix's and El-Baradei's reports were carefully phrased in that, without being in a position to offer any substantive evidence, they made enough of their suspicions and expectations to keep both sides of the war debate going much as they were. So they did nothing to heal the rift in Europe – or indeed counter very nearly unanimous opposition to war in the rest of the world – and the rhetorical ploys on which the debate was now almost exclusively balanced stayed in place.

On 28 January 2003 in his State of the Union address Bush declared that the US was set to bring 'to the Iraqi people food and medicines and supplies – and freedom'. The rift in Europe manifested itself in an open letter issued on 30 January 2002 calling for European states to maintain good relations with the US for the 'values we share: democracy, individual freedom, human rights and the Rule of Law', signed by the 'new democracy' champions: the heads of states of the UK, Portugal, Spain, Italy, Czech Republic, Poland, Hungary and Denmark. Given that both the US and UK had taken steps to go for unilateral action against Iraq if UNSC sanction was not forthcoming, and had gestured towards this as early as September 2002, the constant invocation of the principle of Rule of Law was beginning to sound invidious. It also emerged by this time that Colin Powell would himself undertake to erase the indeterminacies left by Blix's and El-Baradei's reports by presenting evidence originating from US intelligence directly to the UNSC on 5 February 2003.

On 5 February 2003 Colin Powell made his presentation to the UNSC detailing the evidence in question, equipped with audio and audio-visual material (S/PV.4701). The details of this are not material to this study. Briefly, it can be noted here that Powell had in fact set himself an uphill task if he hoped thereby to convert those who were against military action, because: (a) it naturally seemed presumptuous of the US to present independent evidence to the UNSC when UN inspectors were on the ground in Iraq and should have been party to such intelligence as the US had; (b) the, self-evidently circumstantial, evidence that he did present did not suggest the inevitable failure of inspections as a means of disarming Iraq; and (c) the evidence had to be taken on trust as representing intelligence gathered and presented with full integrity, which could hardly be expected from so vociferously partisan a quarter as the US. Colin Powell acquitted himself as well as could be expected. In the statements from UNSC members that followed the following emerged. Those who felt inspections should continue as constituted included China, Russian Federation, France, Mexico, Pakistan, Chile, Angola, Syria, Guinea and Germany. Among those who more or less explicitly gestured towards a new resolution setting a deadline for military action apart from the US was the UK, Bulgaria and Spain. Cameroon's statement was ambiguous. All looked forwards to the next briefing by the weapons inspectors on 14 February 2003.

The UNMOVIC and IAEA briefings of 14 February to the UNSC (S/PV.4707) added little to the reports of 27 January, except in assuring all that further progress was being made. Blix's report said categorically that UNMOVIC had not found any weapons of mass destruction yet, but that further inspections and verifications were necessary; addressed the matter of extrinsic intelligence originating from governments (clearly in the light of Powell's presentation of 5 February) and the role this might play; and warned against jumping to conclusions without verification through the inspections process (casting doubt on one of the contentions in the evidence presented by Powell); and ended by saying, 'Today, three months after the adoption of Resolution 1441, the period of disarmament through inspection could be short if immediate, active and unconditional cooperation with UNMOVIC and IAEA were to be forthcoming' (p. 6), which suggested that there was still something lacking in Iraqi cooperation (thus, given the wording of Resolution 1441, still allowing some legalistic credence to the US–UK position). El-Baradei's report suggested that Iraqi cooperation was satisfactory and confirmed that nothing had yet been found. In the statements that followed the issues of maintaining evenness, such as it is, in the implementation of the multilateral democracy of the UNSC, and the appearance of double standards, came up again. More interestingly, the 'old and new democracy' rhetoric that had been effervescing in the public domain since January 2002 surfaced here. As noted above, in the 16 and 17 October 2002 UNSC open debate on Iraq this had only appeared once, when Israel sought to defend its position as a democratic country. In the statements of the 14 February 2003 meeting, this was a more general theme. It was deployed, in an ironic allusion to recently reported sentiments expressed by Powell, Rumsfeld and others, by Villepin of France: 'It is an old country, France, of an old continent such as mine, Europe, that speaks before the Council today, that has known war, occupation, barbarity – a country that does not forget and that is aware of all it owes to the fighters of freedom who came from America and elsewhere' (p. 13). Villepin's allusion to the 'oldness' of France however was not associated with the idea of representative/participatory democracy as a moral position, more as an affirmation of France's understanding of the multilateral process. In a similar spirit Tang Jiaxuan's statement on behalf of China also alluded to the 'oldness' of China: 'China is an ancient civilization. Our ancestors proposed long ago the idea of peace being the best option' (p. 15). These grandstanding claims of national experience drew on some loose idea of the legitimacy drawn from learning the lessons of history. The moral legitimacy drawn from being ostensibly democratic in some majoritarian/representative way in the domestic domain was used here, as previously by Israel, primarily by those seeking military action most aggressively in Iraq. Jack Straw of the UK alluded to Villepin's use of 'old' in a witty riposte ('I speak on behalf of a very old country, founded in 1066 by the French': p. 17), but much in the same spirit. A more humourless intervention within this strand of exchange, but inserting the moral claims of domestic democracy with international effect, came from Colin Powell:

> I am very pleased to be here as the Secretary of State of a relatively new country on the face of the Earth. But I think I can take some credit sitting here as the representative of the oldest democracy represented here around this table. I am proud of that. It is a democracy that believes in peace, a

> nation that has tried in the course of its history to show how people can live in peace with one another. But it is a democracy that has not been afraid to meet its responsibilities on the world stage when it has been challenged and, more importantly, when others in the world have been challenged, when the international order has been challenged or when the international institutions of which we are a part have been challenged. (pp. 18–19)

This gives a somewhat different turn to this strand of the exchange. It pushes the advantages of historical experience aside in favour of the moral legitimacy derived from representing democracy. It doesn't accept lessons, it gives lessons; it is not simply *a* democracy which speaks of its experience, it takes on democratic responsibility for the rest of the world. Implicitly, little space is left for multilateral democracy here. Also worth noting is the change of tone, from the ironic, witty, slightly distanced turn of Villepin's or Straw's allusions to this, to the unambiguous manner in which Powell seeks to *embody* democracy – '*I* take credit', '*I* am proud'. After this point, to some extent the statements turned into a debate between multilateralism and the ethics of democracy. Ivanov of the Russian Federation referred to the importance of multilateralism, as did Gaspar Martins of Angola. Tafrov of Bulgaria came back to the claims of 'new democracy': 'I have the privilege and great honour of speaking on behalf of another old European country represented in this Chamber, but also on behalf of the sole new European democracy represented on the Security Council. I must add that we are very happy to be so' (p. 28). The aggressors, so to say, in this exchange tended to push the democratic legitimacy line.

Since the tabling of a second UN Resolution with a concrete deadline for military action seemed now imminent, another open UNSC debate along the lines of the one on 16–17 October 2002 was called by South Africa on behalf of the Non-Aligned Movement. This took place on 18 and 19 February 2003 (S/PV.4709, summarized in Press Release SC 7666), and 62 speakers expressed their views on the occasion. It was understandably more troubled than the previous one; but, from the perspective of this study, nothing relevant that hasn't been covered already came up here. In fact, nothing much that is relevant to the concerns of this study emerged in the remainder of the UNSC meetings before military intervention officially began on 19 March. The rest of this story is largely a matter of rounding up the details of developments in the UNSC and outlining the fate of the draft second resolution. As a matter of maintaining a sense of the manner in which multilateral opinion developed – or was subverted – in this period, and the kind of unilateral interests which played within the process (constantly reported through the period), I briefly indicate the official positions taken by different states in following UNSC meetings. On 18 and 19 February, those who expressed doubts (with different degrees of moderation) about the effectiveness of the inspections process, and therefore favoured (to different degrees) a second resolution setting a deadline for military actions, included representatives of the following: Australia, Japan, Macedonia, Nicaragua, Albania, Uzbekistan, Marshall Islands, Georgia, Latvia. The other 53 speakers (representing a significantly larger number of states through different alignments) spoke in favour of continuing inspections as they were currently constituted and in process. Also of interest here were the remarks made by a significant number of speakers about the vast number of anti-war protest marches that were taking place all around the world – but more of that in the next chapter.

A similar pattern of meetings as in February 2003 was repeated in the first half of March 2004. But, by this time, it was reasonably clear that a second resolution was unlikely to be adopted at the UNSC, and in fact it was indicated that the US had already assumed it wasn't necessary. In his address to the American Enterprise Institute of 26 February 2003, Bush discussed at length plans for rebuilding a 'liberated' Iraq. No mention was made of the UN in this, apart from a brief statement: 'In confronting Iraq, the United States is also showing our commitment to effective international institutions. We are a permanent member of the United Nations Security Council. We helped to create the Security Council. We believe in the Security Council – so much that we want its words to have meaning.' A great deal more was said about the US's mission of spreading democracy:

> The world has a clear interest in the spread of democratic values, because stable and free nations do not breed the ideologies of murder. They encourage the peaceful pursuit of a better life. And there are hopeful signs of a desire for freedom in the Middle East. Arab intellectuals have called on Arab governments to address the 'freedom gap' so their peoples can fully share in the progress of our times. Leaders in the region speak of a new Arab charter that champions internal reform, greater politics participation, economic openness, and free trade. And from Morocco to Bahrain and beyond, nations are taking genuine steps toward politics reform. A new regime in Iraq would serve as a dramatic and inspiring example of freedom for other nations in the region.

It was pretty clear that the weapons inspectors' reports had already been pushed into oblivion by US–UK and others who were determined to initiate military action.

Nevertheless Blix and El-Baradei presented another set of reports on 7 March 2003 at the UNSC (S/PV.4714). Blix noted an acceleration of Iraqi initiatives towards full cooperation, and suggested that the inspections process would take months to complete. El-Baradei confirmed this and stated that no evidence of nuclear capability or attempts to develop this had yet been found. In the statements that followed, the reports were only alluded to opportunistically; the question on which positions were taken was whether the second resolution should be adopted or not. On 7 March too, Spain, the US and UK released a draft resolution – the second resolution – setting 17 March 2003 as the final deadline by which Iraq had to demonstrate full, unconditional and immediate disarming or become open to military action. The statements at the UNSC meeting were naturally more impassioned than before. Of the 14 UNSC member states, the following declared unambiguous support for a new resolution: the US, UK, Spain, Bulgaria. More interesting developments with regard to the draft resolution had already occurred before that meeting. A joint declaration came from Russia, France and Germany which affirmed their complete confidence in the UN inspections, and in which the former two pledged to use their veto against the passing of the second resolution. Hectic and widely publicized horse trading, promises of gifts and threats from the US and UK to less influential UNSC members, exchange of invectives with the French and Germans, offers of concession on the wording of the draft resolution were already underway. On 11 and 12 March 2003 yet another open UNSC debate took place (S/PV.4717). A total of 58 representatives of UN member states and other alignments attended this in addition to the usual UNSC members. In this, those advocating the adoption of the second draft resolution were: Kuwait, Australia, Iceland, Republic of Korea, Albania, Japan, Philippines, Dominican Republic, Latvia, El Salvador, Georgia, Nicaragua, Bolivia, Macedonia, Peru, Colombia (i.e. 16 in all). Amongst many expressing similar opinions, Zainuddin of Malaysia noted that: 'It is clear that the well-being of the world would be better served by a strong multilateral system revolving around the United Nations that is more representative and democratic, rather than a unilateral system based on the dominance of one Power, however benign that Power may be' (p. 7); Baali of Algeria made a spirited speech to the same effect; and Rodriguez Parrilla of Cuba felt that a unilateral war against Iraq 'would be the end of democracy in international relations' (pp. 25–6). The significant number of South American countries amongst supporters of a second resolution cannot but be noted. It should also be remembered that voting for a second resolution did not necessarily imply support for military action without the adoption of such a resolution in the UNSC.

But all that was really an academic exercise. The performances at the UNSC were, in a sense, being kept up only apparently to obscure details of the beginning of unilateral military action without UNSC sanction. It was, for the US and UK and Spain at any rate, apparently a fairly translucent cloaking device while preparation for serious and official military action was underway (action over no-fly zones and military build-up were ongoing since September 2002). The spirit in which Bush viewed the UNSC deliberations was wonderfully apparent in a National Press Conference on 6 March 2003:

> Q. As you said, the Security Council faces a vote next week on a resolution implicitly authorizing an attack on Iraq. Will you call for a vote on that resolution, even if you aren't sure you have the vote?
> Bush: Well, first, I don't think – it basically says he's in defiance of 1441. That's what the resolution says. And it's hard to believe anybody is saying he isn't in defiance of 1441, because 1441 said he must disarm. And yes, we'll call for a vote.
> Q. No matter what?
> Bush: No matter what the whip count is, we're calling for the vote. We want to see people stand up and say what their opinion is about Saddam Hussain and the utility of the United Nations Security Council. And so, you bet. It's time for people to show their cards, to let the world know where they stand when it comes to Saddam.
> Q. Mr President, are you worried that the United States might be viewed as defiant of the United Nations if you went ahead with military action without explicit and specific authorization from the UN?
> Bush: No, I'm not worried about that. As a matter of fact, it's hard to say the United States is defiant about the United Nations, when I was the person that took the issue to the United Nations, September the 12th, 2002. We've been working with the United Nations. We've been working through the United Nations.
> Secondly, I'm confident the American people understand that when it comes to our security, if we need to act, we will act, and we really don't need United Nations approval to do so.

As it happened a UNSC vote on the draft second resolution was not called. Blair, Bush and Aznar held a summit in Azores, Spain, and issued statements on 16 March 2003 congratulating each other on their resolve to assume their responsibilities even in the face of worldwide scepticism. In an Address to the Nation on 17 March, Bush demanded that Saddam Hussain leave Iraq within 48 hours. On 18 March Bush asked all UN personnel to leave Iraq, and Kofi Annan, the UN General Secretary, issued orders to that effect. It was reported on 18 March too that a poll conducted by NBC News–*Wall Street Journal* showed that 65 per cent backed military intervention in Iraq in the US.[5] Ironically, on 19 March 2003, the day Bush announced: 'On my orders, coalition forces have begun striking selected targets of military importance to undermine Saddam Hussein's ability to wage war' (many commentators have noted the unusual use of the personal pronoun there), a UNSC meeting was scheduled to receive a draft work programme for UNMOVIC from Blix (S/PV.4721). This proceeded in the midst of despondency and bitterness. However, it became perfectly clear that none in the UNSC would propose any resolution about the unilateral action against Iraq initiated by US–UK. Almost with one voice, UNSC members asserted the need to rebuild solidarity within the body, put the past behind them, and focus on the humanitarian issues arising out of military conflict. A final open UNSC debate on 26 and 27 March 2003 (S/PV.4726) saw more bitterness: several statements argued the illegality of the unilateral action, most pleaded for focus on the humanitarian situation in Iraq and unity among UNSC members.

INFERENCES AND OBSERVATIONS

The manner in which ideas of democracy with different nuances were deployed/assumed/received with international/transnational effect in this story is self evident. Since I have chosen to examine the *surface* of this narrative, so to say, or to focus on the ostensible claims that were publicly made and highlighted in this network of exchanges, the political economic considerations that were all too materially simmering just beneath that surface have not been taken up. What is apparent even at the surface is, however, germane to the manner in which democracy has been conceptualized with regard to borders and at an international/transnational level. The arguments regarding democratic legitimacy in the above network of exchanges recall conceptual positions outlined in Part I (with their contradictions) in two ways. The first has to do with theorizations of democratic norms, the other to do with democratization studies – both discussed in Part I.

The connection to democratic norms

The key debate in the above story is between the principle of multilateral democracy embodied in the UN (albeit imperfectly) and a notion of normative democratic legitimacy (connotatively democratic) which applies with transnational effect but derives from a domestic majoritarian/representative democratic constitution and process (denotatively democratic).[6] The domestically ensconced ethical notion and the multilateral notion do not intersect at any point; on the contrary, these appear to be pitted against each other in irreconcilable ways. Victory for the one simply undermines the other. In this instance, multilateral democracy is (imperfectly) institutionally operative in an international domain in a way that domestic democratic legitimacy with transnational aspirations cannot be. The paradox is that the transnational aspiration is unilaterally exerted with narrowly procedural domestic legitimacy, and the international balance is held by a prevailing multilateral arrangement – and in both of these the connotations and denotations of democracy are implicated *without* overlap but with plenty of scope for confusion. The former involves a leap from the contextual to the acontextual, from the domestic to the transnational, from the microcosmic to the macrocosmic, to implicitly assert the paradigmatic status of certain domestic arrangements. This leap occurs through a, so to say, inward-out process, emanating from an increasingly self-assertive democratic context (or group of contexts in a position to make such a claim) that celebrates its perfectness, and its superiority to other contexts. There is contained within it a Judaeo-Christian sense of chosen peoples taking on their burdens. In the above story *domestically (denotatively) ratified democracy with (connotatively weighted) transnational effect* simply defeated *the institutional principle of multilateral democracy in international politics.* The questions and recriminations that followed this victory, as discussed in the previous story (Chapter 10), were conducted in the terms of the moral discourse – the normative rhetoric – of the former. Self-contradictions were sought, and easily found, in the actions of those who championed the former, but not particularly because of the undermining of the latter. Nevertheless, clearly the status of the multilateral principle has thereby been severely, perhaps irrevocably, damaged.[7] Clear precedents have now been set for the continued assertion of domestically ratified democratic legitimacy with transnational effect. There is no longer much need to worry about rectifying existing imbalances in the application of the multilateral principle; the multilateral principle itself has been demonstrably defeated.

Of course, domestic ratification in this instance is itself open to question – but that's the subject of the next chapter. And certainly the securing of domestic ratification has something to do with political economic considerations – that is the subject of the chapter after that. The conceptual inferences and observations made in the previous few paragraphs draw a line under the above story.

This conceptual aspect of the story is significant because the rhetoric of domestically ratified democracy with transnational effect is in fact remarkably close to some of the currently in-favour conceptual positions discussed in Part I. Cosmopolitan democrats who formulate an alignment of democratic states with transnational alignments for a revitalization of democracy, and who envisage adjustments to the multilateral arrangements in the UN to effectively remove multilateralism, effectively play the same overt tune as Blair and Bush. So do Rawlsian liberal democratic theory or deliberative democratic theory or radical democratic theory, all of which make explicit the unilateral inward-out expansion of normative democracy from so-denoted democratic state to transnational domain. There are echoes of Bush and Blair especially when these theories confuse the denotative and connotative understandings of democracy, and formulate the emergence of true democracy (fulfilling connotative expectations) within the frame of existing liberal democracy (so denoted) or by extending the boundaries of such frames. In many ways, Bush and Blair and their functionaries speak the same language as Held and Archibugi and Rawls and Habermas and Laclau/Mouffe and others. The register is the same. All strive to be friendly to and draw upon and appeal to the prevailing environment, with all its deeply embedded confusions about the denotative and connotative aspects of democracy – and with its anxieties about political boundaries that are fluid, polarized, reduced, dispersed and reified with mind-boggling simultaneity. The conceptual positions in question mark the rational limits of this prevailing environment; Blair and Bush work adroitly within and with effect on this prevailing environment. Conceptualizations test power politics just as power politics test conceptualizations, and together they characterize and concretize the ideological bent of the prevailing international/transnational domain.

It is incorrect to think of Bush and Blair and others as unthinking proponents of power politics; they are proponents of power politics, but far from unthinking. Their power politics is persuasively framed within the terminology and implications of the most carefully thought-out and well-intentioned conceptual positions, and exploits the contradictions that are contained in those positions. That they won their arguments domestically, and divided the international body and eventually undermined it, was largely due to the underlying conceptual seriousness of their rhetoric. It is the same sort of seriousness which characterizes the work of the above-named theorists discussed in Part I. They deliberately exercise a certain affinity of seriousness and a certain akinness of terminology to the conceptual positions of cosmopolitan, liberal, deliberative and radical democracy. This affinity and akinness extends, it appears to me, to similar kinds of conceptual fractures and contradictions. It is through these fractures and contradictions that the conceptual and the political real come together: that the stories narrated in Part II meet with the general and abstract ideas discussed in Part I.

The notion of chosen peoples that is implicit in the Bush–Blair rhetoric of domestic democratic legitimacy with transnational effect is implicit in the difficulties with negotiating borders discussed for some of the conceptual positions in question. That rationalizations of majoritarian/representative democracy, however pluralistically and open-endedly conceived, nevertheless inevitably return to some sort of closure (within transnational cosmopolitan institutions, postnational constellations, well-ordered societies, radical discourse constructions), and therefore some sort of exclusion, in most conceptual positions examined in Part I, is part of the problem. Inevitably, these conceptual positions seek relevance across borders by dint of unilateral assertion, despite announcing themselves as open and pluralistic.

The connection to democratization studies

Another link to discussions of Part I appears in the above story in the deployment of the rhetoric of 'new and old democracies'. This was introduced to bolster the cause of those asserting an ethical democratic mission, primarily against those who could also claim domestic democratic ratification but in favour of adhering to the principle of multilateral democracy that is unevenly followed in UN procedures. But, again, this was not simply an insubstantial rhetorical ploy: the fact is that it was based on a perceivable situation. It was the case that amongst those who were prepared to support the claims of a moral democratic mission were a significant number of so-called 'newly democratized' states – in Europe the post-1970 democracies of Portugal and Spain, and some of the post-1990 Eastern European democracies; but also South American political states. It was obvious that the alignment of these states with the US and UK had more to do with existing political economic interests and geopolitical spheres of influence than with shared ideologies. But the fact that such factors could be hidden away behind the appearance of an ideological alignment, much as the political economic interest that arguably underlay the US–UK drive to invade Iraq was hidden away behind claims of an ethical democratic mission, is worth unpicking.

The rhetoric of 'old and new democracy' is also not simply the careless manoeuvre of power politicians and their spin doctors; again, it is that, but it is framed within a developed field of current thinking and research. The terminology in this instance is obviously linked to that used in expressing conceptualizations of 'democratization'. I observed in Chapter 7 that 'democratization studies', at different stages, have often assumed a comparative political methodology and a politically realist perspective to occasionally perpetuate questionable ideological polarizations. It has provided to a significant extent an apparently rational basis to prevalent and popular reductive oppositions. I do not mean to denigrate the oppositional politics and emancipative struggles of so-called 'new democracies' in South America, East Europe and elsewhere, or cast doubts on the salutary manifestations of 'new democratic' civil society and collective action. My observation is entirely with regard to the presumptions with which the *conceptual field* of democratization studies has been developed. In Chapter 7 I also observed that comparatively neutral and thought-provoking directions in democratization studies have become available. But that development of democratization studies which I regard as suspect, which generates ideological polarizations to serve a tacit political agenda, appears to me to be linked to the manner in which 'old and new democracy' appeared in the above story. It was calculatedly used to create non-existent polarizations between otherwise similarly oriented (at domestic levels) political states with regard to their roles in the international/transnational domain. In this calculated use there was considerable experience at play: democratization studies and the ethical democratic mission politics (since the Korean and Vietnam Wars) evolved simultaneously in a period that engraved the ideological polarizations of the Cold War in the popular imagination. What is interesting about the deployment of the 'old and new democracy' rhetoric again in the context of debates about Iraq in 2003 is that it worked without the obvious and constantly hammered polarizations of the Cold War – it succeeded in *creating* polarizations that were not already in the popular imagination. This is not political discourse reacting with or even constructing the political context (now well known and much examined relationships), but political discourse becoming political context, morphing into political context.

These kinds of slippages and links between real political deliberations and conceptual positions that enjoy wide currency at present have occasionally been remarked, but with little apparent effect on the development of those conceptual positions and no effect whatever on the conduct of political deliberations. Similar observations have been made explicitly in some of the politically realistic, theoretically nuanced and responsive writings of Danilo Zolo; and these are implicit in some of the responsive political commentary and analysis that comes with interventionist effect, such as Noam Chomsky's. But these points seem to me to be always worth repeating in new contexts and with ever greater attention to theoretical nuances.

NOTES

1 All the UNSC documents referred to here are openly available through the United Nations online documentation service: www.un.org/Depts/dhl/resguide/scact.htm; and all UNMOVIC documents are available at www.unmovic.org/. All were downloaded for reference here between June and September 2003.

2 Several kinds of UNSC documents are referred to here: records of meetings (indexed as S/PV.[number of meeting]), press releases (indexed as SC/ . . .), reports (indexed as S/[year]/ . . .). Page numbers in-text refer to the document most recently mentioned.

3 Quotations from speeches, interviews and statements by George W. Bush are mostly from transcripts placed on www.whitehouse.gov/news/. Quotations from Tony Blair's speeches, interviews and statements are largely from www.number-10.gov.uk/. Other government websites have been used here to access statements by these and other US and UK government figures, such as www.fco.gov.uk/; www.labour.org.uk/speeches; www.dod.gov/speeches/; www.state.gov/. All were downloaded for reference here between June and September 2003.

4 The literature on US–Israel relations and the role this has played in the workings of the UN is voluminous, and is spectacularly polarized. Those books that regard the US–Israel relationship and its impact on the UN with unease (to put it mildly) include: Noam Chomsky, *Fateful Triangle: The United States, Israel and the Palestinians* (New York: South End, 1983), Naseer Aruri, *The Obstruction of Peace: The US, Israel and the Palestinians* (Monroe, ME: Common Courage Press, 1995) and Naseer Aruri, *Dishonest Broker: The Role of the United States in Palestine and Israel* (New York: South End, 2003). A defence of Israel's position has been recently attempted by Alan Dershowitz, *The Case for Israel* (Hoboken, NJ: Wiley, 2003).

5 For the larger picture here, the PEW Research Centre report of 20 February 2003, 'Post-Blix: Public Favors Force in Iraq, but US Needs More International Backing' (people-press.org/reports/), is useful. This gives figures on US backing for various specific questions in relation to US military intervention in Iraq at regular intervals.

6 In the context of an examination of the ethics of George Bush, the particular UNSC deliberations detailed here and their relationship to ethical notions of participative/representative democracy and multilateralism, have been examined briefly – and with similar effect – in Peter Singer, *The President of Good and Evil: Taking George W. Bush*

Seriously (London: Granta, 2004), pp. 154–77 and pp. 184–7. The tension between the kind of unilateralism and multilateralism that is picked up here has been anticipated and observed in numerous scholarly works on the role of the UN after the Cold War: e.g. Karen A. Mingst and Margaret P. Karns, *The United Nations in the Post-Cold-War Era* (Boulder, CO: Westview, 2000); W. Andy Knight (ed.), *Adapting the United Nations to a Postmodern Era* (Basingstoke: Palgrave Macmillan, 2001); David P. Forsythe, Roger A. Coate and Thomas George Weiss, *The United Nations and Changing World Politics* (Boulder, CO: Westview, 2001); Ian Clarke, *The Post-Cold War Order: The Spoils of Peace* (Oxford: Oxford University Press, 2001).

7 In another report presented by the PEW Research Centre on 3 June 2003, 'Views of a Changing World 2003: War with Iraq further Divides Global Publics' (people-press.org/reports/), based on a 2003 survey of 22 countries and a 2002 survey of 44 countries, it was found that: 'public confidence in the United Nations is a major victim of the conflict in Iraq. Positive ratings for the world body have tumbled in nearly every country for which benchmark measures are available. Majorities or pluralities in most countries believe that the war in Iraq showed the UN to be not so important any more. The idea that the UN is less relevant is much more prevalent now than it was just before the war, and is shared by people in countries that backed the war, the US and Great Britain, as well as in nations that opposed it, notably France and Germany.'

12 *Protest Rallies*

THE THIRD STORY

On Saturday 15 February 2003 I was in the London rally protesting against impending military action in Iraq. An impressive magnitude and diversity of individuals and interest groups participated in this. The *mood* of that rally was best gauged by experience (hence this brief digression into personal narrative): it was an orderly, purposeful, enthusiastic and optimistic rally rather than a bitter and angry one. To some extent, this was due to the satisfaction of having confirmed what many involved in the rally suspected all along: this concrete embodiment of a mass of dissent simply gave democratic affirmation to fractured expressions and feelings of dissent. Not insignificantly, one of the constant chants in the London rally exhorted Bush and Blair to note that, 'This is what democracy looks like.' Not a little of the enthusiasm came from some subliminal assuaging of guilt that the gesture of being in the protest allowed for those in Britain – the guilt of complicity by formal democratic citizenship. All the newspaper and broadcast reports on these protests at the time noted that the largest rallies took place within those Western European countries the governments of which were pushing for military action in Iraq most single-mindedly: particularly in London, Rome, Barcelona and Madrid. Briefly, during that weekend of worldwide anti-war rallies, through the manifestation of a mass gesture of such scale, it appeared that the drive towards military action in Iraq might conceivably be checked. Every public statement by Bush and Blair and others, every twist in the saga of UN weapons inspections and UNSC debates, pretty much every mass media analysis and report that dealt with this until this point seemed imbued with a sense that the invasion was *fait accompli.* Even a staunch spokesman for military intervention like Jack Straw was reportedly momentarily shaken by the magnitude of these rallies (though not for long). To the highlighting that happened in the exchange of public statements and mass media reports/analyses apropos these protests I come soon in this chapter.

My sense of the mood of the London rally of 15 February 2003 is similar to another impressionistic account of the anti-invasion march that took place that day in New York. David Manning's account of this, contrasting it with the sombre mass exodus or 'march' away from uptown Manhattan after the terrorist attacks of 11 September 2001 (weather-wise a 'strangely beautiful day'), reads as follows:

> By contrast, the more recent march took place on a chilly winter day, yet the mood was exuberant, and terribly comprehensible – a spilling forth of opposition to the dangerously misguided, misled, response to the cause of the first march. . . . Though the moods and goals were quite different on 9/11 and 2/15, the sense of community was the same. Although the anti-war march was certainly purposeful, energized and vocal, there was also, as on 9/11, a sense of quiet self-containment within each individual. There was never a feeling in either crowd of mob mentality or impending loss of control.
>
> Neither event was supposed to be a march in the first place – in one case an aberration of the day's homeward commute, in the other an inevitable outcome of the impractical, unenforceable, possibly unconstitutional stick-to-the-sidewalks rule. In each instance, the course flowed as naturally as a stream seeking gravity.[1]

He also compares the 15 February march to anti-Vietnam War protest marches:

> Back then we were bound by a sense of self-selected minority identity, sociological martyrs united in spirit against the misguided mainstream. The anti Iraq-attack demonstration, however, encompassed a much fuller demographic spectrum – all ages, incomes, ethnic groups . . . a slice of New York's full mosaic, along with those who travelled from their own corner of the mainstream to join in. Many veterans.[2]

Manning, obviously a veteran himself of many protest marches, notes the 'exuberance' and orderly purposiveness of the 15 February 2003 march in New York with an experienced eye. The words he uses to describe this mass gesture are tacitly suggestive of an instinctively formed and transient democratic ideal: both spontaneous (not 'supposed to be a march in the first place') and purposive ('terribly comprehensible'); both undirected ('spilling forth') and orderly (no 'mob mentality', following 'stick-to-the-sidewalk rules'); both collective (the march acts as a coherent whole) and yet composed of distinct individuals (with 'the quiet self-containment within each individual', evidencing the presence of a 'fuller demographic spectrum'); both gesturing towards and looking for the right direction ('a stream seeking gravity').

The worldwide coordinated marches of the weekend of 15 and 16 February 2003 to protest against the forthcoming attack on Iraq were the largest ever seen (size definitely matters here), both as a whole, and in many cases in the specific locations where marches actually took place. This international gesture was also notable for failing completely in its objective. To come to grips with the nuances of this in this study of democracy in the international/transnational domain the impressionistic is not adequate, a more conventionally measured and studied approach is necessary.

As I just said, numbers matter here – but numbers in this instance are not a matter of being accurately measured, but a matter of political perception and effect. Accustomed as we are to thinking of parliamentary democracy in domestic domains as a majority matter, numbers attributed to a political position is loosely understood as extent of democratic legitimacy for that position. It was reported that the London rally of 15 February 2003 had 500,000 to 750,000 protesters (according to police estimates) and between 1.5 to 2 million (according to organizers' estimates). The consensus now appears to be that there were at least 1 million protesters marching in London that day. According to a brief survey of protests in the *Guardian*[3] on the Monday after that weekend, of the other cities mentioned above, rallies in Barcelona and Madrid were estimated as bringing together 1 million people each on the 15th, in Rome campaigners claimed 3 million people had converged (though police put the figure at 650,000), and in New York organizers counted 400,000 demonstrators marching in defiance of a court order. Over the weekend it was estimated that more than 600 cities and towns around the world had witnessed protest marches, with about 30 million persons participating. A more cautious estimate doing the rounds now for 15 February alone is 12 million worldwide, with 6 million in Europe. In every recorded instance that I have come across, police estimates differ widely from organizers' estimates (police estimates in the region of half or less that of organizers' estimates), and estimates favoured in Western liberal newspapers are the organizers' (e.g. the *Guardian* in the UK) and those favoured by more conservative broadsheets are the police's (e.g. *The Times*,[4] the *Daily Telegraph* in the UK). It was generally agreed that no consensus was possible on numbers, simply because the methods for measuring these are very far from perfect, but it was also agreed that whatever the different estimates the numbers in question represented the largest protest marches ever recorded worldwide, or in the specific locations mentioned above. Another *Guardian* report[5] quoted a London police spokesperson agreeing that the 15 February march brought together 'one of the largest [crowds] in living memory' – while defending police estimates against charges of manipulating figures.

Despite the undependability of the numbers on offer and the general agreement that the marches of 15 February were the largest ever recorded, the differences in numbers offered do serve a significant symbolic function. The very fact that obvious state functionaries like the police, supported by the conservative mass media, go for smaller estimates can be understood to be indicative of a desire to underplay democratic legitimacy. Similarly, the very fact that obviously oppositional parties like protest organizers, supported by a liberal-left mass media, offer large estimates can be interpreted as a claim of adequate democratic legitimacy. Numbers are used here primarily for effect, much as numbers are counted up for determining election victories in domestic democratic processes, but without the dependable basis that is available in the latter. Numbers are symbolic then, in this context, but paradoxically, numbers are also touted with the *appearance* of being definite indicators: the symbolic suggestiveness of numbers in these marches can be played on in various ways both because of their undependability and because of their simultaneous appearance of being definite. These patterns of tacit ideological manipulation of claims to democratic legitimacy have been manifest for as long as protests have taken place and numbers put on protesters – and especially so for the series of so-called anti-globalization protests that have taken place in various places around the world over the last decade, and for anti-war protests that have taken place regularly (and with increasing participation) since late 2001. In the rare instances where rallies are not seen to be critical challenges to government policy, and can be used to argue the contrary, organizers and the police are evidently able to come up with agreed numbers. This was the case for the Countryside Alliance rally of 22 September 2002 in London, where organizers and police agreed that 400,000 people had participated. In the first major rally in London protesting against possible military action in Iraq that took place on the following weekend, 28 September 2002, estimates were however divided along the usual lines: organizers claimed 400,000 people had participated, the police said they counted 150,000. It was widely felt at the time that the Countryside Alliance rally had been used in some way – certainly by the dominant mass media – to marginalize the anti-war protests. In every major newspaper in the UK, and in most news broadcasts, the former had occupied headlines and front pages while the latter had been relegated to inside boxes and within domestic news features, if mentioned at all.

The agreement on the part of all parties about the *large* scale of the protest marches of 15 February is worthy of consideration in that context. The scale was (however the numbers were manipulated or presented) regarded as sufficient for these marches to capture the headlines and front pages of virtually every newspaper in the West, whatever its ideological orientation. Something had changed between the, perfectly noteworthy but comparatively disregarded, rally of 28 September 2002 and those of 15 February 2003. In fact numerous protest marches (and other gestures) had taken place worldwide over this period, of increasing intensity and frequency, and numerous have taken place since, but none received the kind of media attention or immediate political response that the 15–16 February weekend marches did. It is probably fair to say that the scale of these marches was anticipated and proved to be such that they forced their way into the network of exchanges in the mass media and public statements – they compelled their own highlighting.

Apart from the symbolic play on numbers, there are other, arguably more revealing, ways of coming to grips with the significance of these protest marches. Speculations about who would participate in these marches, and the reality of who did participate; the manner in which participants were represented in an anticipatory fashion and after the fact – in brief, exchanges about the composition of the marches allows for the fleshing out of the political nuances of the protest gesture.

Both the relative neglect of anti-invasion marches in the mainstream mass media prior to 15 February 2002, and the anticipation of the scale of the marches that weekend therein (leading up to their briefly dominating media exchanges), derived from perceivably contrary observations. On the one hand, the association of such protest action (most coherently with recent 'anti-globalization' marches) with oppositional left or socialist alignments seemed to fall in with a mainstream mass media frame that is customarily applied in reportage and analysis. Such action is presented generally as a fringe matter, the exaggerated posturings of a discredited and unpopular ideological position in various guises; association with the left is now customarily treated with scepticism if not aversion in the mainstream mass media. On the other hand, it was also clear by early 2003 that those opposing the invasion of Iraq, and prepared to align themselves with protest marches (despite or with left associations), could not really be regarded as *of* the left – often the contrary. Indeed the main organizing groups clearly incorporated a wide ideological spectrum. Writing about the British Stop the War Coalition (STWC), a report of 12 February 2003 in the *Guardian* observed:

> More than 450 organisations, including such disparate groups as Greenpeace, Americans against the War and Britons versus Bush – a group of Bedford cabdrivers – have joined 11 political parties including SNP, the Liberal Democrats, Plaid Cymru and the Greens, and affiliated themselves to the STWC.[6]

It was also observed that there were separate anti-war groups that had come together outside the STWC because of the predominantly left make-up of its steering group, such as Our World Our Way (which registered its protest by placing advertisements in major national dailies), members of which may also join protest marches. The International ANSWER (Act Now to Stop War and End Racism), United for Peace and Justice and Not in Our Name Project, the main protest organizations based primarily in the US, listed in their websites a range of endorsements from representatives of groups that embraced positions far outside the remit of left associations. A report of 15 January 2003 in the *New York Times* mentioned a number of groups with no specific ideological position other than a humanitarian one (such as Win Without War and September Eleventh Families for Peace), Church-based groups, and even Republican and business associations (Business Leaders for Sensible Priorities) coming together with an anti-war agenda. A quotation therein of a statement by an anti-war organizer, Kevin Martin, for Peace Action (which had joined United for Peace), seemed to capture the moment: 'It's like the 60s is the only lens through which many people grasp protest, but in many ways we have moved on.'[7]

Attempts to reconcile the given frame of scepticism about and marginalization of such left-associated protests with the evidence of broader involvement led to some interesting manoeuvring in features about the scale of the anti-invasion protests, particularly those that anticipated the concrete revelation of that scale on the 15–16 February weekend. The mainstream liberal news press in the UK, represented by the *Guardian*, carried analyses of the current position of the left and its relation to the growing anti-invasion protests. A feature published there on 11 February 2003, 'Left Over?',[8] reflected on the apparent paradox of the post-September 11 unpopularity of left political positions and the increasing scale and diversity of the anti-invasion movement (which seemed willing to channel their protests through events organized by left alignments). That this was presented as a paradox is indicative of prevailing mainstream attitudes to the left (which broadly equates socialist alignments of various hues). Another feature, published in the *Observer* on 17 January 2003, noted this too – clarifying the customary rhetoric of the mainstream British press to the left as follows:

> In the British press alone, [the left] have been described as 'defeatist' and 'unpatriotic', 'nihilist' and 'masochistic', and both 'Stalinist' and 'fascist'; as a 'Prada-Meinhof gang', 'the handmaidens of Osama' and 'an auxiliary to dictators'; as 'limp', 'lofty', 'wobbly', 'heartless and stupid', and 'worm-eaten by Soviet propaganda'; as 'full of loose talk', 'wilful self-delusion' and 'intellectual decadence'; as a collection of 'useful idiots', 'dead-eyed zombies', and 'people who hate people'.[9]

Such pondering in the liberal press reflected at least the unease at the manner in which the customary mainstream framing of the ambiguously and broadly understood left was being complicated by evidence of the scale and diversity of the anti-invasion gestures. In the conservative British mainstream press, primarily (somewhat gently) *The Times* and (more hardnosed) the *Daily Telegraph*, features struggled to cope with the diversity of factions, not simply the congenital left protester but the other groups that were aligning themselves with protest gestures. Take, for example, a brave attempt to throw vitriol on all protesters of the 15 February marches in London in an anticipatory fashion, in a feature of 12 February 2003 in *The Times*. This berated all those contemplating marching in the following words:

> London and Glasgow will echo to the slogans of the morally deluded and the self-consciously caring. Papoose-wearers, manic recyclers, the priggish, the cranky, nudists and Woodcraft folk will march this Saturday in a cloud

> of outrage. Peaceniks, marshalled by the Stop the War Coalition, claim to march for the majority. They do not. Marches automatically cut themselves off from Mrs. Typical (nee Apathy). Activism, like writing letters to The Daily Telegraph about sodomites, is an unlovable eccentricity.[10]

The feature went on to group the would-be marchers into the following categories, which notably went well beyond the dreaded left, and ironically undermined its claim for speaking for the majority itself (not much was left out): Committee Man, Poshniks, Tricoteuses, Angry Young Muslims, Angry Old Lefties, students. The harder conservative *Daily Telegraph* published a much larger number of similar features, without bothering to express repugnance at those who complain about sodomites.

The mainstream news press in the US evidenced roughly similar exchanges apropos protest marches – but was, as may be expected, on the whole more emphatically anti-left, more determinedly pro-invasion, and less inclined to give coverage to protests.

After the marches of the 15–16 February 2003 weekend had taken place, anticipatory pondering on paradoxes and struggles to place the scale of participation within an appropriate ideologically oriented rhetoric died down briefly in favour of the numbers game outlined already. Accusing the left of not playing the game and misleading people continued in the expected spaces, but in a more defiant than taken-for-granted tone. For a brief period of about a week the ideological proclivities and polarizations of the Western mass media converged on more or less neutral noting of the scale of the marches, or on shrouding ideological positions behind the insinuations of the numbers in question – or noting laconically, as in a report in *The Times* of 16 February 2003: 'The appeal of the march went well beyond the left-wing activists who organised it,'[11] or in a report in the *Telegraph* of 17 February 2003: 'Many "hard-Left" groups dominated the front of the march. . . . There were, however, tens of thousands of "moderate" protesters.'[12] Very soon however, though vehement protest marches and other protest gestures continued, these were relegated to neglect; they became, or were made, cold news through disregard.

The relationship of the left to the anti-invasion marches of 15–16 February 2003 was only one strand in considerations of whom the marchers consisted of. It was one that seems to me to have been particularly highlighted in the Western mainstream mass media. The negotiations and shifts in the manner in which this was highlighted in an anticipatory fashion and after the fact was easier to gauge when the debate was ongoing, than to gauge through retrospective documentation. A systematic study of the mainstream Western mass media exchange in this regard requires a much larger collation exercise than I have provided; the above points are made more impressionistically than rigorously, with a few symptomatic references. Such a rigorous research exercise yet awaits us; but more to the point, and I believe largely as a result of the recognition of the scale and diversity the protest marches which did get conveyed in the mass media (arguably despite itself), there have appeared some retrospective academic research and analyses of those marches. These do not deal so much with the media idea of the left, as with the reality of who was or was not in the protests and how certain *segments* of protesters were represented in the media. Some of the points made therein are worth noting here to gain a clearer sense of the protests in question.

An International Peace Protest Survey[13] was undertaken on 15 February 2003 by a group of researchers, coordinated by Stefaan Walgrave of the University of Antwerp, which involved distributing more than 10,000 survey questionnaires to protesters across eight countries: the UK, Italy, the Netherlands, Switzerland, the US, Spain, Germany and Belgium. The questionnaires were designed to gauge who the protesters were (what sort of demonstrators' profiles was involved), how they were mobilized, why they chose to demonstrate, what sorts of differences exist in such data between countries, and why these differences exist. At the time of writing this (end-2004), the overall findings and comparative analysis of this research is yet to appear in the public domain. Some preliminary results and analysis, drawn from the surveys returned by demonstrators in Glasgow, have been placed on the Internet by Wolfgang Rüdig and Catherine Eschle of the University of Strathclyde.[14] The Glasgow demonstration was comparatively small: police estimated about 27,000 participants, while organizers put the number at 80,000 to 100,000. How typical the Glasgow march was will only be revealed when all the results become available, but some of the statistics about the composition of marchers that have been made available could be taken as indicative until then. Rüdig and Eschle found that, judging from their survey, in Glasgow 35 per cent of the demonstrators on 15 February had never been to a demonstration before, and of the remaining 65 per cent about 30 per cent hadn't been to a demonstration in the five years before that. It is not clear from the report whether those who said they had been to a demonstration before meant they had been to another demonstration on the same issue, the impending invasion of Iraq. Men and women took part to roughly the same degree – 52 per cent were men, 48 per cent women. Demonstrators in the age groups 25–40 and 41–59 were equally represented and accounted for about a third each, and 22 per cent were in the 14–24 age group. In terms of proportions of age groups in the Scottish population, the 17–24 age group was overrepresented, and the above-60 age group underrepresented. In terms of occupation, professionals accounted for 42 per cent, those in full-time education for 23 per cent – both hugely overrepresented in terms of proportions of the Scottish population, and proportionally the less qualified in terms of formal education were underrepresented. Interestingly, more than 60 per cent of the demonstrators had a university degree, and 13 per cent were in full-time education studying for a university degree (the report points out that in the 2001 Scottish Census only 19.5 per cent of the working population was found to have a university degree or equivalent qualification). Only 30 per cent of the respondents admitted to belonging to a particular religion, of which 4 per cent were Muslims (a significant number given that according to the 2001 Scottish Census only 0.84 per cent of the Scottish population is Muslim).

Caution naturally needs to be exercised in reading these figures: for instance, the quirks of who chooses to fill in questionnaires and who doesn't are not factored in there. These are indicative figures. But at least some of these figures coincided with what was impressionistically observed in mass media reports on other such marches in the UK, especially in London: the number of demonstrators who were new or very rare participants in demonstrations was large, and the number of youth participants was also large. The latter had received significant media attention at the time: the protests organized by school and university students, and the measures taken in educational institutions to deal with such protests (particularly for school students), had been the matter of numerous British news reports and features at the time. Stephen Cushion has published an interesting article on the representation of youth demonstrators at this event in the media.[15] The participation of young people, he observes, militates against another conventional media frame (like the media frame that comes with considerations of left politics), which works on the assumption that young people are generally not interested or involved in politics.[16] According to Cushion the dominant mass media has therefore attempted to downplay genuine political understanding and involvement among the youth with regard to the Iraq invasion, by explaining/presenting their large-scale participation in the protests in other (usually belittling) ways. The latter includes: presenting youth as victims of adult anxieties (about truancy and transgression); representing youth in sexualized terms; playing up consumerist tendencies among young people (following pop idols, following a vogue without understanding it, trying to get media attention, etc.); and as expressing anxieties about their powerlessness.

The kind of general and academic observations that I have referred to so far is primarily with regard to the UK context. While I am on the issue of the composition of anti-invasion protesters, it is worth widening this discussion outside the UK and the 15 February marches particularly, and considering some relevant observations with regard to anti-war protests in the US.

In mid-2003 Barbara Epstein published some observations on the anti-war protests in the US until that time.[17] Amongst other observations, she feels that the participation of young people in the movement in the US 'represented only a small minority of their generation' (she contrasts this to the anti-Vietnam War protests, but it also contrasts with perspectives in the UK). She puts this down primarily to the fact that: 'Today's young people grew up in the conservative culture of the last two decades which has promoted individual material success, and in which collective action for a better world has often seemed like a faint memory, or a far-off dream.' She also observes – and this is interesting in being especially pertinent to the US context – that:

> The most glaring weakness of the movement against the war in Iraq was the limited involvement of people of color, especially African Americans. According to many polls, blacks opposed the war in roughly the percentages in which whites supported it. . . . there is a striking contradiction between the racial composition of the antiwar movement and the racial breakdown of opposition to the war.

Though she doesn't cite it, one of the polls she may have been referring to was the PEW Research Centre report of 20 February 2003 (shortly after the 15–16 February weekend protests), which gave figures based on surveys of US support for war.[18] The relevant figures here are the following responses to the question 'Take military action in Iraq?' (see Table 12.1).

The difference between white and black opinion in this regard is striking. It is all the more striking given the peculiarity of the US context: support for military action was uniquely high in the US. To get a comparative sense of this, the situation can be compared to the UK where it was relatively high. To keep this comparison in perspective, I should note that a factor that plays with the above-cited PEW report is figures on whether the respondents felt a UN resolution is needed or not: of the total, 58 per cent felt a UN resolution favouring military action was needed, and 33 per cent felt it wasn't in the US. A MORI telephone poll published somewhat later (17 March 2003)[19] but covering a similar period in the UK, asking whether respondents supported or opposed British involvement in military action in Iraq in the event that a UNSC resolution for such action was secured and in the event that it was not secured (and given that no WMD were found), came up with the results shown in Table 12.2.

Across Europe opposition to the war was far more emphatic, as a series of opinion polls reportedly demonstrated.[20] In the climate of sympathy for

Table 12.1. PEW Opinion Poll of 20 February 2003: Support for War by Ethnic Category in the USA

	Favour (%)	*Oppose (%)*	*Don't know (%)*	*(Number surveyed)*
Total	67	26	7	(1,254)
Race				
White	73	21	6	(1,060)
Non-White	45	45	10	(179)
Black	44	47	9	(109)
Hispanic	67	32	1	(74)

Table 12.2. MORI Telephone Poll of 17 March 2003: Support for Military Action in the UK

With UNSC resolution		
	28 Feb–2 Mar (%)	*14–16 Mar (%)*
Support	42	46
Oppose	46	41
Don't know	12	12
Without UNSC resolution		
	28 Feb–2 Mar (%)	*14–16 Mar (%)*
Support	24	26
Oppose	67	63
Don't know	10	11

military action that apparently prevailed in the US the indicative figures of lack of sympathy among blacks was striking. Striking also was, if Barbara Epstein is correct, the observation of low black participation in anti-invasion protests.

This situation has naturally been the subject of some reflection in the US. A revealing paper on the subject by Lisie Montano appeared in late 2003, which makes several points that are worth noting in this context. Montano reflects on the powerfully militarized environment that youth of colour experience in the US, where becoming part of the military often seems to be the 'most accessible career path' available. As military fodder for the US 'war on terror' minority students in schools had been particularly targeted as a matter of policy:

> Bush's education reform bill, the No Child Left Behind Act, helped open up the war on terror's soldier supply channel even more with a hidden provision that makes federal education contingent upon schools' submitting access information to military recruiters. In order not to have their information given to recruiters, students must submit an 'opt-out' form, which in many cases also opts them out from receiving information about colleges. Six months later, in July 2002, Bush issues an executive order stating that non-citizens who enlisted after 9/11 could apply immediately for citizenship so long as the war on terror continued, broadening the military track on which low-income immigrant youth are already placed.[21]

Montano also notes that in schools with high numbers of coloured students particularly abrasive measures were assumed to check participation in anti-invasion protests (citing the instance of Rio Grande School in Albuquerque and a school in Oakland, California). Under the circumstances, it is argued, the opposition to the invasion of Iraq among blacks in the US was as much an opposition to their situation in the domestic domain as a gesture about something that was happening abroad. The fact that this opposition didn't get channelled in a proportional fashion into actual protest activities was probably indicative of the fact that those activities were organized in a manner, and by alignments, which were unable to reflect the particular anxieties that fuelled that opposition in the first place.

If nothing else, such observations show that a complex series of domestic factors intertwined with perceptions of the international/transnational domain in determining the inclusions and exclusions of anti-invasion protests, such as those of 15–16 February 2003. Apart from indications of the composition of those protest rallies, other kinds of information need to be addressed in this story to come to grips with the relevance of these for this study. In particular, some information on the organizational aspects of these, and the public statements and reactions that followed from these, are likely to be useful.

Though most of the details I have given so far, and continue to refer to below, are with reference to the UK context, and to some extent the US context, what was remarkable about the 15–16 February 2003 protests was their international scale: 600 towns and cities and millions of protesters worldwide were involved. Quite apart from the number of local to international organizations that made it possible, it instinctively appears that an enormous financial outlay must have been necessary for a gesture of this scale to be put together. If accounted as a whole this is no doubt true, but what is interesting is that such information in the public domain as is available suggests that no particularly large centralized fund was involved: the expenses had been dispersed across a wide range of local to international sources. Indeed, in accounting terms expenditure by significant discrete organizations from their discrete funds appears to have been extraordinarily low. Consider, for instance, what is known of the Stop the War Coalition's expenditure for primarily organizing what was undoubtedly one of the largest rallies seen that weekend.[22] The London march was organized largely by two STWC employees and a small number of volunteers from a former brewery in Brick Lane (a comparatively less affluent area in East London with a large number of immigrants). According to Lindsey German, one of the members of the STWC steering committee, there were two main sources of funding: small individual donations, the largest of which were in the region of £5,000, and gifts from the unions (the Fire Brigade Union, the National Association of Teachers in Further and Higher Education, etc.), who are unlikely to be able to afford large payments. Since January 2003 the STWC had also run a national membership scheme with a £20 fee (£12 for the unemployed), which was taken up by 3,000 to 4,000 people (a maximum of £80,000 came from that source). The main expenses involved were given as follows: £6,000 for hiring the stage in Hyde Park; £5,000 for 15,000 placards with wooden handles for distribution, £10,000 for hiring a big screen and further leaflets (this was borne by the *Daily Mirror* group, the only UK tabloid which had taken an explicitly anti-war stance); undisclosed employee costs (low, given the numbers of volunteers); and transport costs which were footed by local organizations from where people converged on London. The total organizational costs were probably significantly lower than the policing costs which were largely – and entirely uncomplainingly – paid by London taxpayers. In other words, the costs of organizing this were minuscule compared to any average corporate public relations initiative. It was reported later that for their outlay of £10,000 the *Daily Mirror* gained over £100,000-worth of free publicity, according to PR advisor Eugen Beer of Beer Davis.[23]

Actually this interesting aspect of the organization of the 15–16 February protests was not particularly highlighted in the mainstream mass media. In the US media the matter of costs of organizing protests mainly came up in the conservative press, as another link to the dreaded 'hard left' with which every effort was made to associate the protests. A feature in the *National Review* of 24 February 2003[24] linked the Not in Our Name Project to a foundation called the Interreligious Foundation for Community Organization (IFCO), 'set up by several New Left leaders of 1967', and which had reportedly been the fiscal partner of an organization called the National Coalition to Protect Political Freedom, 'until recently the group's president was Sami Al-Arian, a University of South Florida computer-science professor who has been suspended for alleged ties to terrorism'.[25] Further articles in the media in March 2003, in Fox News and *Insight Magazine*,[26] made similar points. IFCO came up again, as 'a million-dollar-a-year non-profit that supports Cuban dictator Fidel Castro and once sponsored a group headed by Sami Al-Arian'.[27] International ANSWER was presented as an offshoot of the International Action Centre which 'intelligence sources say is a front for the Worker's World Party'[28] – which, in turn, 'supports North Korea's brutal regime'. '$200,000 per demonstration' was the generous figure cited in one of these, which is a drop against the many millions spent on each public relations drive in the 'war on terror' by the US government.[29]

For an international protest gesture of the scale seen on 15–16 February 2003 the most significant cost could have been expected to be in international communications and publicity, and yet these have been the least considered elements. To some extent, as I have observed above, the mainstream print and broadcast mass media undoubtedly served the purpose of publicity in a relatively cost-free fashion by anticipating that the event would be of a scale and at a moment which cannot but be important and saleable news. Had these means been targeted for publicity, the expenses would undoubtedly have been astronomical. But that still begs the question – when the protests were anticipated as a mainstream newsworthy event they had in a sense already become a widely discussed and anticipated public matter; they had been publicized already and yet in a not-too-expensive fashion. The obvious understanding of how this was achieved is that recent (within the last ten years) information technology developments (such as in the worldwide web, email, instant messages or text messages) have opened up channels of publicity and communication that have been used in a *decentred* fashion to great effect. The decentredness is important: what was involved in the use of the Internet, for instance, in building up towards the 15–16 February 2003 anti-invasion protests was not a concerted and centralized publicity drive, but an accrual and growth of variously located and dispersed and linked and cross-connected – often after the initiation, in process as it were – efforts. Almost all the organizations involved in bringing together the protests of 15–16 February (ANSWER, Not in My Name, Stop the War Coalition, United for Peace and Justice, and numerous others) have websites which served several important purposes: one, they provided focused news and analysis from different anti-invasion perspectives; two, they provided links to larger and smaller, global and local anti-war organizations' websites with different ideological inclinations and agendas; three, they enabled participation by engaging those who went to them and by offering opportunities for making donations or becoming a volunteer or joining protest events. Some Internet protest organizations used web resources to translate Internet activism to activism on the ground. According to a *New York Times* report of 15 January 2003:

> . . . Internet protest organizations like MoveOn.org and TrueMajority.com are struggling to transform Web-based dissent into actual activism.
>
> The MoveOn web site enlists users to sign a petition opposing a pre-emptive strike against Iraq. It then instantly sorts and logs signers by state, to facilitate organizing at a local level. Users can make credit card donations to antiwar efforts.
>
> When the organization decided last month to extend its work online to the production of antiwar newspaper and television advertisements, the site raised more than $300,000 in 48 hours. The average donation, said MoveOn directors, was $30.[30]

Another report in *The Times* on the eve of the weekend of protests, 14 February, described how the Internet was being used in the UK to bring those together:

> More than half-a-million visits have been made [to the Stop the War Coalition website] in the last six months with interest snowballing as tomorrow's march approaches. The busiest day was Wednesday (31,277 hits) but yesterday more than 33,000 visitors were predicted. Most people appear to be logging on from their work computers, with the majority of hits before 4:30 pm. Sixty percent came from the UK but 17 percent are American.

> The Stop the War Coalition lists 321 peace groups, most with e-mail addresses and many with their own websites. . . .
>
> Some come from opposite ends of the political spectrum. The Socialist Equality Party sombrely describes itself as the 'British section of the International Committee of the Fourth International'.
>
> They will make common cause tomorrow with the obscure Capitalists Against War, a Hotmail address whose owner states: 'You don't have to be from the traditional left side of the political divide to think a pre-emptive strike on Iraq is immoral and plain dumb.'[31]

The report also notes that one of the possible reasons for the involvement of large numbers of young persons in the protests was because of their being adept at using web resources, and that the use of the Internet enables an extraordinarily wide reach. Other modes of protest were also reported, such as attempting to block US government servers with dissenting mass emails and spam mails, or blocking fixed line telephones in government offices by coordinated mass telephone calls. A report in the Australian *Sydney Morning Herald* after the invasion began, on 1 April 2003, observed that protests coordinated with the beginning of the attack on Iraq were in places as widely dispersed as Beijing, Cairo, Copenhagen and Qatar, and used mobile phone text messaging (short messaging service or SMS).[32] On this note – though more to do with cross-border communication than anti-invasion activism – the extraordinary web-log (blog) kept publicly by Salam Pax (a pseudonym) in Baghdad from September 2002 to June 2003, and published later by the *Guardian* in book form,[33] is worth mentioning. Something of the fizz and energy of web-based communication and the impact it may have on political and cultural awareness is evident in this.

If the above gives the impression that only anti-invasion protests and the organization thereof capitalized on the Internet and new IT that would naturally be mistaken. On the one hand, UK and US governments and sympathetic organizations/media groups had carried out their own extensively and more centrally controlled and funded publicity drive on the net too. On the other hand, these parties had also used the net as a 'war' arena (as a means of surveillance on the opposition, to spam Iraq during the war, to introduce 'anti-terror' legislation that might enable greater government control on the Internet, etc.).[34] Interestingly, on the day before the planned protests, 14 February 2003, the White House released both *The National Strategy for Combating Terrorism* and *The National Strategy to Secure Cyberspace*.[35] In the former appeared the not insignificant observation:

> By capitalizing on the very technological advance that we use within our country, terrorist organizations learn and share information garnered from our web sites, exploit vulnerabilities within our critical infrastructure, and communicate across the same internet paths we use everyday. (p. 9)

It also observed that terrorist organizations work in a dispersed and decentred manner from local to global levels. *The National Strategy to Secure Cyberspace* advocated several programmes of coordination between private organizations that provide web resources and services, particularly at the level of information sharing. The mechanisms for tackling the dispersed character of terrorist organizations could easily extend to tackling the dispersed character of anti-invasion protest organization; the IT-based channels of communication used by protest organizers mentioned above are indistinguishable from those that are allegedly being used by terrorists in these documents.

Be that as it may, on the whole it seems to me that the anti-war organizers' drive leading up the protest appeared to capitalize on new IT resources more effectively than the UK and US governments did in their state-sponsored publicity drive for invasion (which arguably worked more effectively through the mainstream mass media). This could perhaps be explained by the relative centralization of the state-sponsored publicity drive as opposed to the dispersed coordination of the anti-invasion protesters' efforts.

Ultimately, the anti-invasion protesters' phenomenal success in organizing a gesture of the scale of 15–16 February 2003, a scale that could not be disregarded by either aggressive states or the mainstream mass media, proved to be – in media terms – a brief one, because the US and UK governments are more savvy and well-resourced on the mainstream mass media. Protests of comparable scale continued since, but the presence and visibility these attained on that weekend unquestionably diminished. This was not because the popular sentiment that was expressed in those protests diminished, and nor is it because the mainstream mass media were all unambiguously pro-war. Indeed, if the moral justifications of the invasion of Iraq have been interrogated at some level constantly since, with increasing pressure and attrition in the coalition of aggressors, that too can be laid at the doorstep of the mainstream mass media. The dynamism of the protest marches was punctured because they were so single-mindedly, indeed crudely, disregarded – because they couldn't effect the sought-after result. To gauge how this was conducted, some of the public statements made by Bush, Blair and others in the military action camp with regard to the protests – public statements that were necessarily given maximum exposure on the mainstream mass media – are worth recalling here.

In a press conference after the new Securities and Exchanges Commission Chairman, Bill Donaldson, was sworn in at the White House on 18 February 2004, George Bush gave the following responses when questioned about the previous weekend's protests:

> Q. Thank you, Mr President. What do you make of the fact that millions of people across the globe have taken to the streets to protest your approach to Iraq? And if you decide to go to war, how do you wage a campaign in the face of such stiff opposition?

> Bush: Two points, one is that democracy is a beautiful thing, and that people are allowed to express their opinion. I welcome people's right to say what they believe. Secondly, evidently some of the world don't view Saddam Hussein as a risk to peace. I respectfully disagree. Saddam Hussein has gassed his own people. Saddam Hussein has got weapons of mass destruction. Saddam Hussein has made – defied the United Nations. Saddam Hussein is providing links to terrorists. Saddam Hussein is a threat to America. And we will deal with him.
>
> You know, I – war is my last choice. But the risk of doing nothing is even a worst option as far as I'm concerned. I owe it to the American people to secure this country. I will do so.

And a bit later:

> Q. Given the size of the protests in England over the weekend, do you have any concerns that Tony Blair might pay a serious political price for supporting you on Iraq?
>
> Bush: I think any time somebody shows courage, when it comes to peace, that the people will eventually understand that.
>
> First of all, you know, size of protest, it's like deciding, well, I'm going to decide policy based upon a focus group. The role of a leader is to decide policy based upon the security – in this case, the security of the people. Tony Blair understands that Saddam Hussein is a risk. Tony Blair sees that, you know, a weakened United Nations is not good for world peace. And he is a courageous leader and I'm proud to call him friend.

There are some revealing turns of phrase in these responses. That democracy is the condition whereby 'people are *allowed* to express their opinion' allocates to people a purely passive – indeed infantalized – role. Opposed to that is the first-person leader who paternalistically 'welcome[s] people's right to say what they believe'. It is nevertheless significant that the protest gesture was received as the disagreement of the *people*, with whom Bush emphasizes that it is *he* who disagrees: '*I* respectfully disagree.' Paternalistic too is the underlying logic of the role that Bush allocates himself: in a sense, defending people against their judgement. The view that what people express in a democracy has nothing to do with what a leader does unquestionably offends the deep sense of democracy, the minimum linguistic definition of democracy that now, as I observed in Part I, underlies all modern conceptualizations of democracy at some level. Bush's view that 'The role of a leader is to decide policy based upon the security' makes precisely that point. It smacks of precisely the kind of totalitarianism that is often instinctively posited against the minimum understanding of democracy. However, it wasn't these nuances that were commented on at the time; what did offend some was the attempt to play down the *scale* of the protests by likening them to a 'focus group'. It was the flippant diminution of the gesture that caught attention, but perhaps more than that the lifting of the term from commercial public relations/advertising jargon. It seemed to indicate both a performance and a statement of what Bush was doing: aggressively selling his view, a hard sell.

Bush was effectively defending Blair in one of these (the UK had seen some of the most emphatic anti-invasion gestures ever, much more emphatic than in the US), and Blair was himself doing no less in the UK. Indeed Bush appeared to be echoing Blair above, or perhaps it was really the other way around. Even while the weekend protest rallies were in process, on 15 February 2003, Blair himself said the following in a speech at Labour's Local Government, Women's and Youth conferences in Glasgow:

> I rejoice that we live in a country where peaceful protest is a natural part of our democratic process.
>
> But I ask the marchers to understand this.
>
> I do not seek unpopularity as a badge of honour. But sometimes it is the price of leadership. And the cost of conviction.
>
> But as you watch your TV pictures of the march, ponder this: If there are 500,000 on that march, this is still less than the number of people whose deaths Saddam has been responsible for.
>
> If there are one million, that is still less than the number of people who died in the wars he started.

He went on to read some emails he had allegedly received from Iraqi exiles exhorting Blair to rid Iraq of Hussain. Again the pattern of the rhetoric is revealing. It suggests again an opposition between peaceful protest in a democracy and leadership exerted by the leader. His assuming the moral high ground (saving Iraqi people from Hussain) is presented as an effort to countermand 'your TV pictures of the march' (that *your* was rich with possibilities). But along with that, the conviction and leadership that Blair was in his own terms extending to the Iraqi people against the judgement of the democratic British people who protested, couldn't but touch a disquieting note. It was a disquieting speech, given with a sort of quivering conviction and belief in charismatic leadership. Blair repeated this performance in a Prime Ministerial press conference on 18 February 2003.[36]

By pushing itself on to the mainstream international mass media, by the very scale of its manifestation, the weekend protests of 15–16 February 2003 did have a momentary impact even on the most diehard of aggressors in the UK. It was reported that the protest marches shook Jack Straw, who commented: 'It's very difficult indeed in those circumstances. It is patently more straightforward for governments to take a country to war if they palpably have got the whole population behind them than if not.' But Straw had clearly recovered himself by 20 February when asked for a comment at the doorstep of the Foreign Office while meeting the EU High Representative, Javier Solana, and reacting to a strongly critical public statement on military intervention in Iraq from Rowan Williams, the Archbishop of Canterbury. By 21 February, Straw was laying out the moral case against Iraq with as much verve as ever in addressing the Royal Institute of International Affairs at Chatham House in London. For a brief while after the protests it was reported that Blair's popularity ratings had plummeted, and that Labour's prospects did not look good at the forthcoming local elections in May 2003, but that was only briefly. In the US the worldwide protests made no significant difference to opinion polls on military intervention.

The very obduracy of the public responses of democratically elected leaders in the US and UK, the overtaking of other frames of newsworthiness (UNSC debates, weapons inspections, plagiarized dossiers, etc.) in the mainstream media – the sheer velocity of the flow and highlighting of information – made the impact of the unprecedented international protests of the weekend of 15–16 February 2003 a brief and ultimately ineffective affair. Nevertheless it remains, one hopes, memorable.

Bush declared the beginning of the military action in Iraq, dubbed Operation Enduring Freedom initially and changed to Operation Iraqi Freedom, on 19 March 2003 and declared its end on 1 May 2003. Many would contest these dates – US and UK planes were carrying out sorties over Iraqi no-fly zones since at least September 2002, and if anything violence constantly escalated after May 2003. To get a sense of the scale of the military operation in this period (and in the immediate aftermath), the following figures are helpful.

- Between 19 March 2003 and 17 April 2003 (720 hours), 19,948 guided munitions and 9,251 unguided munitions were dropped, and 16,901 20mm and 311,597 30mm ammunition was used, by US/UK-led forces, 466,985 of whom had been deployed in this period. $917,744,361.55 contingency funds were spent on this operation to that date. Somewhat absurdly, as part of psychological operations, 31,800,000 leaflets were also dropped.[37]
- Between 19 March and 31 April 2003, 212 US–UK military casualties were reported. Between 19 March and 30 October 2003, 417 US–UK military casualties were reported.[38]
- Between 19 March and 20 October 2003, it was estimated in a Project of Defense Alternatives Report that 9,200 (+/– 1,600) Iraqi combatants died, and 3,230–4,327 Iraqi non-combatants died (the constraints and ambiguities under which these figures were reached is explained in the report).[39] According to this it was estimated that between 11,000 and 15,000 Iraqis had been killed in the war over that period, of whom 30 per cent were non-combatants (civilians who didn't take up arms). The Iraq Body Count group, which maintained a website keeping an ongoing count

of Iraqi civilian casualties since the start of the military invasion of Iraq,[40] estimated that 5,450–7,100 civilians had died over the period covered by the above mentioned report. The Defense Alternatives report attributed the difference to their not integrating media reports on casualties with official lists of various sorts.

INFERENCES AND OBSERVATIONS

It might appear that protest marches such as on 15–16 February 2003 are similar to large-scale 'anti-globalization' marches in the last two decades of the twentieth century, and should be understood, as the latter often are, in terms of thinking about social movements. It seems to me that that won't be a productive line to follow here. I examined briefly some of the conceptual positions taken with regard to social movements in Chapter 8, with particular attention to the articulations of democracy therein. My principal observation there is that the convergences of diverse interests that are ostensibly achieved in anti-globalization marches are momentary convergences, though they encourage perceptions of deep coherence and direction (and attempts to theorize them). The articulations of democracy in that field, it seems to me, often possess the very problems and contradictions that they wish to resist, or have limited application and deliberately defer conceptualization (by expecting a spontaneous emergence of democratic practice or waiting for a future clarification of democratic possibilities). Nevertheless, the moments of convergence themselves – the massing of protestors of different persuasions – inevitably comes with an instinctive sense of embodying the minimum meaning and normative connotations of democracy. In that, large-scale anti-globalization marches are obviously analogous to the anti-war protests described in this story. Observations made on the composition of anti-globalization protesters, decentred organizational tactics, funding, etc., overlap to a great degree with those made above. Insofar as the understanding of social movements has focused on moments of convergence (such as massing of protestors) in themselves there are obvious and useful parallels to the anti-war protests described here. However, it also seems to me that insofar as research and thinking on social movements attempt to discern a larger, coherent, grassroots-upwards flow of a 'movement of movements' underlying those convergences, the area becomes less useful to understanding anti-war marches. The purposive convergences of diverse interests in a series of anti-war protests – 15–16 February ones highlighted here – are less amenable to being understood in a 'movement of movements' fashion simply because the convergences here are *not* due to any perceivable or imposable coherence at the grassroots or the base. The convergence in this story is only attributable to the bare purpose (the undesirability of this particular invasion, for whatever reason), not to any kind of equivalence or common direction or ideological sympathy that cuts across or conjoins all the diverse interests (individual and group) represented there. A conceptual frame of social movements does not contain this particular convergence, and other such anti-Iraq invasion convergences. The kind of massing of protestors described in this story needs to be understood in its momentary appearances, irrespective of the coherences sought by organizers and observers – and the articulation of democracy here needs a different kind of analysis from those given by social movements researchers, theorists and activists.

The association between the left (as socialist/communist) and the massing of people in protest (whereby the protest acquires a certain democratic legitimacy) – which was systematically presented as threatening in the mainstream mass media and systematically downplayed by the organizers of the international anti-invasion protests – did come with historical resonances. Though political states based on socialist or communist single-party centralism have almost invariably led to unhappy political and economic outcomes (have, so to say, failed), and political states with formal socialist democracy have met with moderate economic and political success, there is no doubt that in *opposition* socialist and communist ideologies and organizations have been resoundingly successful. That alignments with socialist/communist ideologies were instrumental in overthrowing and taking over from such a large number of authoritarian, repressive, deeply unequal, brutally imperialistic regimes around the world was to a large measure because of their appeal to people, the popular support they garnered, their success in representing the interests of the people – certainly a majority of the people (usually the mass which occupied the lower rungs of social stratifications). By the minimum linguistic definition of democracy and its ethical connotations, such support – which was widely regarded as, and practically available as, manifest – could be thought of as giving the aspiring left movement through much of the nineteenth and twentieth centuries democratic legitimacy. The left has therefore constantly, and often indisputably, claimed democratic legitimacy for its aspirations. This democratic legitimacy was regarded as being manifest because of such large protest gestures as were seen on 15–16 February 2003; the appearance of mass support has historically often been regarded as being as democratically cogent as an accounting of majorities through a formally democratic elective system. This has especially been the case where such massing appeared in protest against or in opposition to a prevailing state apparatus and its policies. The democratic credibility of such massing was all the stronger because under these circumstances no other channel to express the people's disenchantment was available. The massing of people, the popular uprising, internationally coordinated rallies, dispersed disruption of government communications, non-cooperation, etc., are all the stuff of the left movement in opposition, and the stuff which enabled left alignments to claim and often to be seen as having democratic legitimacy. Quite possibly, though, apart from ideological contradictions, the large number of failures of the left movement after taking over the reins of political power also has a relation to the manner in which this form of democratic legitimacy was mobilized. All too often such mobilization of the people by the left drew upon a quasi-religious structure of convictions and authority (not unsurprisingly, massing of people is also associated with religious mobilization – religious mobilization often claims majoritarian democratic legitimacy by the same standards) which have simply been impossible to sustain in a reasonable and open fashion. Ironically, the very evidence of people's support which made the left movement in opposition such a success, also made the movement against it a success. At the end of the twentieth century such images of massing and protest (throughout the Soviet and Eastern Europe) seemed to give democratic legitimacy to the oppositional alignments against centralist socialist and communist states – and again this sense of democratic legitimacy gained from the absence of any other channel to express disenchantment. For the latter, the largely capitalist and formally democratic West hailed these as evidence of 'civil societies' ready for democracy. It is worth remembering that similar gestures by the same 'civil societies' had given the same kind of democratic legitimacy – repeatedly and often – to left alignments and ideologies in opposition (and in some parts of the world, still do). This is so much the case, that this kind of democratic expression is indelibly associated with the left.

Recalling the historically formed associations of such mass protests with the left in this context is useful, but not because there was any substantial basis to the association in this instance. The protests of 15–16 February 2003, and those before and since on this issue, were issue-based rather than ideologically led. It was indubitably the case that the scale of these protests was enormous because a great variety of ideologically oriented alignments and perspectives, even contrary ones, were able to unite with regard to this issue. But recalling those historical associations is useful because it helps clarify the basis on which such gestures can be thought of as having democratic legitimacy. Massing of significant, albeit unaccountable, scale as protest is conventionally understood as having democratic legitimacy, particularly where other channels for the *demos*, the people, to express a position are unavailable. The 15–16 February and other similar protests had democratic legitimacy from that perspective in two significant ways. One, discrete mass protest gestures in discrete domestic domains had such legitimacy in specific ways. For instance, the enormity of the protest marches in London and elsewhere – ultimately unaccountable, but indicative of a large scale according to every play of numbers given by every interested party – was an expression of democratic import about the formally democratic state within which they appeared. It concretely showed that very significant numbers of peoples (which tallied with such opinion polls that were taken at the time) in the UK felt they were left with no other channel of expression. The dislocation between leadership and people that Blair and company were working with, the unilateral morality that was being sold with charismatic fervour, the parliamentary processes that were being manipulated, were all concretely opposed on this issue by this gesture – as a questioning of *their* democratic legitimacy. Two, and more importantly, the scale of the protests was unprecedented because of the international dimensions that they assumed. These protests were not about the people expressing discontent with a domestic event that necessarily affects them directly; these protests were overwhelmingly about people reacting to a matter of international/transnational import. These protests give the *only* kind of democratically legitimate indication of what people wish that is currently possible with regard to the international/transnational domain. For a democratic position on the international/transnational domain this is all that can be referred to; it devolves in some acceptable sense from the people of the world, and is not something that is simply unilaterally asserted by self-appointed champions of democracy, or is legitimized from some formally democratic domestic domain acting as the chosen people.

Along with noting that such internationally coordinated protests are the only available and plausible democratically legitimate expressions that are available in the international/transnational domain, it is also worth simply noting that these have now become organizationally possible. It may have been suspected that technological developments have made it possible for such an international expression to be registered in a coordinated and concerted fashion, but in fact it was only symptomatically gestured toward in a number of late twentieth-century 'anti-globalization' protests.

It is disappointing that democratization studies provide little of use to understanding the anti-invasion protests of this story. It is an area where a politically realist apprehension on massing and 'civil society' protest may have been expected, such as might have had a bearing on gestures like the 15–16 February anti-invasion protests. However, the dependence on ideological polarizations, on comparative-politics methodology facilitating categorizations, on normative- and boundary-defined orthodoxies is still so powerful therein that no suitable conceptual position exists yet that can illuminate this story. But Whitehead's metaphor of the performative in that area which I have particularly noted in Chapter 7, and some of the loose ideas of 'civil society' as applied there, may be wrenched out of their locations to throw some light here. The processes of highlighting and exchange through the mass media, public statements, etc., that I have followed in this part, and particularly in this story, do seem to me to have an obvious bearing on the idea of the performative.

To some extent, the effective failure of the worldwide anti-invasion protest marches can be put down to the lack of conceptual clarity that prevails with regard to them. In the conceptual void, the negating efforts of public figures, the negating effects of mass media frames and superlative information flows, the negating misdirection of dominant legal positivistic and boundary-bound normativity naturally prevail.

An area of academic scholarship which might tangentially inform conceptual efforts which are relevant to this study while embracing the connotations of such coordinated worldwide gestures is to do with technologically enhanced international networks and communications and the impact these have on politics. I have noted above the important role that IT developments have played in the organization of the 15–16 February 2003 worldwide coordinated protests. Some analytical examinations, particularly of Internet activism, are available now which are relevant here. Again, I mentioned these briefly in Chapter 8 in the context of social movements research. The above story shows that the relatively greater efficiency of the protest organizers' use of the Internet and other new communication technologies compared to the US and UK governments', derived from the dispersed and decentred nature of the former in contrast to the centralized efforts of the latter. The centralized efforts of the latter were arguably more successful (despite hitches) in manipulating the mainstream print and broadcast mass media. This coincides with observations made in the context of social movements and global activism – with, for instance, W. Lance Bennett's observation:

> Communications in distributed networks becomes potentially transformative when networks spill outside of the control of established organizations. Networks that are not limited to the agendas of any of their members may, under the right conditions, become sustainable, growing democratic organizations. They may exhibit high volume, simultaneous interactive communication, complete with web-based organizing and planning, and hyperlinked public access to large volumes of politically diverse information.
>
> When networks are not decisively controlled by particular organizational centres, they embody the Internet's potential as a relatively open public sphere in which the ideas and plans of protest can be exchanged with relative ease, speed and global scope – all without having to depend on mass media channels for information or (at least, to some extent) for recognition.[41]

The real and conceptual bases attached to such speculations, it seems to me, need to be expeditiously and seriously integrated into the dominant thinking that addresses (and struggles with notions of) democracy, boundaries and the international/transnational domain. Or perhaps such dominant ideas need to be transformed and redirected substantially.

NOTES

All web pages referred to here were downloaded between June 2003 and March 2004.

1 David Manning, 'The Tale of Two (or Three) Marches', *Bad Subjects* issue 63, April 2003, at eserver.org/bs/63/.

2 Ibid.

3 Angelique Chrisafis *et al.*, 'Millions worldwide rally for peace: huge turnout at 600 marches from Berlin to Baghdad', *Guardian*, 17 February 2003.

4 Writing in the *Sunday Times* of 16 February 2003, Peter Conradi in 'Demos follow sun around the globe', p. 2, for instance, offers 'over 5 million' as a conservative estimate of numbers participating in '600 demonstrations around the globe'.

5 John Vidal, 'They stood up to be counted – and found nobody could agree on totals', *Guardian*, 17 February 2003.

6 John Vidal and Jamie Wilson, '1 million could join grassroots protest', *Guardian*, 12 February 2003.

7 Lynette Clemetson, 'Protest groups using updated tactics to spread antiwar message', *New York Times*, 15 January 2003.

8 Gary Younge, 'Left Over? The left in America was once a powerful force that fought for civil rights and helped to end the Vietnam War. But today, with the US poised to attack Iraq, where are the voices of dissent?' *Guardian*, 11 February 2003.

9 Andy Beckett, 'Kabul fell in five weeks. The Islamic World has not yet erupted. So did the left get it wrong – and does it matter?' *Observer*, 17 January 2002.

10 Robbie Millon, 'March for anything, anywhere', *The Times*, 12 February 2003, p. 22.

11 Scott Millar and Dearbhail McDonald, 'Generations march against Iraq war', *Sunday Times*, 16 February 2003, p. 3.

12 Rajeev Syalm, Andrew Alderson and Catherine Milner, 'One million march against war', *Telegraph*, 16 February 2003.

13 Details of the project and copies of the questionnaire were downloaded from www.uia.ac.be/u/wwwm2p/IIPS/.

14 Wolfgang Rüdig and Catherine Eschle, 'Who Demonstrated on February 15?: Some Preliminary Results of a Survey of Anti-War Protesters in Glasgow', at www.strath.ac.uk/government/awp/demo.html.

15 Stephen Cushion, 'Misrepresenting Youth: UK Media and Anti-Iraq War Protesters', *Bad Subjects* issue 65, January 2004 – at eserver.org/bs/65/.

16 In fact, research suggests that the popular perception of political apathy among youth is at odds with other sorts of protests as well. With reference to the so-called social movements (anti-globalization), John W. Cleveland, 'Does the New Middle Class Lead Today's Social Movements?', *Critical Sociology* 29: 2, 2003, pp. 163–88, argued that it is more appropriate to think of these as led by a 'Young Adult Nucleus' than by the 'New Middle Class'.

17 Barbara Epstein, 'Notes on the Antiwar Movement', *Monthly Review* (New York), Vol. 55, No. 3, July–August 2003 – downloaded from www.monthlyreview.org/0703epstein.htm.

18 PEW Research Centre, *Post-Blix: Public favors Force in Iraq, But U.S. Needs More International Backing*, Washington, DC, 20 February 2003 – downloaded from www.people-press.org. The table here is adapted from a larger table that appears on p. 15.

19 MORI, 'War with Iraq: Trends', 17 March 2003 – www.mori.com/polls/trends/iraq.shtml.

20 See William Horsley, 'Polls Find Europeans Oppose Iraq War', BBC News, 11 February 2003 – at news.bbc.co.uk/.

21 Lisie Montano, 'Would America Fight for Me? What Does Organizing Against

Militarism Mean for Youth of Color?', *ColorLines Magazine*, Vol. 6, No. 4, Winter 2003, p. 16.

22 Most of the details in this regard are taken from John Vidal and Jamie Wilson, 'One million could join grassroots protest', 12 February 2003, *Guardian*.

23 Julia Day, 'Mirror profits from protests', *Guardian*, 17 February 2003.

24 Byron York, 'Follow the Money: The antiwar money, that is (finance of the antiwar group Not in Our Name)', *National Review*, 24 February 2003.

25 Professor Sami Al-Arian was employed at the University of South Florida. On 28 September 2001 he appeared on Fox News's 'O'Reilly Factor' to discuss Muslim perspectives on current events, and found himself lambasted as a terrorist for connections with Muslim think tanks dating back 15 years, and none within the last 5 years. As a result he was suspended from his job by USF President Judy Genshaft three days later, and then dismissed. This was widely regarded as a threat to academic freedom and free speech, and the conservative media's campaign against Al-Arian was regarded as a political affair with little basis in fact. On 16 December 2002 a court ruled that USF did not have the right to dismiss Al-Arian. On 19 March 2003 Al-Arian was arrested and charged for his alleged links to Palestinian terrorists. The case continues at the time of writing this. For informative sceptical examinations of the evidence against Al-Arian see Eric Boehlert, 'Is Sami Al-Arian guilty of terrorist plots?', *Salon Magazine*, 21 February 2003, and on the media's campaign against Al-Arian, Eric Boehlert, 'The Prime Time Smearing of Sami Al-Arian', *Salon Magazine*, 19 January 2002 – both at www.salon.com/. The other side of the controversy is best gauged from features such as Joel Mowbray, 'No *Mea Culpas*: The pre-arrest Al-Arian defense team has fallen silent', *National Review*, 19 March 2003, at www.nationalreview.com/.

26 The quotations are from Dan Springer's report 'Anti-War Protests Have Big Price Tags', Fox News, 18 March 2003. Similar information was given in Michael J. Waller, 'Who's Paying for it All?' *Insight Magazine*, 4 March 2003. A common source referred to in both articles was Herbert Romerstein, described as 'a veteran investigator for the House Permanent Select Committee on Intelligence and former head of the Office to Counter Soviet Active Measures at the US Information Agency'.

27 On its website, www.ifconews.org/, the IFCO describes its purpose as: 'to advance the struggles of oppressed people for justice and self-determination', and its Cuba programme in the following words: 'Our work in Cuba centers on our US-Cuba Friendship Caravans, as well as our ongoing program of solidarity with the people of Cuba, which began in 1992 at the request of the Martin Luther King, Jr. Memorial Centre, in Havana, Cuba. Together with our international partners, we organize study tours, construction brigades and delegations for our members, bring Cuban religious leaders to the US, and educate US citizens in their work with Congressional representatives.'

28 On its website, www.workers.org/, the Workers World Party describes its basic view as follows: 'We're for socialism. We think that ownership of the tremendous productive wealth built up by hundreds of millions of workers can't remain in the hands of a privileged few.'

29 E.g., for a PR campaign coordinated by Charlotte Beers to improve America's image abroad in the context of the 'war on terror' in 2002, which eventually failed, US Congress was asked for $595 million – Sheldon Rampton and John Stauber, *Weapons of Mass Deception: The Uses of Propaganda in Bush's War on Iraq* (London: Robinson, 2003), p. 30.

30 Lynette Clemetson, 'Protest Groups Using Updated Tactics to Spread Antiwar Message', *New York Times*, 15 January 2003.

31 Dominic Kennedy and Ben Hoyle, 'Protesters use internet as weapon to stop a war', *The Times*, 14 February 2003, p. 13.

32 AP, 'Anti-war protesters use technology to organize', *Sydney Morning Herald*, 1 April 2003 – at www.smh.com.au/articles/.

33 Salam Pax, *The Baghdad Blog* (London: Guardian Books, 2003).
34 An informative feature on the use of the web in the Iraq conflict in broader terms, considering all sides, is Jim McClellan, 'War on the Web', *Guardian*, 20 February 2003.
35 *The National Strategy for Combating Terrorism*, February 2003, downloaded from www.whitehouse.gov/news/releases/2003/02/counter_terrorism/counter_terrorism_strategy.pdf and *The National Strategy to Secure Cyberspace*, February 2003, from www.whitehouse.gov/pcipb/cyberspace_strategy.pdf.
36 For an account of this see Matthew Tempest, 'Tony Blair's press conference: minute-by-minute highlights of the prime minister's monthly televised press briefing', *Guardian*, 18 February 2003.
37 These figures are taken from T. Michael Moseley, *Operation Iraqi Freedom – By the Numbers*, USCENTAF, 30 April 2003 – downloaded from www.globalsecurity.org/military/library/report/2003/uscentaf_oif_report_30apr2003.pdf.
38 These figures are based on the Iraq Coalition Casualty Count which was maintained at lunaville.org/warcasualties/Summary.aspx.
39 Carl Conetta, *The Wages of War: Iraqi Combatant and Noncombatant Casualties in the 2003 Conflict* (Defense Alternatives Research Monographs 8), 20 October 2003 – downloaded from www.comw.org/pda/0310rm8.html#3.3.%20Total%20Iraqi%20non combatant%20death.
40 At www.iraqbodycount.org.
41 W. Lance Bennett, 'New Media Power: The Internet and Global Activism', in Nick Couldry and James Curran (eds.), *Contesting Media Power* (Lanham, MD: Rowman and Littlefield, 2003), p. 33.

13 *Reconstructing a 'Democratic' Iraq*

THE FOURTH STORY

This chapter concludes the politically realistic consideration of conceptualizations and applications of democracy in the international/transnational domain in the context of the invasion of Iraq between September 2002 and June 2004. In taking up the occupation scenario in Iraq (May 2003–June 2004) – where the occupying US–UK forces allegedly initiate a 'democratization' process from outside – two areas are briefly outlined below: the political economy of reconstructing Iraq; and the establishment of an internal democratic structure and environment in Iraq. Together these make the fourth story of the context in question that is examined here.

I have noted at several points in the previous three chapters that political economic considerations appear to be neglected or carefully side-stepped in the deliberations surrounding the invasion of Iraq. They are side-stepped *within* the deliberations summarized above but not in the mass media; they are however located in the mass media in a manner which doesn't encourage widespread and informed debate. This is not so much the result of a deliberate propaganda strategy, as due to the conventional disposition of financial and economic matters therein and the characteristics of the discourses that pertain to that area. Some significant moments in developments on this front were in fact reported in the main news and analysis sections of US and UK print and broadcast media (the no-bid Iraq contracts awarded by USACE, the large amounts of US public money directed to the Iraq invasion and reconstruction, state–industry links that played in favour of companies like Halliburton and Bechtel, etc.). But more significantly, important links between these have only been reported and analysed in specialist business and finance sections. Business and finance section reporting often occurs with a particular audience in mind: it is assumed that readers would be aware of the different measures of the health of corporations and national economies that exist, and would recognize the general significance of specific items in an ongoing fashion. These are designed, in other words, to cater to the interests of business professionals and economic analysts rather than the interests of a broad politically informed public. Relevant events that are reported in the main political interest sections lack cohesion without the ongoing business section reportage; the general consumer's (who is rarely completely on top of the complexities of even domestic economic processes) sense of political economic considerations is often fragmentary as a result, and apprehended through the sensational rather than the continuously developed. Further, few general consumers – even when particularly politically conscious – have the leisure to pursue a wide range of mass media outlets; most make do with reading one or two newspapers and listening to television/radio broadcasts or surfing through some pre-selected Internet-based news sites. Insofar as I have been able to consult political economic reporting *vis-à-vis* the Iraqi invasion, no one mass media information provider had developed anything near a well-linked and comprehensive picture. Reporting had been uneven in all newspapers and broadcast channels that I have referred to, and often (this is where an implicit propaganda model may be discerned) selective in consonance with the declared ideological proclivities of such providers.

My own brief take on this below is in fact based entirely on information which has been reported somewhere or the other in the mass media, and is therefore in the public sphere. The main elements therein are condensed in the table of Iraq contracts offered by the US government between March 2003 and March 2004 (an obviously limited chart, in ways that I clarify below) that appears below (see Table 13.1). In bringing these and some ancillary reported events together, and considering them in a synthetic and joined-up fashion, it is possible to grasp the political economic situation that pertains to the invasion of Iraq and indubitably has a very significant bearing on this discussion of democracy in the international/transnational domain. I present this picture as an interpretation of the table of some of the major reconstruction contracts given here, as answers to five questions that arise with regard to it: (a) whose money is being represented in the table?; (b) what was done with this money according to the table?; (c) how were the contracted companies mentioned in the table selected?; (d) what sort of environment was created for these contractors?; and (e) what are the overall implications and effects?

(a) Whose money is being represented in the table?

First, let me try to get some perspective on those not inconsiderable sums mentioned there. The contracts highlighted here are a fraction[1] of what's called Iraqi *reconstruction* contracts given over a period of one year, from March 2003 to March 2004, and have little to do with the services relevant to and the export of Iraqi oil. It had been, in my view largely correctly, understood that the second largest oil reserves in the world and control over them was at the heart of military action in and occupation of Iraq: there is a somewhat distinct story there,[2] which connects to the UN oil-for-food programme since 1995, much longer-standing corporate interests

Table 13.1. Major Iraq Reconstruction Contracts/Grants awarded by US and Iraqi government, March 2003–March 2004

Date	*Given by*	*Given to*	*Purpose*	*Amount funded in $ (information available at May 2004)*
24/3/03	USAID contract	Stevedoring Services of America, Seattle, US	Seaport administration	14,318,985
25/3/03	USACE contract	Kellogg, Brown and Root (Halliburton subsidiary), Arlington, VI, US	Fight oil fires, reconstruct oil fields	Max. 7 billion
28/3/03	USAID grant	World Health Organization	Strengthen health system	10 million
28/3/03	USAID grant	UNICEF	Water, basic health, sanitary services	8 million
8/4/03	USAID grant	UNICEF	Basic education	1 million
11/4/03	USAID contract	Research Triangle Institute, North Carolina, US	Restructure local governance	236,911,000
11/4/03	USAID contract	Creative Associates International, Washington, US	Primary and secondary education	56,503,000
17/4/03	USAID contract	Bechtel San Francisco, US	Capital construction	1,029,833,259
18/4/03	US State Department	Dyn Corp. Aerospace Operations, UK (subsidiary of Computer Sciences Corp., US)	Set up law enforcement, judicial and correctional agencies	22 million
30/4/03	USAID contract	Abt Associates Inc., Cambridge, MA, US	Public health	20,995,000
5/5/03	USAID contract	Skylink Air and Logistical Support Inc. US	Airport administration	27.2 million
27/5/03	USAID grant	Cooperative agreement of 5 NGOs	Community action projects	35 million
25/6/03	USAID contract	Management Systems International, Washington, US	Monitoring and evaluation	5.5 million

25/7/03	USAID contract	BearingPoint Inc., McLean, VI, US	Economic recovery, reform and sustained growth	62.8 million
3/10/03	USAID grant	University-based research groups, US and Iraq	Higher education and development	11, 729,732
6/10/03	CPA-IGC contract	Asia-Cell (Kuwait/Bahrain) Orascom (Egypt) Atheer Telecom (Kuwait)	GSM mobile phone network	
8/10/03	USACE contract	Perini Corp. Farmingham, US	Rebuild power lines and electrical facilities in southern Iraq	66 million – increase to 220 million in December
8/10/03	USACE contract	Washington Group Int., Idaho, US	Rebuild power supplies	Max. 500 million
8/10/03	USACE contract	Flour Corp. California, US	Rebuild power supplies	Max. 500 million
21/10/03	USAID contract	Development Alternatives Inc., US	Agriculture reconstruction and development	12,397,156
16/12/03	USACE contract	Kellog, Brown and Root (Halliburton subsidiary) US	Restoration of oil infrastructure	222 million – through Development Fund for Iraq
4/1/04	USAID contract	Bechtel, San Francisco, and Parsons, Pasadena, US	Power projects	1.8 billion
9/1/04	Defense Contracting Command for CPA	Harris Corp, Melbourne Florida, US	Rebuild Iraq's TV and other media networks	96 million
16/1/04	USACE contract	Kellog, Brown and Root (Halliburton subsidiary) US	Restoring oil infrastructure in southern Iraq	Max. 1.2 billion Min. 500,000
16/1/04	USACE contract	Parsons Iraqi Joint Venture (Parsons of Houston, TX, US, and Worley Group of Australia)	Restoring oil infrastructure in northern Iraq	Max. 800 million Min. 500,000
21/1/04	CPA-IGC	Raytheon Co., Waltham, MA, US	Air traffic management systems for Iraqi airports	10.5 million + 38.9 million equipment option

Table 13.1.—*continued*

Date	*Given by*	*Given to*	*Purpose*	*Amount funded in $ (information available at May 2004)*
29/1/04	CPA	NourUSA, Vienna, VA, US	Equip new Iraqi army	327,485,798
6/2/04	CPA-IGC	Engineered Support Systems US	Satellite-based Command and Control IT infrastructure support	17.6 million
10/2/04	IGC – Ministry of Communication	Zhangxing Telecom Co. China	Supply telecommunication equipment	5 million
17/2/04	CPA-IGC	Tehnoforestexport Romania	Furnish schools	18 million
17/2/04	USACE contract	Flour Corp., CA, US	Restore power	154 million
10/3/04	US Ministry of Defense contract	AECOM Los Angeles, US	Programme Management Office Support	21,610,501
10/3/04	US Ministry of Defense contract	CH2M Hill, Englewood CO, and Parsons Water Infrastructure Inc., Pasadena, CA, US	Public works and water sector programme management office support	28,494,672
10/3/04	US Ministry of Defense contract	Louis Berger Group Inc./URS Group Inc. US	Transportation/communications sector programme management office support	8,458,350
10/3/04	US Ministry of Defense contract	Louis Berger Group Inc./URS Group Inc. US	Security/justice sector programme management office support	8,458,350
10/3/04	US Ministry of Defense contract	Louis Berger Group Inc./URS Group Inc. US	Buildings/education/health sector programme management support	10,754,664
10/3/04	US Ministry of Defense contract	Iraq Power Alliance Joint Venture (bet. Parsons Energy and Chemicals Group, US, and Parsons-Brinkerhoff Ltd., UK)	Electrical services sector programme management office support	43,361,340

10/3/04	US Ministry of Defense contract	Foster Wheeler UK	Oil sector management office support	8,416,985
11/3/04	US Ministry of Defense contract	Flour AMEC LLC, Greenville, SC US	Electrical sector – power generation	500 million ceiling
11/3/04	US Ministry of Defense contract	Washington International Inc./ Black & Veatch Joint Venture US	Public works and water support sector	600 million ceiling
12/3/04	US Ministry of Defense contract	Washington International Inc, Princeton, NJ, US	Construction services for electrical sector in northern Iraq	500 million ceiling
12/3/04	US Ministry of Defense contract	Perini Corp., Framingham, MA, US	Construction services for electrical sector in southern Iraq	500 million ceiling
23/3/04	US Ministry of Defense contract	Flour AMEC LLC, Greenville, SC, US	2 contracts – for construction services for water and sewer systems; solid waste management systems	1.1 billion total (600 million & 500 million ceilings)
23/3/04	US Ministry of Defense contract	Contrack/AICI/Archirodon Joint Venture, Arlington, VA, US	Construction services for transportation and communication sector	325 million ceiling
23/3/04	US Ministry of Defense contract	Lucent Technologies World Services Inc., Whippany, NJ, US	Repair and modernization of existing Iraqi communications systems	75 million ceiling
25/3/04	US Ministry of Defense contract	Parsons Delaware Inc., Pasadena, CA, US	Construction services for buildings, education and health sector	500 million ceiling

Sources:

United States Agency for International Development (USAID) – www.usaid.gov
United States Department of Defense – www.defenselink.mil
United States Army Corps of Engineers (USACE) – www.hq.usace.army.mil
Various newspapers and news sites

(particularly US, but also Russian, French, Canadian), the agreements on lifting and shipping oil that have happened since April 2003, the drive to extract oil in that period, etc. The contract list given here is only tangentially related to that story: evidently the biggest deals mentioned here are for oil sector reconstruction – particularly Halliburton[3] subsidiary Kellogg, Brown and Root (a name that comes up often in the following few paragraphs), and to a smaller extent Parsons, and, of course, their subcontractors. This reconstruction element is transparently about taking and exercising control of Iraqi oil services for the foreseeable future; the full implications of that, however, cannot be obtained without looking at the oil trail that is not tracked here. On a different note, the money mentioned in Table 13.1 is essentially US money, approved by US Congress in two significant phases: $75 billion in April 2003 (of which $13 billion could be used towards reconstruction purposes) and $87 billion in November 2003 (of which $20.3 billion was for reconstruction).[4] This was public money, given by US taxpayers, and had largely been handled fiercely independently by the US government; it's worth keeping in mind that the US government over this period was the occupation government of Iraq too in the shape of the Coalition Provisional Authority (CPA) and with the puppet Iraqi Governing Council (IGC) in hand. Somewhere in there were also bits of UK public money: the Chancellor of the Exchequer Gordon Brown had set up an Iraq invasion budget of 3 billion pounds which was reportedly almost spent by October 2003, so that by November 2003 he diverted 100 million pounds to Iraq from the UK overseas aid funds (which left a number of South American and East European beneficiaries suddenly worse off).[5] There were two other sources of revenue that went into reconstruction. One, frozen former Iraqi government assets (estimated at $3 billion) were diverted to reconstruction too – some of it may be reflected in the charted figures.[6] Two, a series of donor meetings culminating in one at Madrid in October 2003 led to another approximately $11 billion (leaving aside US's $20.3 billion) being pledged by various governments and international organizations to the reconstruction effort.[7] Little of that materialized within this period. In February 2004 it was reported that $1 billion of that had been paid into two trust funds run by the United Nations and the World Bank.[8] Monies from most of the above-named sources were lodged in a Development Fund for Iraq set up on 10 June 2003 and controlled by the CPA,[9] which was used for offering a wide range of comparatively smaller reconstruction contracts in Iraq.

Essentially, the bulk of the money that is listed in Table 13.1 was US public money drawn from US taxpayers.

(b) What was done with this money according to the table?

The answer seems to me to be reasonably straightforward: most of this money was handed over to a small selection of large corporations so that they could use it to establish a suitable hold over different sectors of Iraq, generate profits from their extended operation and working capital, and increase their share values. All the corporations that secured these contracts benefited from immediate increases in share values, and, even within the short period represented in Table 13.1, significant profits were shown, often turnarounds. The case of Halliburton, figuring here through its subsidiary Kellogg, Brown and Root, is unusual in the scale of its success in securing these contracts, but in terms of changing fortunes thereby far from unusual. In August 2003 it was reported that due to the Iraq contracts, Halliburton had moved into profit in the second quarter after the losses in the previous year: net profit was \$26 million in contrast to the net loss of \$498 million a year back, with sales rising from \$3.24 billion to \$3.6 billion.[10] By January 2004 it was reported that fourth quarter revenues for Halliburton jumped 63 per cent to \$5.4 billion almost entirely out of Iraq oil contracts.[11] The experience of Halliburton can be generalized: prior to the Iraq war by all indicators the US economy was stagnating, there were reports of diminishing oil reserves, and recession seemed around the corner; the occupation of Iraq enabled public money to be used to subsidize a small number of large corporations so as to change their fortunes and in the hope of kick-starting the faltering US economy. The only slight problem is that whatever effect this has on the US economy as a whole, the benefits will be reaped by the corporations in question and their shareholders; these benefits are very unlikely to come down evenly or at all to US taxpayers in general, or the US public. These corporations are not public-interest bodies. But these private corporations were championed in their profit-making by the state (nothing wrong with that) *using* public money and without any significant guarantee of public-interest returns (something not right there). That the state (understood more or less by definition as the principal public-interest alignment in a country) had given out these contracts doesn't mean – irrespective of what it said – that public interest would thereby be protected. There was no contractual obligation involving public interest in these contracts that anyone is aware of.

The US public was apparently remarkably compliant about this situation. There was very little interrogation of this kind of use of public money. Perhaps this mode of using public money has become so commonplace in the current global capitalist dominance of state–business nexuses, so deeply engrained through the acceptance of privatized public services, that no one raises an eyebrow any longer. But this was different: there was no public interest to be served *for* the American people through these private enterprises; this was outside the domestic domain. And the American people could exert little control on, or even hope to be reasonably aware of, the ways in which their money would be used there. Perhaps the American people are wholly sold out on some notion of trickle down ('corporations profiting in Iraq will eventually profit all of us'); or possibly some notion of transnational democratic altruism was at work ('this is how our US public interests are served these days, and we hope this is how the Iraqi people's public interests will also be served').

The only kind of interrogation that did take place of this process of using public money was with regard to the integrity of the companies in question. There was some discussion of whether companies like Halliburton and General Electric, which have long-standing business interests in the Middle East, could be thought of as indirectly supporting 'rogue states and terrorism', and whether shareholders are aware of this possibility. It was averred that shareholders in these instances are akin to the general public, because large pensions schemes had invested in these companies, and anyone with a \$401,000 pension plan or mutual fund in the US is likely to be a stakeholder at some level in these companies.[12] But this is beside the point: irrespective of the vague moral questions, this indirect investment would have returns if the companies remain profitable. The public-interest returns that could come from the investment of public money in these ventures remain wholly unclear. All that could be said was that a very small number of major shareholders and employees in these companies would profit enormously from this expenditure of public money, some indirect and small-scale shareholders might profit moderately, and the rest would have to test their luck.

(c) How were the contracted companies mentioned in the table selected?

Until August 2003 some of the largest contracts given out by United States Army Corps of Engineers (USACE) and United States Agency for International Development (USAID) were no-bid contracts or contracts on the basis of proposals from requested parties – i.e. handed over to amenable corporations rather than won through competitive and open bidding. Table 13.1 focuses primarily on USACE, USAID and US Department of Defense fronted contracts, and only very selectively on smaller contracts given directly by the CPA through the Iraq Development Fund. The no-bid or requested proposal-based contracts did naturally invite attention, and were the subject of much pondering in business pages of the mass media. The biggest beneficiaries of the early contracts were Kellogg, Brown and Root (KBR), the Halliburton subsidiary (which received a stunning up-to-five-years up-to-7-billion-dollars oil sector reconstruction contract on 25 March 2003, and carried on receiving lucrative contracts thereafter), and Bechtel (which got a phase I reconstruction contract in 17 April 2003 which had been funded to over 1 billion by March 2004, and had received another large contract of 1.8 billion in January 2004 in partnership with Parsons). The choice of both smacked of collusion with business interests involving US government officials and the Republican Party. Almost all of Halliburton's contribution to the previous election campaign (95 per cent) was directed to the Republicans, as was the larger part of Bechtel's contributions (59 per cent). Both companies made contributions to Bush's personal campaign.[13] It is well known that Vice President Dick Cheney, one of the prime movers for the invasion of Iraq, was the Chief Executive Officer of Halliburton for five years till 2000 (when he took up public office) – it is not clear whether, through what means and how much he stood to gain from Halliburton's rising share prices.[14] Lawrence Eagleburger, a former US Secretary of State under Bush Sr., was a board member of Halliburton. The 'war on terror' from 2001 as a whole had proved to be very useful to KBR; as a *Business Week* report put it, apart from the Iraq contracts:

> KBR is in line to earn tens of millions of dollars more to maintain the archipelago of U.S. military bases that now arcs from the Balkans south to the Horn of Africa and east to Afghanistan and Kyrgyzstan. Closer to home, KBR built the detention camps at Guantanamo Bay, Cuba, that house Taliban and al Qaeda prisoners. All in all, no corporation has played as central a role in America's global anti-terrorism campaign – or profited as handsomely from it – as KBR.[15]

Bechtel's ties with Republicans are deep and of long standing. Dena Montague of the Arms Trade Resource Centre was quoted as saying in April 2003:

> Key Bechtel alumni are Reagan Secretary of Defense Caspar Weinburger former Bechtel general counsel, and Reagan Secretary of State, George Schultz former Bechtel President, and current board member. W. Kenneth Davis, former vice-president for nuclear development became Reagan's deputy secretary of Energy and head of the Atomic Energy Commission [ACE] under Reagan. William Casey, Chairman of the Security and Exchange Commission under Nixon, head of the Export-Import Bank under Ford, Reagan campaign manager and head of CIA under Reagan was also a Bechtel consultant . . .[16]

The list carries on. Interestingly, in the process of administering the contracted work these companies were able to secure or lobby for useful concessions. Bechtel was reported in October 2003 as having received Republican support for a significant tax break, which would reduce its company tax from 35 per cent to 32 per cent[17] – a reduction that could be claimed by Halliburton too, among other key Iraq contractors. On 1 January 2004 KBR was given a waiver by USACE, relieving it from providing certified costs or pricing data for fuels obtained from Kuwaiti contractors on specific orders[18] (the significance of this will become clear soon). All major contracts in the first phase of contracting went to US companies, with companies from the UK, Kuwait, Australia and a few other partner countries in the invasion of Iraq figuring primarily at subcontracted levels.

The first open and competitive bids offered by USACE on oil sector reconstruction contracts were opened on 23 June 2003 with a deadline of 14 August 2003, with results due to be declared in October. These were announced as being open to: 'Companies from countries qualifying under the Trade Agreements Act, Balance of Payments Act and Coalition members that are not qualified under the Acts'.[19] The deadline was pushed back several times and, in fact, the results were not announced till mid-January 2004. On 9 December 2003 Paul Wolfowitz issued a Pentagon directive which banned all but those companies based in the US, Iraq and 61 other countries designated as 'coalition partners' in the invasion of Iraq from bidding for key Iraqi contracts (though subcontracting was left open). This effectively left out such opponents of the unilateral invasion as Russia, France, Germany and Canada – which had substantial business interests and agreements in Iraq dating back from before the invasion. In fact, it appeared now that just as the US and UK were transparently motivated by economic considerations in the drive for invasion, quite possibly both the opposition to invasion and the keenness to contribute to reconstruction after the invasion on the part of the above-named countries was influenced to a significant degree by their existing economic interests in Iraq, in addition to conviction in multilateralism and international law. Anyway, the directive naturally was strongly condemned by those countries that found themselves left out of the rewards of post-invasion reconstruction, and doubts about it expressed by Kofi Annan of the UN. Bush, ostensibly a vocal proponent of global free markets, defended the move in the following words:

> Our people risked their lives. Coalition, friendly coalition folks risked their lives and therefore, the contracting is going to reflect that, and that's what the U.S. taxpayers expect.[20]

Not surprisingly, this also found the support of the UK government, through the voice of Jack Straw:

> The United States Congress is fully entitled to say the tax dollars are spent in one way, which in this particular case is contracts limited to those active allies in Iraq, rather than another way. We have talked to them about it, but the decision is for them, not ours.[21]

It is interesting that this was the only (indubitably strategic) point at which the US taxpayers' public-interest claims were raised. Unfortunately, the nature of this public interest and how it was expected to be served by issuing these contracts was not interrogated further. As it happened the next successful contractors to be declared by USACE were, again, KBR and Parsons on 16 January 2004. Throughout this period other bidders had expressed disgruntlement at the manner in which the bidding process had been designed to advantage companies like KBR, by writing into the invitation to bid conditions which closely resembled those that already obtained with regard to KBR.

While I am discussing the process of contracting, another point which is worth picking up here has to do with several media reports suggestive of corruption in the administration of contracts. One of the companies, for instance, that had attracted such media attention was the Halliburton subsidiary and largest beneficiary from Iraq contracts, KBR again. From about October 2003 reports emerged of the Pentagon suspecting that KBR had overcharged the US military for oil supplies through Kuwaiti subcontractors. An investigation was launched by the Pentagon in December 2003, when a Pentagon audit suggested that KBR had overcharged the government by about $120 million. In January, in fact, Halliburton admitted irregularities in their accounting, fired two KBR employees for taking bribes of $6 million from a Kuwaiti firm, and offered to pay back $27.4 million.[22] Even while this investigation was underway, however, KBR received both the no-bid contract (through the Iraq Development Fund) of $222 million on 16 December 2003, and the very lucrative contract of $1.2 billion from USACE on 16 January 2004. Another example of a contract which seemed to smell of corruption was the $327.5 million contract that was awarded by the CPA to NourUSA in January 2004 for supplying the new Iraqi army with equipment. The award was immediately followed by challenges from unsuccessful bidders, expressing doubts about NourUSA's ability to deliver on such a large contract at the stated amount (it appeared that competing bids had largely ranged from $500 million up to $1 billion) and its lack of experience in dealing with such large contracts. It appeared in fact that the company had been set up only in March 2003 in anticipation of precisely such deals arising out of the Iraq invasion, and was led by Huda Farouki, a close friend of IGC member and Iraqi National Congress head, Ahmed Chalabi. In March 2004, the US military took the extraordinary step of cancelling this contract, while explaining that this in no way reflected adversely on NourUSA, which would be able to bid again when the contract was reopened.

(d) What sort of environment was created for these contractors?

The brief answer is, from an outside corporation's point of view, unusually favourable, certainly more so than anywhere else in the Middle East, or in the US and Europe themselves. A few reported details of how the US government and the CPA in Iraq went about preparing this environment speak for themselves.

Shortly after the downfall of the Saddam Hussain government, on 17 July 2003 it was reported that the CPA had unilaterally (by Order Number 20) set up the Trade Bank of Iraq (TBI) with authorized capital of $100 million to facilitate the country's imports and exports and the transition of state-owned enterprises to greater privatization.[23] It was unclear at the time who the shareholders were, though it was understood that the CPA and the transitional IGC were in control of it. It was also understood that its operations and management would be outsourced, to which end bids had already been invited from banking consortiums. By September 2003 it had emerged that a consortium of 13 international banks (none Iraqi), led by J.P. Morgan Chase and Co, had been chosen to lead the TBI, and that it has an initial lifetime of 12 months with the option to extend for another three years.[24] A press release of 5 December 2003 from Export-Import (EX-IM) Bank of US announced that it had joined export credit agencies (ECA) from 15 other nations in signing framework agreements with the TBI and CPA providing for support of over $2 billion for TBI[25] – by January two more ECAs had joined and export guarantees stood at $2.4 billion.[26] According to a CPA press release of 7 March 2004, Paul Bremer, Administrator of CPA, also announced a new law regarding the governance of the Central Bank of Iraq (CBI), whose objectives are to 'maintain domestic price stability and to foster and maintain a market-based financial system' independently from the government.[27]

On 8 August 2003 it was reported that Thomas C. Foley had been appointed Director of Private Sector Development for the CPA, and would be overseeing 194 Iraqi state-owned businesses' transition to the private sector.[28] Foley had been Chairman of the board of directors of T.B.Woods, and was one of the main fund-raisers for Bush's election campaign. In a conference organized by the US Department of Commerce on 11 February 2004, 'Doing Business in Iraq', Thomas Foley had the following advice for US businesses: 'US companies big and small should be taking advantage of opportunities in Iraq and should be doing so now. You should be doing it not just because you will have very good returns on your investments, but because there won't be another situation any time soon when a market with this much potential opens up after such a long sleep.'[29] He also tried to allay fears about growing insecurity and widespread disaffection in Iraq following reports in the mass media. On 13 March 2004 Michael Fleischer, entrepreneur and brother of former White House press secretary Ari Fleischer, succeeded Foley as Director. He had been Deputy Director of the CPA's Private Sector Development since September 2003.[30]

In September 2003 it was reported that a firm, New Bridge Strategies, had been set up to advice businesses that wished to extend their interests to Iraq. Its website announced its aim as: 'assisting clients to evaluate and take advantage of business opportunities in the Middle East following the conclusion of the US-led war in Iraq. Its activities will seek to expedite the creation of free and fair markets and new economic growth in Iraq, consistent with the policies of the United States Government.'[31] This was headed by Joe Allbaugh, who had been Bush's campaign manager in 2000 and the Director of the Federal Emergency Management Agency until March 2003. Other directors included Edward Rogers, Jr. and Lanny Griffith, both assistants to Bush Sr.

On 6 October 2003 it was reported that the Centre for International Private Enterprise (CIPE), an organization funded through the National Endowment for Democracy (NED – of which more later) and affiliate of the US Chamber of Commerce, had opened a Baghdad field office. According to its press release, the task of the field office 'will be to provide an on-the-ground presence for CIPE's programme to build greater democratic awareness within Iraqi society of market and democratic values and to work with the Iraqi business community to strengthen its leadership role in the country's democratic transformation'.[32] It also announced the launch of two programmes: one, a monthly business review in Arabic highlighting best business practice and economic reforms for Iraqi entrepreneurs, in partnership with *Al Alahi* newspaper; and two, a survey of business conditions and barriers to entrepreneurship in six regions of Iraq. The CIPE Office was set up to follow an Iraqi American Chamber of Commerce and Industry (IACCI) survey of August 2003, sponsored by CIPE, which came up with recommendations for moving towards a free-trade agreement between Iraq and US.[33]

In September 2003 Order 39 on Foreign Investment,[34] accompanied by orders on the tax regime and bank law (Orders 37 and 40) signed by the IGC and the CPA chief Paul Bremer, came into force. By these 100 per cent foreign ownership of all Iraqi sectors except natural resources was permitted; restrictions of trade, capital flows and foreign investment were removed; foreign banks were allowed to open businesses and buy Iraqi banks; import tariffs were cut to 5 per cent; and the top tax rate in Iraq was cut from 45 per cent to a flat rate of 15 per cent for both individuals and corporations. Over 200 Iraqi state-owned enterprises had been privatized. Ihsan al-Titenchi, Director of the IACCI, reportedly complained that in passing this law the Iraqi business community was not consulted. The latter were understandably unhappy about this (especially the 100 per cent foreign ownership possibility) and felt it was not, after an extended period of sanctions and the continuing instability, in a position to compete with foreign companies on a level playing field yet. Michael Fleisher of the CPA's private sector development office reportedly said: 'The entire Republican Party in the United States would like to have the new Iraqi law.'[35] On 1 April 2004 Bremer signed Order 64 to restructure Iraqi Company Law, which, according to the CPA press release, 'removes the remnants of Iraq's centrally planned and controlled economy, and officially opens the door for foreign investment in Iraq by making the company law consistent with CPA Order No. 39'.[36]

(e) What are the overall implications and effects?

What the above details gesture towards is the creation of an environment enabling comprehensive privatization of an unprecedented level, unilaterally conducted by the US-led occupying force. It was in this environment that the contractors listed in Table 13.1 were invited to operate.

There are a couple of points that are noteworthy here. The first concerns the extent of this privatization and establishment of control through private companies – it is *comprehensive.* It included every sector of the Iraqi economy and of Iraqi public interest imaginable: not just oil resources, but banking, healthcare, education, military, policing, housing, foodstuffs, power generation, water and sewage, waste disposal, transport and communications, information and the media, community services and welfare, every kind of productive industry and exports and imports, management of government and administration. All of those came under 'reconstruction'. It also included something deeper: a comprehensive level of ideological re-education and re-moulding, through 'community action' together with 'humanitarian' activities, 'restructuring' of education, and media-based programming and branding practices. Relevant here were the contracts given by USAID to Research Triangle Institute on 11 April 2003 to 'restructure local governance' (on which Naomi Klein has written a revealing article[37]) and to NGOs for 'community action projects' on 27 May 2003. Probably more relevant here were the activities of bodies funded through the National Endowment for Democracy (NED), particularly the International Republican Institute (IRI) and the National Democratic Institute (NDI). I come back to their activities later in this chapter. The comprehensiveness of these changes, through privatization and a sector-by-sector mapping of external control of the Iraqi people and economy, is arguably more pervasive and permanent than straightforward colonization. Straightforward colonization is at least a transparently iniquitous step, which confers on a colonizing government some of the responsibilities of maintaining public interest (in however self-serving a fashion), for which the colonizing power is answerable at least to the people of the home country. In this instance, the comprehensive extrinsic control of Iraq was devolved through private agencies and contracts and a network of closed interests therein in such a manner that only the self-serving element of colonialism is left, without either any long-term responsibility towards the Iraqi people, or answerability to Iraqi *or* the American/British people. The arrangement was such that even within a brief period of direct control through occupation (effectively the role of the CPA and its puppet the IGC), and through limited contracting periods, the extrinsic interests could be made embedded enough for them to be served for the foreseeable future. This mode of setting up comprehensive extrinsic control was organized so that by the time direct occupation was ostensibly withdrawn the necessary embedding of economic control would have been effected; the withdrawing of direct occupation would only mean a withdrawing of such public interest as is enjoined on an occupation government, without losing the advantages gained through occupation. As Naomi Klein put it in an article written as early as 15 April 2003:

> . . . by the time the Iraqi people have a say in choosing a government, the key economic decisions about their country's future will have been made by their occupiers. . . . The process of getting all [the] infrastructure up is usually called 'reconstruction'. But the American plans for Iraq's future economy go well beyond that. Rather, the country is being seen as a blank slate on which the most ideological Washington neoliberals can design their dream economy: fully privatized, foreign-owned and open for business. . . .
>
> Entirely absent from this debate are the Iraqi people, who might – who knows? – want to hold on to a few of their assets. Iraq will be owed massive reparations after bombing stops, but without any real democratic process, what is being planned is not reparations, reconstruction or rehabilitation. It is robbery: mass theft disguised as charity; privatization without representation.[38]

The other point relevant to the details given above has to do with the legality of these proceedings in terms of existing international law. Insofar as it is understood, the proceedings detailed above were obviously a violation of the then existing Iraqi constitution (which prohibited foreign ownership of immovable property, and investment in and establishment of companies in Iraq by foreigners who are not resident citizens of Arab countries), and of both the Hague Regulations of 1907 and the Geneva Convention of 1949. In UNSC Resolution 1483 of 22 May 2003, where the US–UK's status as occupying power was recognized and sanctions withdrawn, the occupying powers were enjoined to comply with the Hague Regulations and the Geneva Convention. According to Article 53 of the Hague Regulations:[39]

> An army of occupation can only take possession of cash, funds, and realisable securities which are strictly the property of the state, depots of arms, means of transport, stores and supplies, and, generally, all movable property belonging to the state which may be used for military operations. All appliances, whether on land, at sea, or in the air, adapted for the transmission of news, or for the transport of persons or things, exclusive of cases governed by naval law, depots of arms, and, generally, all kinds of munitions of war, may be seized, even if they belong to private

> individuals, but must be restored and compensation fixed when peace is made.

And Article 55:

> The occupying State shall be regarded only as administrator and usufructory of public buildings, real estate, forests and agricultural estates belonging to the hostile State, and situated in the occupied country. It must safeguard the capital of these properties, and administrate them in accordance with the rules of usufruct.

Legally, a 'usufruct' may enjoy/use/profit from a property belonging to another without altering the substance of that property. Article 53 of the Geneva Conventions states:

> Any destruction by the occupying power of real or personal property belonging individually or collectively to private persons, or to the state, or to other public authorities, or to social or cooperative organisations, is prohibited, except where such destruction is rendered absolutely necessary by military operations.

And Article 54:

> The occupying power may not alter the status of public officials or judges in the occupied territories, or in any way apply sanctions to or take any measures of coercion or discrimination against them, should they abstain from fulfilling their functions for reasons of conscience.

Whatever interpretation is applied to these, it is self-evident that the process of comprehensive economic, political and social structuring by the US-led CPA in Iraq described above contravened all of these.

The ability to implement the enactment of reconstruction contracts, the installation of a suitable legal and political environment, and the apparent maintenance of a democratizing mission for the world and the media to keep track of, rested to a great extent on the administrative authority in place in Iraq over the official period of occupation (May 2003–June 2004). I have mentioned the Coalition Provisional Authority (CPA) and the Iraq Governing Council (IGC) so far with little introduction. A few details about the CPA in the official occupation period might help in clarifying its relevance for this study.

Initial responsibility for overseeing reconstruction in post-invasion Iraq fell on the Office of Reconstruction and Humanitarian Assistance (ORHA), established in early 2003 and headed by Lieutenant General Jay M. Garner of the US Army. By mid-May this responsibility was taken over by the CPA, headed by L. Paul Bremer III, and the ORHA was dissolved or absorbed within the CPA. CPA Regulation 1, which effectively announced and defined itself, was signed by Bremer on 16 May 2003. The CPA announced itself therein as follows:

1. The CPA shall exercise powers of government temporarily in order to provide for the effective administration of Iraq during the period of transitional administration, to restore conditions of security and stability, to create conditions in which the Iraqi people can freely determine their own political future, including by advancing efforts to restore and establish national and local institutions for representative governance and facilitating economic recovery and sustainable reconstruction and development.
2. The CPA is vested with all executive, legislative and judicial authority necessary to achieve its objectives, to be exercised under relevant UN Security Council resolutions, including Resolution 1483 (2003), and the laws and usages of war. The authority shall be exercised by the CPA administrator.
3. As the Commander of Coalition Forces, the Commander of US Central Command shall directly support the CPA by deterring hostilities; maintaining Iraq's territorial integrity and security; searching for, securing and destroying weapons of mass destruction; and assisting in carrying out Coalition policy generally.[40]

Paul Bremer, a former assistant to Henry Kissinger and Alexander Haig, was appointed Ambassador to Holland by Reagan in 1983 and became Ambassador-at-Large for Counterterrorism in 1986. After retiring in 1989 he was Managing Director of worldwide consulting firm Kissinger Associates founded by Kissinger, and then CEO of the risk and insurance services firm Marsh Crisis Consulting. In 1999 he was appointed Chairman of the US National Commission on Terrorism. His expertise in security and diplomatic matters, his extensive political (Republican) and corporate connections and the fact that he wasn't a military person seemed to make him the ideal choice for the post. It was observed that most of the key appointments made to the CPA had profiles with strong Republican Party connections (with official appointments under Republican presidents and significant records of fund raising) and equally powerful roles in the corporate sector. These included Bremer's senior advisor Tom Korologos; in charge of privatization of Iraq's state-sector corporations, Tom Foley (and later Michael Fleischer); the chief advisor of the Agriculture Ministry, Dan Amstutz; senior advisor for organizing Iraq's media, Dan Senor; and chief advisor to the Minister of Education, Williamson Evers.[41] Richard Henry Jones, US Ambassador to Kuwait, and Sir Jeremy Greenstock, UK Special Representative in Iraq, were

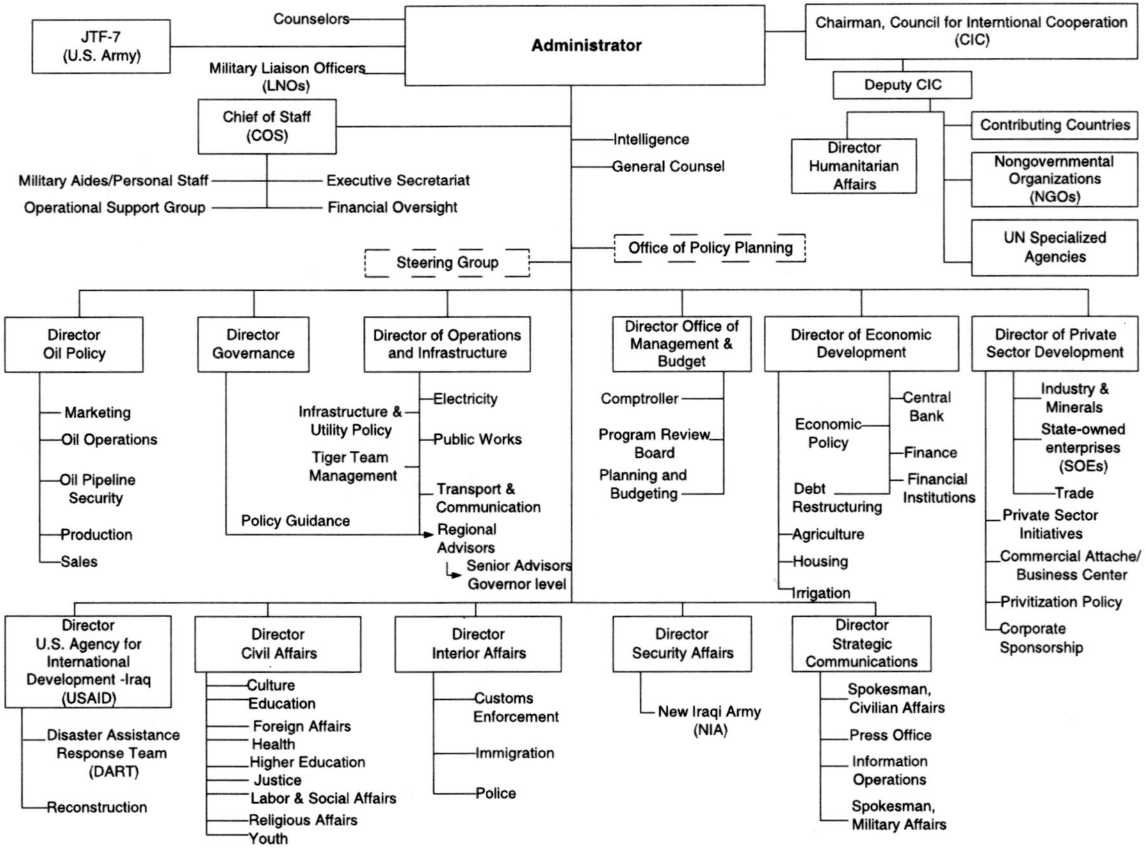

Figure 13.1. Coalition Provisional Authority

Source: L. Elaine Halchin, 'The Coalition Provisional Authority (CPA)', *CRS Report for Congress*, 29 April 2004, Order Code RL32370, CRS-26

deputies to the CPA Administrator. Figure 13.1 gives a sense of the organization of the CPA.

More interestingly, the official status of the CPA was carefully left unclear all through; it has been difficult to determine from where its authority was invested for legal purposes. It wasn't clear whether it could be regarded as a federal agency of the US government appointed by the President or whether it was an agency of the US Department of Defense answering to the Secretary of Defense; whether the UNSC was instrumental in its institution, through Resolution 1483 (constantly cited by Bremer in CPA Orders and Regulations) – so that it can be regarded not as a federal agency but a multinational coalition agency. If thought of as a US federal agency it was unlike most others in that it was neither an executive department (which are identified by statute) nor a government corporation (which are solely controlled by the US government). A Congressional Research Service Report for Congress by L. Elaine Halchin of April 2004, which goes through the ambiguities of the CPA's establishment and functional legitimacy, concludes that these have the following positive and negative effects (an informative if longish quotation this):

> Perhaps this ambiguity allows the authority to perform multiple roles, each with its own chain of command, stakeholders or constituents, funding, and accountability policies and mechanisms. . . . Possibly, this mix of arrangements allows CPA to operate with greater discretion and more authority, and have access to more resources than if it was solely a federal agency, or an arm of the United Nations. CPA personnel might also be able to work more efficiently under this mix. By operating under more than one set of laws, regulations and policies, CPA possibly could expand the scope and reach of the organization's authority beyond what it would be otherwise. . . .
>
> Potential drawbacks of this arrangement are that the lines of authority and accountability could become tangled, or even obscured. CPA personnel possibly could find it difficult to understand and delineate clearly – on a daily basis – the organization's different roles and associated funds, laws, and rules. Personnel might be hampered by this tangle of resources, laws and documents, and could find themselves engaging in questionable, if not unethical or criminal, activities. This scenario also could prove challenging for organizations that are attempting to monitor CPA and its activities. When the authority makes a decision or expends funds, it might not be clear to external parties under what authority it is acting. Without transparency, the CPA might give the appearance of shifting funds, personnel, and tasks among different roles. Further compounding the problem, oversight initiatives might be met with the response that the activity in question was carried out under an authority over which the oversight body – Congress – has no jurisdiction.[42]

Clearly, the advantages and the disadvantages noted here could be thought of as complementing each other; from the CPA administration's point of view, extended scope of resources and activities and the difficulties posed for external monitoring are both advantages.

Some of the key moments of the CPA-controlled period of occupation help to break that period up into progressive phases. The Iraqi Governing Council (IGC) was appointed by Bremer on 13 July 2003. The council consisted of recently returned exiles, tribal leaders, women, religious Muslim conservatives, and secular political leaders. Shiites, who account for 60 per cent of the Iraqi population, were allotted 13 seats on the US-appointed council; 12 seats were divided among Iraq's main minorities: Sunni Arabs, Kurds, Assyrians and Turkmen. In the course of the occupation year two members of the IGC were assassinated and replaced with like candidates. Of the 25 members 12 were recently returned Iraqi exiles – a disproportionate number, it was observed in the media. The IGC had powers to appoint diplomats and ministers, approve budgets and propose policies, but the CPA had a veto on all these areas.[43] On 1 September 2003 the IGC announced the names of 25 ministers for its first cabinet. On 15 November 2003 the CPA and the IGC signed an agreement[44] giving a timetable for the restoration of Iraqi sovereignty, the creation of a new constitution and the holding of elections. The IGC was expected to have a significant role in the appointment of the transitional government for Iraq after restoration of sovereignty and the dissolving of the CPA on 30 June 2004, but this was undermined by the UN's taking over of this process under the leadership of Lakhdar Brahimi early in 2004 (who was appointed Special Advisor to the UN Secretary General in January 2004, and UN Special Envoy to Iraq – he was already so for Afghanistan). An Iraqi Transitional Administrative Law was drafted by the CPA, passed without changes by the IGC after consultations, and came into force on 8 March 2004.[45] This law defined a legal framework for the functioning of government over two phases: the first from the handover of power by the CPA and IGC to an interim Iraqi government on 1 July 2003 to the election of a National Assembly by 1 January 2004, and the second from the election of a National Assembly to the establishment of a permanent constitution approved by a nationwide referendum by 15 December 2005. Article 26(a) of the Transitional Law ensured that the laws in force in Iraq on 30 June 2004 shall continue to remain in effect over the transition period. The IGC was dissolved on 1 June 2004 when members of the interim Iraqi government were announced. A UN team headed by Brahimi was instrumental in the appointment of members of the interim government; nevertheless it was the CPA (the US government) which dictated terms, as became apparent in some much-reported differences about the naming of the interim government's Prime Minister and President. Ayad Allawi was named Prime Minister and Sheikh Ghazi al-Yawar President of the interim government. On 19 April 2003 it was announced that Bush had appointed the then US

Ambassador to the UN, John D. Negroponte, US Ambassador Designate to Iraq, to take charge of the US embassy through the period in which the interim government would be in place. Negroponte had fronted the aggressive US position during the pre-occupation UN Security Council debates in late 2002 and early 2003. He had also been US Ambassador to Honduras between 1981 and 1985, a controversial period of US collusion with a military dictatorship. In a Washington briefing on transition from the CPA to the US Mission of 9 June 2003, given by Francis J. Ricciardone (US State Department Coordinator for Iraq Transition) and Lt. Gen. (ret.) Mick Kicklighter (US Department of Defense Director of Iraq Transition), some pertinent details emerged about the post-CPA US role in Iraq. It emerged that the US embassy in Iraq would be the largest in the world, with about 1,000 permanent Americans directly under the mission in place, many continuing from offices under the CPA. Outside Baghdad, the embassy would have regional offices in Mosul, Kirkup, Hilla and Basra and work with military units. Two hundred foreign (155 US, 111 already in place) experts would advise ministries. As regards the reconstruction fund and contracts, Ricciardone had the following to say:

> The CPA's Project Management Office will go out of business, if it has not already. It's in the process of transitioning. And there will be a project management staff for the Ambassador called IRMO, the Iraq Reconstruction Management Office. It will be a temporary office of the embassy, meaning lasting for a few years, as long as the 18.4 billion [US dollars reconstruction in the Iraq Development Fund] needs oversight and planning and spending.
>
> Then there will be, under that staff, the implementing agencies. There will be the US Army Project and Contracting Office, which will implement the majority of those things. It will do a degree of project management also across other agencies that are doing construction. USAID will be another implementing agency. The Department of State has various elements that will implement contracts, such as State's Bureau of International Narcotics and Legal Affairs that will assist in training programs. The Department of Justice is another implementing agency. So there is a series of implementing agencies, each with their respective inspectors general that are involved.[46]

Evidently, the dissolving of the CPA would make little difference to effective US control of Iraqi economic and relevant infrastructural processes; however, US's accountability in terms of Iraqi public interest would thereafter disappear.

From the perspective of this study, apart from creating a suitable economic environment one of the important areas of the CPA's activities in Iraq over the period of occupation was to create an environment that is amenable to parliamentary democracy (such as would go hand in hand with the economic environment in question). This involved an extraordinary effort to impose wholesale political democratization of the Iraqi polity from outside; unprecedented in the degree of unilateral extrinsic input into such a process and in the concentration of the planned operation of such a process. The process was planned by US agencies that were set up for precisely such purposes, and that have worldwide experience of promoting their ideological version of democratization. These agencies, in this instance, worked through and with the CPA on a programme of total extrinsically controlled ideological transformation of a nation. The organizations funded by the National Endowment for Democracy (NED) – especially the International Republican Institute (IRI), the National Democratic Institute for International Affairs (NDI) and the Centre for International Private Enterprise (CIPE) – had a significant role in setting up an ambitious planned process of democratization through re-education and infrastructural change. These were all formed after President Ronald Reagan set out an agenda of 'foster[ing] the infrastructure of democracy'[47] in a speech at the British Parliament, Westminster, of 8 June 1982. Two decades later in 2003 Bush recalled Reagan's speech in an address to NED on 6 November, and made the invasion of Iraq appear to be part of Reagan's plan. However, Bush's perspective of democratizing Iraq (not unlike Reagan's own foreign policy) clearly had a somewhat more confrontational approach than the word 'fostering' might suggest:

> The failure of Iraqi democracy would embolden terrorists around the world, increase dangers to the American people, and extinguish the hopes of millions in the region. Iraqi democracy will succeed – and that success will send forth the news, from Damascus to Teheran – that freedom can be the future of every nation. (Applause.) The establishment of a free Iraq at the heart of the Middle East will be a watershed event in the global democratic revolution. (Applause.)[48]

The threatening tone of these remarks in the context in which they were made (at the NED anniversary) is not irrelevant. It is now well known that despite their status as independent non-partisan organizations, the NED-funded bodies have a distinctly right-wing Republican agenda (an agenda of global market liberalization and extension of US influence at the expense of national self-determinism, *through* a drive towards global democratization), and their international programmes have been largely conducted to that end. On the ground in Iraq, this meant that first the NDI carried out an assessment mission in Iraq between 23 June and 6 July 2003.[49] On the basis of a broad region-by-region survey of existing political alignments in Iraq, and with some opinion polls in hand, this came up with a recommended programme of 'levelling the political playing field', i.e. assisting individuals and groups to develop organizations that could be regarded as viable alternatives to ethnic and religious alignments; and of 'increasing democratic knowledge, strengthening democratic values and improving democratic skills', i.e. a systematic programme of ideological and level-by-level re-education. Implementation of these through four planned phases was outlined. The extent to which this programme was implemented by the NDI with the IRI and CPA is evidenced in the weekly reports on governance that appeared on the CPA website between February and June 2004.[50] These weekly reports detailed programmes of 'refreshing' provincial councils; of distributing vast numbers of leaflets and booklets to impart 'education in democracy' to peoples of different categories; of organizing workshops and conferences targeting particular strata of the population (teachers, tribal leaders, women, etc.) as part of a 'civic education campaign'; IRI, NDI and CPA meetings and exchanges with various political parties and groups; of propaganda to garner support for the de-Ba'athification policy and the democratic credentials of the CPA; of gathering opinion polls on various issues and interpreting them in ways that justify these programmes; and so on.

All these moves, however, took place against a backdrop of ever-intensifying violence and disaffection in Iraq. The incidents were too numerous to chart out here, and I won't attempt a grim litany of all the violence that took place over this period. Mass media reports daily detailed resistance against occupying US and UK forces in various parts of the country. Devastating bombing attacks were carried out in several cities, claiming numerous Iraqi civilian and not insignificant US–UK military victims. The kidnapping of foreigners, especially those associated with coalition countries, became rife – and some executions of kidnapped persons were reported. Media features on the prevailing lawlessness and disorder in Iraqi cities undermined efforts at publicizing the democratization that the CPA was allegedly carrying out. Early in 2004 reports of widespread torture and abuse of Iraqi prisoners by US and UK soldiers – all too visually evidenced in the photographs of torture that were published – caused outrage both within the Middle East and in the West. As reports of Iraq's falling into chaos continued to accumulate, criticism of Bush's and Blair's drive towards and conduct of the invasion of Iraq was being viewed with increasing bitterness in the world. Whereas the US and UK had been resistant to the input of the UN in the reconstruction and political restructuring of Iraq through most of 2003 after invasion, in 2004 incremental gestures brought the UN gradually onto the scene (naturally, in a fashion that wouldn't disturb the economic arrangements that had already been put in place). This occurred in a peripheral fashion, primarily by giving way to Brahimi's plan for the UN overseeing the transition towards a democratically elected government in Iraq. Opinion polls in the US and UK seemed to come out squarely against the military action in Iraq as the summer of 2004 approached. The 30 June 2004 deadline for withdrawing the official occupation of Iraq approached in the midst of both a sense of failure and of relief in the US and UK, and passed with a quiet formal handover of 'sovereignty'. Bremer's exit from Iraq was without ceremony.

INFERENCES AND OBSERVATIONS

A reasonably systematic look at the economic manoeuvrings during the occupation of Iraq shows that though these were carried out in the name of democracy and ostensibly for the sake of democratization, these had no understandable basis in democratic processes themselves. At various levels economic processes unravelled at odds with what are commonly (connotatively and denotatively) regarded as democratic processes. Within the arena of market opportunity itself, the closed interests and doubtful or absent bidding procedures cited above themselves undermined any principle of a level playing field for comparable corporations (or democratic openness of opportunity for corporations). The lack of consultation of stake-holding peoples – particularly the Iraqi people, but also the US and UK peoples whose money was used to fund both military action and reconstruction contracts – suggests dissociation between the economic processes described above (which favoured certain established and limited corporate and private interests) from democratic public interest. The mode in which the economic environment in Iraq was moulded to enable almost total extrinsic control of that economy and its existing revenues and resources undeniably severely limited the scope of its future democratic self-determination. On the whole, the political economic picture briefly drawn in this chapter gestures towards a deliberate, and successful, delinking of ostensibly democratic politics (denotatively at the level of governance, administration and legislation) from the economic processes that (allegedly inevitably) accompany them.

The question that arises is whether this is a situation peculiar to the particular context of Iraq under invasion, or whether this reflects a larger and general reality wherein capitalist economy and liberal democratic politics are apparently linked or (paradoxically) operate together with mutually dissociated and contradictory effect. This is a difficult question to answer without further examination of comparable contexts. As it happens, loosely comparable situations are legion, though there are some ways in which the Iraq invasion is, I believe, unusual at this point in time. This is the first concerted *unilateral occupation* in modern times, with *no significant and effective pre-existing internal support base*, that has been carried out ostensibly *for the sake of a democratizing mission.* Nevertheless, there are loosely comparable situations in the so-called democratization of certain South American and Eastern European countries since the 1980s with US involvement (I have mentioned some of the relevant research in the chapter on democratization research) which can and no doubt will be examined in this regard. This is not the subject of this study and here I won't press on with this point further.

On a related note, but from a slightly different perspective, it does instinctively appear that the kind of dissociation of capitalist economic logic and democratization that is evidenced under the distorted situation of Iraq occupation described above, is related to a larger reality of global capitalism. This relationship pertains not merely to comparable situations of extrinsic control but to the manner in which the economic logic of contemporary corporate capitalism is working increasingly everywhere, with ubiquitous effect. Analyses of the slippages between global capitalism and democratic politics (in terms of contradictions within parliamentary democratic governments' responsibility towards public interest) are numerous already (I have looked at this to some extent myself elsewhere[51]). It instinctively seems to me that there are affinities between such research and the situation that pertains to Iraq outlined above – but again, this is a matter that requires more rigorous examination than I am prepared to devote to this issue here. In passing I may as well mention that I have presented the story of reconstruction contracts in Iraq as given above in a couple of discursive forums.[52] In both, the feedback I received suggested that the audiences largely regarded the described situation as being an exacerbation of or logical extension of political economic developments experienced elsewhere – or rather, to some degree, everywhere.

At any rate, the dissociation of economic manoeuvrings from democratic process described in this chapter falls in with a point made in Chapter 10 above: the normative associations of democracy were deployed and used to attract a range of concerns both for and against invasion, so as to distract any significant attention being given to the political economic reality that underlay it.

The other and final point that comes to mind given the story of this chapter is a more complicated one. The attempt to import from outside a wholesale democratization of a domestic context – both by *instituting* structures and processes of parliamentary democracy from local to national level, and by *creating* a civil society through re-education and ideological moulding – left little space for domestic legitimacy for democracy to emerge and make its claims *within* Iraq. The conceptual position underlying this situation appears to be that democracy does not have to depend on the *spontaneous emergence* of democratic legitimacy from within (which would always situate the domestic sphere as the prime legitimizer of democracy), but that democracy depends on *creating* democratic legitimacy within (which puts the onus of creating democracy on any extrinsic agency that has the wherewithal to do so). This is a most perplexing situation, since the predominant mode of conceptualizing democracy denotatively has historically been and continues to be, as I have constantly observed in Part I, pre-eminently in terms of national or transnational boundaries where legitimacy comes from within. The difficulties that this position presents are all too evident; they are manifest in the throes of violence that were experienced within Iraq and the bitter divisions and dissent that were expressed worldwide while this ostensible importation of democracy was underway. Irrespective of the success or failure of this experiment in comprehensive democratization from outside (with the somewhat obscured political economic picture), there appears to exist in the politically real sphere a model of democratization – a normatively potent and pragmatically effective *formula of democracy*, so to say – that is dislocated from its internally legitimizing boundaries, and apparently freely afloat in the arena of transnational politics, just waiting to be grabbed by whoever finds it useful.

This abstract formula for democracy apparently doesn't need pre-legitimation from an internal constituency that would be subject to it – this floats freely in the domain of transnational politics – this is somehow outside the boundaries of nation-states or any other formal organization but waiting to be imposed within them through a quick violent process. Such a formula cannot but play on absolute and universal and decontextualized norms. Its legitimacy is drawn from the assertion of a chain of normative terms (human rights, plurality, freedom, etc.) that can be endlessly adjusted for content depending on who is doing the adjusting and where. The legitimation is not drawn from those who would be subject to this formula, the *demos* itself. That may seem very strange, but that is how it is. There are three inevitable consequences to this, all manifested in the story outlined in this chapter. One, the legitimation of democracy given by the people themselves (in politically realist terms through some sort of elective system), is a forced democratization exercise. In Iraq, it was set up as a military operation and a guilt-assuaging-for-the-West publicity exercise for 2005: it is a *figment* of the process, not part and parcel of the process itself. Two, the formula for democracy has to be rigorously and narrowly *managed* to keep the chain of normative associations intact: it shouldn't actually be allowed to fit in with the inclinations of the people in a particular social-cultural-historical context who will be governed by this system. In any majoritarian democratic system it is possible that a range of possible positions can get democratic legitimacy. Worryingly, fundamentalist religious and fascist alignments can win and assert themselves through a democratic process – through elections, and through democratic institutions. Equally, however, a desire for government with strong investment in public interest and welfare, or a desire for more equalitarian economic and social policies, can exert themselves through those processes too. To a large extent the free-flowing formula for democracy in question is designed to resist a range of such possibilities, thus narrowing down democracy to a very particular ideological position that sustains itself through normative claims of a quasi-religious nature. In Iraq this has meant an attempt to manage what people think, feel, do – so that they can vote in a predetermined *democratic* way. They have to be taught to be democratic, they have to be skilled in democracy, they have to be prepared for democracy; they cannot be expected to be able to give shape to their democratic order by dint of being the *demos.* They should not be allowed to give way to their religious and gender prejudices. They should not be allowed to give way to their desire to control their resources and markets. A chain of absolute democratic norms are spun together outside the domestic domain in the expectation of a certain kind of ideological homogenization.

My final (the third) point is more a reasonable (and hopeful) expectation following from the above than an observation. However strongly one may feel attached to some of the norms that are thus promoted in the name of democracy (human rights and tolerance and gender equality, for instance), this mode of formulating and imposing democracy will always be open to the charge of being imperialistic – culturally and materially. It will be seen as self-contradictory and self-defeating. And since it is deployed from the transnational domain, it will also be resisted at the transnational level. That doesn't mean that such resistance will necessarily be conservative or against norms of human rights and justice and equality; ultimately such resistance must search for and come up with a more rational mode for embracing those norms.

NOTES

All web documents were downloaded between August 2003 and August 2004.

1 In May 2004 it was reported that a report to the House of Representatives committee on government reform stated that $88 billion had been awarded for contracts to do work in Iraq, out of a total of $107 billion-worth of contracts awarded without open competition – see Suzanne Goldenberg, 'Email shows Cheney "link" to oil contract', in the *Guardian,* 1 June 2004, p. 10. This figure far exceeds the sum of figures gleaned together from news reports in the appended chart.

2 Several books address the oil story: Stephen C. Pelletiere, *Iraq and the International Oil System: Why America Went to War in the Gulf* (Washington, DC: Maissonneuve Press, 2004 – updated from 2001 edition); Stephen C. Pelletiere, *America's Oil Wars* (Westport, CT: Praeger, 2004); Larry Everest, *Oil, Power and Empire: Iraq and the U.S. Global Agenda* (San Francisco, CA: Common Courage Press, 2004).

3 The article cited in note 1 also states that Halliburton had obtained $17 billions-worth of such contracts, far exceeding any other company.

4 The first of these was drowned in the midst of interest in the politics of the war effort in Iraq, but debates and negotiations leading to the second were extensively reported in the US mass media.

5 Owen Bowcott and Grace Livingstone, '£100 m in aid funds diverted to Iraq', in the *Guardian,* 7 November 2003 – on www.guardian.co.uk.

6 'Iraq's Central Bank asks UN to urge countries abroad to hand over frozen Iraqi assets', *SFGate,* 4 August 2003 – at www.sfgate.com.

7 For a breakdown see 'FACTBOX – Contributions to reconstruction in Iraq', Reuters reports of 15 October and 24 October 2003 – at www.forbes.com.

8 'Donors commit $1bn to Iraq funds', BBC News (Business), 29 February 2004 – at news.bbc.co.uk/1/hi/business/. In this context see report on 'Financial Reconstruction in Iraq' of 12 February 2004 by John B. Taylor, Under Secretary of the Treasury for

International Affairs before the Senate Banking, Housing and Urban Affairs Committee Subcommittee on International Trade and Finance, at www.iraqcoalition.org/press-releases/20040212_taylor.html.

9 This was done by CPA Regulation Number 2 of 10 June 2003 (CPA/REG/10 June 2003/02) – the full text can be accessed at www.iraqcoalition.org/regulations/20030615_CPAREG_2_Development_Fund_for_Iraq.pdf.

10 'Iraq work helps Halliburton return to a profit', *International Herald Tribune*, 1 August 2003 – at www.iht.com.

11 'US firms enjoy the spoils of war', *Evening Standard*, 30 January 2004 – at www.thisislondon.co.uk.

12 Lesley Stahl, 'Doing Business With the Enemy', CBS News, 25 January 2004 – at www.cbsnews.com.

13 This was naturally suspected almost as soon as news of the first round of contracts were made public – see 'Rebuilding Iraq – the Contractors', 28 April 2003, at www.opensecrets.org.

14 The already cited report – Suzanne Goldenberg, 'Email shows Cheney "link" to oil contract', in *The Guardian*, 1 June 2004, p. 10 – cites possible evidence that shows that Cheney had personally played a role in the award of Iraq contracts to Halliburton. It also points out that in 2003 he received $178,437 in deferred compensation from the company.

15 Anthony Bianco and Stephanie Anderson Forest (with Stan Crock and Thomas F. Armistead), 'Outsourcing War: An Inside Look at Brown & Root, the Kingpin of America's New Military-Industrial Complex', *Business Week*, 15 September 2003 – at www.businessweek.com. Also informative here is a book published in the run-up to the 2004 US elections, with a clear anti-Bush/Cheney line: Dan Briody, *The Halliburton Agenda: The Politics of Oil and Money* (Hoboken, NJ: John Wiley, 2004).

16 Quoted in Erik P. Sorensen, 'Bechtel in Iraq: Weapons of Mass Construction', 18 April 2003 – at www.neilrogers.org.

17 Edmund Andrews, 'Bechtel gets GOP support for a potential tax break', *New York Times*, 28 October 2003 – at www.nytimes.com.

18 Details of this waiver of 1 January 2004, 'relieving KBR of providing certified cost or pricing data for fuels obtained from its Kuwaiti subcontractor for Task Orders 5 and 7', appear in the USACE website – www.hq.usace.army.mil.

19 Details here too are available on the USACE website, ibid.

20 Quoted in 'Bush defends restrictions on Iraqi contracts', CNN, 11 December 2003 – www.cnn.com/.

21 Quoted in 'Bush sticks with Iraqi contract ban; Annan sides with France, Germany, Russia and others', Associated Press release, 11 December 2002 – at msnbc.msn.com.

22 See 'Criminal probe into Halliburton', BBC, 24 February 2004 – at www.bbc.co.uk.

23 The full text of Order No. 20 (CPA/ORD/17 July 2003/20) is available – at www.iraqcoalition.org/regulations/20030717_CPAORD_20_Trade_Bank_of_Iraq.pdf.

24 See WSJ report from Washington, DC, of 1 September 2003 on www.leasecoach.com/.

25 See report 'Ex-Im Bank Provides $500 million in support of Trade Bank of Iraq', 8 December 2003, which quotes the press release in full – at usinfo.state.gov/.

26 'Trade Bank of Iraq gets $2.4 bln export guarantees', Reuters, 24 January 2004 – at www.forbes.com.

27 Press release 'New Law Governing the Central Bank of Iraq', 7 March 2004 – at www.cpa-iraq.org/pressreleases/20040308_central_bank.html.

28 See, in this context, Ahmad Mustafa, 'Economic Outlook: Privatizing Iraq will have dire results in the country and its people', *Gulf News*, 14 August 2003 – www.gulf-news.com.

29 Thomas Foley, 'Doing Business in Iraq: Opportunities in Investment, Trade and Reconstruction', p. 5 – downloaded from www.export.gov/irqq/pdf/foley_ remarks_02/104.pdf.

30 See press release 'Michael P. Fleischer named Director, Private Sector Development' – at www.cpa-iraq.org/pressreleases/20040313_fleischer_psd.html.
31 The URL of the website is www.newbridgestrategies.com/.
32 Press release 'US Chamber of Commerce Affiliate Establishes Field Office in Baghdad', 6 October 2003 – at www.cipe.org/whats_new/press/oct_6_2003.htm.
33 The survey was entitled 'Conditions and Expectations for Private Enterprise in Iraq: Findings from a survey of Iraq's small and medium sized business owners and managers', compiled by Raad Ommar and Sabah Khesbak, August 2003, for IACCI, with CIPE sponsorship – downloaded from www.cipe.org/regional/mena/iraq.htm.
34 The full text of Order 39 (CPA/ORD/19 September 2003/39) on Foreign Investment, which was discussed at length in various newspapers at the time, can be found at www.iraqcoalition.org/regulations/20031220_CPAORD_39_Foreign_Investment_.pdf.
35 Both al-Titenchi's and Michael Fleischer's views are taken from news feature 'Competition scares Iraqis', *Al Jazeera*, 6 December 2003 – at english.aljazeera.net.
36 Press release 'Restructuring of Iraqi Company Law', 1 April 2004 – at www.cpa-iraq.org/pressreleases/20040401_company_law.html.
37 Naomi Klein, 'Democracy and Robbery: Washington wants to outsource Iraqi sovereignty, but its grip on the country is growing weaker', *Guardian*, 10 February 2004 – at www.guardian.co.uk.
38 Naomi Klein, 'Iraq: Privatization in Disguise', *The Nation*, 15 April 2003 – at www.thenation.com/. Also relevant in this context is another article by Naomi Klein, 'Iraq is not America's to sell: International law is unequivocal – Paul Bremer's economic reforms are illegal', *Guardian*, 7 November 2003 – at www.guardian.co.uk/.
39 The quotations from the Hague Regulations and Geneva Conventions here are given following the lead of Aaron Mate, 'Pillage is forbidden: Why the privatisation of Iraq is illegal', *Guardian*, 7 November 2003 – at www.guardian.co.uk/.
40 CPA/REG/16 May 2003/01, on the CPA website: www.iraqcoalition.org/regulations/20030516_CPAREG_1_The_Coalition_Provisional_Authority_.pdf.
41 An article on the implications of these appointments: Joshua Micah Marshall, Laura Rozen and Colin Soloway, 'Who's Who in the Coalition Provisional Authority', 4 December 2003 – at www.informationclearinghouse.info/article5338.htm.
42 L. Elaine Halchin, 'The Coalition Provisional Authority (CPA): Origin, Characteristics, and Institutional Authorities', Congressional Research Service (CRS) Report for Congress, Library of Congress (Order Code: RL32370), 29 April 2004, pp. 32–3.
43 For further details of the IRG's composition and activities see the Council for Foreign Relations (New York and Washington) website at www.cfr.org/background/background_iraq_council.php.
44 A copy of this is available at www.iraqcoalition.org/government/AgreementNov15.pdf.
45 The entire text of the 'Law of Administration for the State of Iraq for the Transitional Period' was placed on the website www.iraqcoalition.org/government/TAL.html.
46 'Transcript of Briefing on the Transition from Coalition Provisional Authority to US Mission, Baghdad, Iraq', Washington, DC, 9 June 2004, on the US Department of State website www.state.gov/p/nea/rls/rm/33359pf.htm.
47 The full text of Reagan's speech at Westminster of 8 June 1982 is available on the IRI website www.iri.org/newreaganspeech.asp.
48 Transcript of 'President Bush Discusses Freedom in Iraq and Middle East: Remarks by the President on 20th Anniversary of NDI', NDI, US Chamber of Commerce, Washington, DC, 6 November 2003 – at www.whitehouse.gov/news/releases/2003/11/20031106–2.html.
49 Les Campbell and Amy Thayer (eds.), *NDI Assessment Mission to Iraq, June 23 to July 6, 2003*, Washington, DC, NDI, 2003 – the full text can be downloaded at www.ndi.org/ndi/library/1625_iq_report_072503.txt.
50 At www.iraqcoalition.org/government/weekly-updates/.

51 Suman Gupta, *Corporate Capitalism and Political Philosophy* (London: Pluto, 2002).
52 I presented this as a keynote lecture at the Lebanese American University in Beirut, Lebanon, in a conference on 'Violence in the Middle East', 26 May 2004, and in an International Development Centre seminar at the Open University, Milton Keynes, UK, on 23 June 2004.

Conclusion

14 *Iraq-Invasion-Democracy*

The presumptions and convictions that were presented, acted upon and played out in all four stories in Part II can be drawn together into some sort of conceptual schema itself. We can think of this as the conceptual position regarding democracy in the international/transnational domain devolving from the invasion and occupation of Iraq, 2002–2004 (and other such recent and future actions) – a conceptual position that is implicit in the stories of this real world context. This can be regarded as a spontaneous democratic theory of such political practice, just as philosophers are sometimes able to discern a spontaneous philosophy underlying scientific practice.[1] Seen as such, this conceptual position can be located *vis-à-vis* those discussed separately in Part I, and referred to in an ongoing fashion in Part II. The conceptual position of Iraq-invasion-democracy goes roughly as follows.

There is a particular set of formal arrangements involving elective and consultative procedures (involving majority legitimisation) for political policy- and decision-making and the enactment thereof that is denoted as democratic. Such arrangements, ostensibly through formal involvement of all its membership, are implemented within states and other organizations, which are thereby denoted as democratic. Concurrently, there is a wide – almost universal – acceptance that democracy has normative connotations which are related to its minimum meaning. These normative connotations seem to embrace every individual everywhere equally. By any standard, it is questionable whether the formal arrangements that are denoted as democratic come close to realizing the normative connotations of democracy even with regard to those whom it involves directly. But by dint of being denoted as democracies, states and organizations with the above formal arrangements often claim to embody the normative connotations of democracy, and such claims are often accepted widely.

Given that, there are two ways in which internationally/transnationally effective political action can be taken which can claim democratic legitimacy.

One, an international organization can be put in place, the membership of which (representatives of all states and representatives of other transnational alignments, bodies, interest groups) replicates the kind of formal arrangements that operate for citizens of a denotatively democratic state. Just as citizens of a denotatively democratic state cannot in principle be seen as having different rights, so no member of this international organization (irrespective of its ideological, economic or regional status) can be seen as having different rights. Inevitably, some members in such an organization would be such as cannot be formally denoted as democratic. This is an organization following a principle of multilateral democracy. The UN appears to aspire to some such principle in its procedures, but in fact allows a level of pragmatic unevenness which undermines its claim to being multilaterally democratic. Nevertheless, it is widely accepted as representing something like multilateral democracy. The UN itself goes further, and claims to champion the normative connotations of democracy too.

Two, denotatively democratic states (and other denotatively democratic organizations) which claim to embody the normative connotations of democracy can extend that claim with international/transnational effect and undertake political actions accordingly. All such states need to do this is to ratify their claims by the means through which such states acquired their denotative status – the formal mechanisms which apply to their domestic spheres. This implicitly seems to accord those who happen to be within those domestic domains the advantage of deciding on actions which potentially affect everyone outside that sphere. Two ideas provide a way out of this excessive prerogative. One, in claiming to embody the normative connotations of democracy, a denotatively democratic state thereby transforms itself from a specific formation to a universal ethos. Of course it is materially and boundary-wise *there*, but it thereby also is more than *there* – it spreads metaphysically everywhere. Its material and border-demarcated place takes on a decontextualized universal symbolic significance. As a universal ethos the reach of this denotatively democratic state permits no outside and no opposition; everything that protests that it is outside is illegal, is its opposite, and is bent on the destruction of good norms. Two, by taking on such a symbolic significance it also justifies the need to protect its material and border-bound presence, and justifies the superior prerogatives of its members and representatives in the international/transnational domain, i.e. justifies its assertion of its members as chosen people. There remains no distinction between protecting the boundaries and defending universal human rights and equality and freedom. There both are boundaries that have to be hardened to embody democracy better, and there are, at the same time, no boundaries and therefore no limits on where democratic claims can apply. Or, to put it briefly, such democratic states become themselves (singly and together) transnational bodies which can conduct political action in the international/transnational domain with democratic agency (by dint of *embodying* the normative connotations of democracy so that whatever they do is presumptively democratic). Unilateralism is the rather weak term that usually applies here (and I have used it accordingly in Chapter 11).

According to Iraq-invasion-democracy, the second mode of political action with international/transnational effect has greater democratic legitimacy than the first mode.

The arguments here are simple and therefore evidently effective. The first mode of legimitizing political action in the international/transnational domain is lacking because it is not more like the second. The international organization that assumes the principles of multilateral democracy is, after all, modelled on the same formal procedures as the denotatively democratic state. If it is failing to *embody* the normative connotations of democracy (rather than just championing them – let's forget that in real politics the UN is *not* adhering to multilateral democracy), it must be because it is not sufficiently like denotatively democratic states. Denotatively democratic states (in themselves and together) as transnational entities are an agglomeration that supersede boundaries far more effectively than the multilateral organization, and claim democratic legitimacy from their chosen people and for their universal ethos with much greater force.

Iraq-invasion-democracy is able to present useful ways of accommodating the malaise of underhand operations of multinational corporations and global capitalism and the evidence of popular international dissent (in the form of massing of protest).

Denotatively democratic states (and other organizations) that embody the normative connotations of democracy and become agglomerated into – individually and jointly active – transnational entities, and which thereby both harden borders and reify their universal significance at the expense of borders, can consistently be seen to both reiterate themselves and embrace everything without any contradiction in the international/transnational domain. Multinational corporations are the channels of such reiteration and expansion of the borders of denotatively democratic states as transnational entities; and the global capitalist regime that is now so well established and understood is an expression of such reiteration and expansion. Globalization in its entirety, with the concordant infrastructure of transnational bodies – private corporations, banks, investment and speculation facilitators, as well as the IMF, the World Bank, the WTO, and a host of transnational regional alignments, as well as the military and intelligence apparatus that goes with it, as well as controlled and uncontrolled demographic shifts and exchanges – could be regarded as the *modus operandi* of denotatively democratic states embodying normative connotations of democracy as transnational entities. The unstoppable momentum of globalization is regarded as much as justification for what I have understood unilateralism to be, as at the behest of such unilateralism. Iraq-invasion-democracy brings forth the concrete possibility of enacting the extension of globalization to such dispossessed and benighted areas as Iraq for the Iraqi people's (democratic) benefit and for the (democratic) benefit of denotatively democratic states as transnational entities. It simply shows that their transnational status in the international/transnational domain is a condition and a harbinger of universal normatively connoted democratic modernity.

If this kind of falling in with globalization entails the unilateral imposition of democracy from outside by denotatively democratic states embodying the normative connotations of democracy and therefore acting as transnational entities, that is no more than a natural replication of the denotatively democratic state in its own image and yet less than its own image (by an analogous rationale, the Judaeo-Christian-Islamic God created man in his own image and yet lesser than himself). I observed in Chapter 13 that democratization of Iraq in economic and administrative terms (that is, denotatively) was conducted as an imposition of a free-floating model of democracy that loosely resembles some aspects of American or European democracy but in ways that don't obtain in those states. It doesn't, for instance, derive internally from Iraq – not from the *demos* of Iraq. It allows the resources of and the market of Iraq to become a free-trade and property zone for whoever can waltz in (in principle anyway, in practice of course it was a much smaller set of interests that was allowed to waltz in). This free-floating model is the replication of denotatively understood democracies as transnational entities, but with the *demos* removed from the equation. The *demos* only exist – perhaps – as the chosen people who gave democratic legitimacy to the states which thereby claimed to embody the normative connotations of democracy and become transnational actors.

Iraq-invasion-democracy also contains internationally coordinated multi-interest convergences of protest within itself, as no more than an aspect of Iraq-invasion-democracy. Such protests are first and foremost no more than an expression of the very normative terms that denotatively democratic states claim to embody to become transnational entities. When Bush and Blair commended the international protests of 15 and 16 February as salutary democratic dissent that simply proved their claim of embodying democracy, they knew what they were about. Whatever claims protesters make become a competition for the same normative connotations that are presumptively embodied by the opponents. The disregard for such protest is also within the frame of Iraq-invasion-democracy – it just involves the merest shift of emphasis. Ultimately the only mode of connotatively democratic legitimation that is embraced is the one that comes through formal arrangements that pertain in denotatively democratic states (and concordant organizations). We all accept those formal arrangements as democratic. The very informality of international protest gestures permit them to be disregarded. That they happen, from the perspective of Iraq-invasion-democracy, is a good thing because they show that democracy – connotations intact – is indeed a universal transnational affair; that these are informal is a better thing because it is the formalization of denotative democracy reifying normatively connoted status and acting as transnational agents that is widely accepted and constantly asserted. The only disjuncture in the matter of protests and their international scale is in that shadowy presence that just cannot be accommodated in Iraq-invasion-democracy – the association of such protests, and the organizational hand in such protests, with an ideological other: an embattled and flickering materialist socialist left.

At the heart of Iraq-invasion-democracy is the possibility of switching the normative connotations and legislative denotations of democracy, and the magical process through which borders can be hardened and dissolved in the same breath.

The conceptual position of Iraq-invasion-democracy is the stream into which most of the current conceptual positions (regarding democracy in the international/transnational domain), surveyed in Part I, converge through various tributaries,[2] and through which they may through various means be channelled towards an ephemeral ocean of universal democracy (uniting the connotative and denotative therein). Iraq-invasion-democracy achieves a sort of not irrational (but rationally unsustainable) compromise and synthesis of numerous elements and overall tendencies manifest in those conceptual positions.

Cosmopolitan democracy makes prescriptions for the modification of institutions of international governance to embrace a transnational character which is consistent with the connotations and denotations of democracy that usually attach to existing liberal democratic states. This entails an extension of citizenship on a global level along the lines of citizenship within democratic states (and at the expense of state-wise representation in existing international bodies), without dissolving the boundaries of existing liberal democracies and the prerogatives of citizenship therein. It seems pretty clear to me that this is a mode of extending denotatively democratic states with connotative effect as transnational entities, while preserving their boundaries. Rawlsian liberal democracy, especially in laying out a 'law of peoples', describes and prescribes a polarized world view wherein denotative democratic states, connotatively ascribed, place anything outside that sphere as departures from its embodiment of ethical norms. The decent hierarchical regimes and authoritarian (potentially outlaw) regimes that are definitively outside are either open to absorption into its own well-orderedness or are candidates for elimination through just wars. Rawls, in other words, provides the *raison d'être* for the all-embracing normative transnational presence of denotatively liberal democracies to be asserted. By maintaining that universal norms are embodied sufficiently in the constitutional liberal democratic state, and conceptually abstracting and extending those norms to a post-national constellation that is nevertheless geopolitically located, deliberative democrats fall in with Iraq-invasion-democracy – or become amenable to its appropriations. The institutional configurations that are accordingly envisaged, and the boundaries that are coherently but fluidly maintained (despite embodying universal applicability) for post-national constellations, foretell the possibility of merging deliberative democracy with both cosmopolitanism and Rawlsian liberalism to join the stream. Radical democracy's aspiration to linguistically perform the radicalization of democratic participation and dissent *within*, and without radically challenging the liberal regime, effectively draws in and overcomes international protest while embracing it much as Iraq-invasion-democracy does. It dislocates the possibility of dissent and emancipation from the liberal democratic state – which remains untouched – by playing on endlessly replicated and materialized boundaries of identities. The discourse of multivocal pluralism defines and hardens the boundaries of the liberal regime, while extending its normative reach with transnational effectiveness here. Democratization studies attend to real political processes whereby the transnational effectiveness of denotative and connotative democracy is allegedly demonstrably extended. Often here ideological divides are reiterated and measures of legislative denotation are comparatively employed to present real world processes as efficaciously subsumed by Iraq-invasion-democracy. Political economics are only tangentially or prescriptively considered in these current conceptual positions, as constitutive ripples in the stream of Iraq-invasion-democracy. The usual bent is to defer consistent and rigorous normative analysis of real world political economics in terms of the normative connotations of democracy, or to assume that what applies in existing denotatively democratic boundaries must apply to the international domain.

Close attention to the politically real domain is the only perspective that disturbs the conceptual – and crassly real – imperialism of Iraq-invasion-democracy. That, of course, is why consideration of political economic evidence causes unease. Political realism that questions normative absolutes, examines real world happenings, and does not leap to prescriptive or visionary analysis is, in general, least amenable to merging with Iraq-invasion-democracy – even where it is sympathetic to or even accepts some of the tributary conceptual positions mentioned above. Thus, it is not simply the declared political realists who take an iconoclastic position *vis-à-vis* prevailing views on democracy in the international/transnational domain – this is not confined to Waltz, Chomsky, Zolo and others. Attention to the inequities and dispossessions involved in the reality of Iraq-invasion-democracy clearly disturbs Habermas, Held, Archibugi and a few others who champion some of the tributary conceptual positions. But this does not seem to lead to radical rethinking – only incremental adjustment within existing terms, or deferment, or myopia.

I do not need to state my reservations about Iraq-invasion-democracy further; these are written in my attempt to summarize it above, and extensively through Parts I and II. The politically realist methodology I have assumed above clarifies these reservations amply. In Chapter 1 I had mentioned that my politically realist methodology, while nor accepting any given normative strictures *a priori*, is nevertheless and necessarily sensitive to the norms that cut across the prevailing normative field, and, more importantly, cultivates an ethical understanding. The problems with Iraq-invasion-democracy are problems that arise from the interstices of and contradictions within the prevailing conceptual field itself. These problems are concretized in the real political processes that devolve from Iraq-invasion-democracy – amply demonstrable through the stories that attach to one real world application thereof, in the invasion and occupation of Iraq, September 2002–June 2004. In the real world application, Iraq-invasion-democracy is seen concretely to contravene both the normative connotations and the legislative denotations of democracy as these are understood now, while claiming both. Finally, an implacable ethical opposition to Iraq-invasion-democracy is justified by the real politics of the invasion and occupation of Iraq itself: as the stories of Part II and numerous documents and researches show, this has involved lies, bullying, illegalities, injustices, mass killings and brutality, untold suffering, social instability, robbery, waste of resources at an international scale and of transnational scope – and achieved little else.

It is not my intention to draw this study towards prescriptive or visionary analysis. But there are a couple of inferences which can be made from the above in suggestively prescriptive ways. In closing this study, I would like to briefly draw attention to these.

Much of this study has centred on the repercussions of switching the connotations and denotations of democracy, and the boundary negotiations and equivocations that are conducted in conceptualizing democracy in the international/transnational domain. It appears that overemphasis on normative discourses in this area can lead to a playing down of political realities and materialist considerations; that Iraq-invasion-democracy can seep reasonably coherently through these moves; and most importantly that this involves a web of complicities – often unwitting and unthinking complicities – wherein even the most vociferous and obstinate dissent can be appropriated and co-opted. There are clearly significant forces of dissenting activism and gestures being expressed in the international/transnational domain; equally evidently the mechanisms for dispersing or disregarding these are often implicit in their enactment and self-positionings. It seems to me that all who sense the malaise of current conceptual and institutional arrangements pertinent to this domain suffer to greater or lesser degrees by their immersion in them – in, so to say, the ethos they are part of and at odds with. At the level of practice the dissenting gestures, such as they are, can be expected to accrue and develop further momentum while at every moment struggling against and acceding to the appropriations and co-optations of the prevailing ethos. But they have, at any rate, enough conceptual weight and material basis to continue to gather momentum in the near future. It is possible that such momentum of dissent would be able to acquire a more meaningful thrust if it was accompanied, contingently and in a contextually sensitive fashion, with a wide-ranging and concerted conceptual effort. Such a conceptual effort may consist in no more than a strict and rigorous revisiting of the increasingly normativized teleologies and histories of constitutional democracy and transnational globalized democracy. If even some of the observations of this study are provisionally accepted, there follows a possible project which no one person can undertake and no one context can contain and no one set of political actions can exemplify. This would involve a rigorous socio-historical examination of the normative connotations and legislative denotations of democracy (perhaps held apart by such significations as c-democracy and d-democracy). The relationship between these, the distinctions between these, the applications where these enter, the different knowledge and geopolitical spheres where these are encountered, the different boundaries where these apply or transgress are all open to a somewhat defamiliarized and politically responsive and, I believe, necessary re-examination.

Finally, it appears to me that there is promise in one of the observations made above: that the main point of unease regarding such mass international, and arguably democratically (in connotative terms) valid, protest gestures as those of 15 and 16 February – and analogous anti-globalization protests – has been the shadow of the ideological other of capitalist liberal democracy (which merges into Iraq-invasion-democracy) therein. I have loosely characterized this as a materialist socialist left; with which informal mass dissent is inextricably associated, which has the *locus standi* to uncompromisingly critique its past affiliations, and which has a salutary materialist and realist leaning. And since it is a spectre that still haunts the capitalist world, some reconceptual and organizational flesh will make an impact. I associate the materialist socialist left, in contextually specific ways, with the transformative Marxist formations that still resist deep inequalities and oppressions in certain contexts; with democratic socialist principles of economic development and redistribution that enjoin certain states to administer public interest sectors of industry and enterprise; and with the comprehensive restructuring of economic arrangements and governance sought in the international public sphere by some elements of the so-called anti-globalization movement. There already exist the seeds of a broad-ranging alignment in there, which may not get immediate consensus or majority support, and has the uphill task of interrogating the prevailing ethos from base to superstructure before it, but which may have enough conceptual and organizational impetus to provide meaningful transnational opposition against Iraq-invasion-democracy.

NOTES

1 As Louis Althusser is able to do in *Philosophy and the Spontaneous Philosophy of Scientists* (London: Verso, 1990).

2 *Position* (static) and *flow* (active) in this and following paragraphs may convey the confusion of mixed metaphors. There is a discursive paradox here, but no confusion. What appears as a position in a conceptual field may well be thought of as processes of intellectual and practical development. The natural sciences are replete with instances where flow and position coincide in the same framework.

Index

This index lists the following: names of authors whose ideas and texts are discussed (titles of texts are not listed), names of key actors in the events covered, names of alignments and organizations that figure in a significant fashion, events that are referred to more than once, a few key conceptual terms that do not figure in or are not sufficiently covered by the different levels of titles and subtitles.

Printed in the United States
75590LV00002B/1-108

9 780826 496386